VOID
Library of
Davidson College

CICERO: VERRINES II. 1

CICERO:

VERRINES II.1

with translation and commentary by

T. N. Mitchell

ARIS & PHILLIPS LTD

© T.N. Mitchell 1986. All rights reserved. No part of this publication may be reproduced, stored in a retrieval system, or transmitted in any form or by any means without the prior written permission of the publishers.

Latin text: Reproduced by kind permission of Oxford University Press from *Ciceronis Orationes* III edited by William Peterson, 2nd edition 1917.

British Library Cataloguing in Publication Data
Cicero, Marcus Tullius
 Verrines II, Book 1 -- (Classical texts)
  I. Title   II. Mitchell, T.N.   III. Series
  875'.01   PA6282.A5

ISBN 0 85668 252 7 *cloth*
ISBN 0 85668 253 5 *limp*

Cover photograph by coutesy of the Trustees of the Victoria & Albert Museum.

Printed and published in England by ARIS & PHILLIPS LTD,
Teddington House, Church St., Warminster, Wiltshire. England.

CONTENTS

PREFACE		vii
INTRODUCTION:		
	1. The Extortion Court	1
	2. The Career of Verres	5
	3. The Trial	6
	4. The Political Implications of the Trial	10
	5. The Transmission of the Text	12
NOTES TO THE INTRODUCTION		14
ABBREVIATIONS		17
BIBLIOGRAPHY		19
SIGLA		23
CICERO: VERRINES II, BOOK 1		
	TEXT and TRANSLATION	24
	COMMENTARY	159
INDEXES		225

PREFACE

The Verrine Orations have many claims on the attention of classical students and scholars. They deal with a sensational criminal trial that helped establish Cicero not only as the leader of the Roman bar but as a rising politician of unusual energy and ability. They provide a wealth of information about Roman provincial administration and a detailed look at the system's weaknesses and the harsher face of Roman imperialism. Finally, they constitute a major literary achievement, a rhetorical tour de force that represents the maturation of Cicero's skills as an orator and prose stylist.

There are surprisingly few editions of the speeches available in English, and the present work is intended to help bridge that gap. It seeks to provide all relevant historical information and sufficient stylistic comment to illustrate and explicate the literary and rhetorical texture of Ciceronian oratory. It is hoped that the edition will be of use not only to students of Latin but to the many who nowadays study the Classics chiefly in translation.

I am indebted to Professors A.E. Douglas and P.G. Walsh and to my colleague Mr A.E. Hinds for valuable assistance with a number of Latin passages. I also wish to thank Rosemary Doran, secretary of the School of Classics at Trinity, for her cheerful and efficient help in preparing the manuscript. My greatest debt, as always, is to my wife Lynn, who provides unfailing help and encouragement in all my endeavours.

INTRODUCTION

1. The Extortion Court

The system of provincial administration that emerged during the great era of Roman expansion following the Second Punic War made little provision for the protection of provincials against abuse of power by governors and their staffs. When instances of such abuse arose, as they did with increasing frequency in the first half of the second century, they were dealt with by a variety of improvised expedients. The more egregious forms of wrongdoing brought prosecutions before the people, generally on the initiative of tribunes. Occasionally such cases were dealt with by special courts established by statute for the occasion.[1] In instances where unjust exactions of goods or money were the chief complaint, a form of civil procedure might be employed, under which a praetor, acting on instructions from the senate, appointed a panel of senatorial assessors (*recuperatores*) to adjudicate the charges and estimate the damages.[2]

But these makeshift responses to particular cases proved totally inadequate, and in 149 a more systematic attempt was made to deal with malfeasance in the provinces in a law, the *Lex Calpurnia*, introduced by a tribune, L. Calpurnius Piso. Under this law injured provincials were given access to a praetor (presumably the *praetor peregrinus*), who, if satisfied that there was a *prima facie* case, appointed from a standing panel a board of senatorial judges and conducted a hearing in accordance with the civil procedure known as *actio sacramento*. The case of the provincials was argued by Roman advocates (*patroni*), and the penalty on conviction was simple restitution. The measure built on the earlier uses of senatorial *recuperatores* and retained existing procedures of the civil law, but it represented a significant advance in that it gave legal definition to the charge of extortion and established a specific, permanent legal machinery to deal with it.[3]

The next major development in the history of the extortion court occurred during the tribunates of Gaius

Gracchus in 123-22, when a new extortion law, known as the *Lex Acilia*, was enacted by the tribune, M'. Acilius Glabrio, who was most likely a political collaborator of Gracchus.[4] Portions of this law have been preserved on a bronze tablet, commonly referred to as the *tabula Bembina*.[5] It gave Rome's allies and subjects the right to initiate a prosecution against former magistrates, or against senators or their sons for the recovery of property unjustly seized. They could conduct the prosecution themselves or could request Roman *patroni*. A successful prosecution brought a reward of citizenship and exemption from military service for those who were the main agents of it.

The procedure prescribed for the trial was as follows. The accusation was made to the praetor in charge of the court, a process termed *nominis delatio*. The praetor, after obtaining a sworn statement that a false charge (*calumnia*) was not being made, instituted a judicial inquiry (*quaestio*) before a jury of 50 selected from a standing panel (*album*) of 450, which was to be drawn up each year by the praetor appointed to the court. The selection of the jury from the *album* was made by the plaintiff and defendant. Relatives and close associates of both sides were excluded; the plaintiff nominated 100 from the remainder, and the defendant selected from those the final 50. Jurors were no longer to come from the senate. Under the new law they had to be between the ages of 30 and 60, could not be magistrates or ex-magistrates, and could not be senators, or fathers, brothers, or sons of senators. The positive qualification is missing from the inscription, but later references describe the new jurors as *equites*, which could mean they had to have the census-rating necessary for enrollment in the equestrian centuries, or had to have been formally enrolled.[6] In any event, they would come largely from the growing business class, comprising financiers and traders (*negotiatores*) and the public companies (*publicani*) who took state contracts. It was a class sharply distinct from the senatorial order and, given its special interests, unlikely always to be in sympathy with senatorial concerns and actions.

After the jury was empanelled, the plaintiff was authorized to conduct inquiries in Italy in connection with his case (*inquisitio*), and was given a certain number of days to do so. The evidence to be presented could come from documents or witnesses. The plaintiff was entitled to summon up to 48 witnesses, who could be compelled by order of the praetor to attend and testify.

After hearing the evidence and arguments, the jury commenced deliberations (*in consilium ire*). If more than one-third were unable to decide a verdict, judgement was deferred pending a further hearing (*ampliatio*), but after two such deferrals, a verdict had to be reached under penalty of a heavy fine. If the verdict was guilty the jury had then to assess the damages. (*litis aestimatio*), which the law decreed should be double the amount estimated to have been illegally extorted.

The *Lex Acilia* was a highly innovative law. It viewed extortion primarily as a crime and devised a legal process that was more suited to the investigation and punishment of criminal acts than were the essentially civil procedures of the *Lex Calpurnia*. The *actio sacramento* was replaced by a criminal indictment, which was brought before a large and carefully selected board of judges, who were *iudices* rather than *recuperatores*, primarily concerned to judge guilt or innocence. Though the initiation and conduct of prosecutions was left to private individuals, the incentives to prosecute, the *inquisitio*, the enforced attendance of prosecution witnesses, and the imposition of punitive damages represented a significant involvement by the state to help insure the conviction and punishment of offenders. The procedure served as a model for other permanent criminal courts that were soon to emerge, and was therefore an important step not only in the development of the extortion court, but in the evolution of the entire system of Roman criminal justice.

Several other extortion laws were passed during the next half-century, but they were mostly concerned with the composition of juries, an issue that became a major source of political controversy as tension between the ruling class and the equestrian order increased in the final decades of the second century, and it became apparent that control of criminal courts that dealt with political crimes was potentially a powerful political weapon.[7] In 106 the consul Q. Servilius Caepio sought to end the equestrian monopoly of jury service in the extortion court by a law (the *Lex Servilia Caepionis*) decreeing that juries should be drawn from a mixed panel of senators and *equites*.[8] The arrangement was repealed a few years later by a law of the tribune C. Servilius Glaucia (the *Lex Servilia Glauciae*), which returned full control of the extortion court to the *equites*. Glaucia's law also abolished *ampliatio* (cf. above p. 3), substituting a compulsory adjournment followed by a full second hearing, after which the jury was required to reach a verdict.[9]

Sulla, in his comprehensive reform and expansion of the system of standing criminal courts in 81, altered the composition of juries once again, prescribing that juries in all the criminal courts should be empanelled from the senate. To meet the increased demand for jurors created by the expanded system, the senate was enlarged from 300 to 600. The jury-list (*album iudicum*) was compiled annually, as under the *Lex Acilia*, the task of selection most likely falling to the *praetor urbanus*.[10] Individual juries were not drawn from the entire panel, but from subdivisions known as *decuriae*, which were apparently arranged in a numbered sequence and assigned in order as prosecutions arose, one *decuria* to each case.[11] The empanellment of the jury from the *decuria* was done by lot, sufficient numbers being chosen to allow for challenges (*reiectio*) by the main accuser and defendant. On the evidence of the Verrines, it would seem that a senator was entitled to reject six names, but a non-senator only three.[12] The final size of a Sullan jury was considerably less than that prescribed by the *Lex Acilia*. Cicero records that 32 jurors sat in judgement at the murder trial of Oppianicus in 74. There is no definite evidence for other courts, but there is no reason to suppose the same size did not prevail throughout the system.[13] Sulla had therefore radically altered the size, composition, and mode of selection of juries, though it does not appear that he made any other significant change in the existing legislation on extortion.

The controversy over juries surfaced again in the latter half of the 70's as part of a broader attack by a succession of dissident tribunes on oligarchic and repressive aspects of Sulla's legislation. The senate was eventually forced to make major concessions to placate burgeoning popular discontent, and in 70 two major reforms were implemented. One, sponsored by the consuls Pompey and Crassus, restored the powers of tribunes, the other (the *Lex Aurelia*), enacted by a praetor L. Aurelius Cotta shortly after the trial of Verres, ruled that juries should be drawn from three groups: senators, *equites*, and *tribuni aerarii*.[14] The *album iudicum* now comprised three distinct and equal groups; each was divided into an equal number of *decuriae*, and one *decuria* from each group was assigned to each case. Larger juries of about 75 resulted, presumably chosen as before from the *decuriae* by lot, with provision for challenges.[15] The *Lex Aurelia* proved a satisfactory and enduring compromise, and brought to an end the major developments in the operation of the extortion court during the Republic.

2. The Career of Verres

C. Verres was born around 115 B.C., and was the son of a senator who was most likely one of the many new men elevated to the senate by Cinna in the mid-eighties. He had previously served as a tribal official responsible for distributing gifts to tribesmen (*divisor*).[16] Verres himself began his public life as a supporter of the Cinnan regime. He was elected to the quaestorship for 84 and served under the consul Cn. Papirius Carbo. He continued in the latter's service, probably as proquaestor, in 83, but in the course of the year deserted him for Sulla, taking with him the funds that had been allotted for Carbo's army. He was rewarded by Sulla with land confiscated from proscribed persons in the area of Beneventum. His next public assignment came in 80 when he served as a *legatus* under Cn. Dolabella, proconsul in Cilicia. His depredations and varied misdeeds in this office are recorded in detail in Verrines II.1 (41-102). He escaped retribution, however, by agreeing to testify against his commander, Dolabella, who was convicted of extortion in 78. He went on to become *praetor urbanus* in 74, after which he governed Sicily until the end of 71.

Verres had fared well in the overcrowded and highly competitive world of post-Sullan politics. His advancement to the praetorship was a considerable achievement for a man of his obscure lineage, in a period when only two out of every five new senators could achieve that office. He had also succeeded in gaining the friendship of a number of leading nobles. Foremost among them was the celebrated orator Q. Hortensius, who dominated the law courts in the 70's and was a prominent member of the Sullan oligarchy and a close associate of many of its most influential leaders, such as Q. Catulus and L. Lucullus. Hortensius became Verres' chief defence counsel, and greatly increased the value of his support by gaining election to the consulship in July of 70.

Verres also enjoyed the friendship of three brothers from

the powerful Metellan clan, Quintus, Marcus, and Lucius. They were grandsons of the great Metellus Macedonicus and sons of Metellus Caprarius, consul of 113. As in the case of Hortensius, their high prestige and influence was given a further boost in 70 when Quintus was elected to the consulship, Marcus to the praetorship, and Lucius became governor of Sicily in succession to Verres. Two other distinguished politicians can be added to the list of Verres' friends in high places: P. Scipio Nasica, a cousin of the Metellan brothers, and L. Cornelius Sisenna, a longtime friend of Hortensius, who had been praetor in 78 and governor of Sicily in 77.[17]

Verres' political success and influence may have been due in part to his father, who had practised a profession that brought contacts and knowledge of the mechanics of political intrigue and who seems to have been a masterful political manipulator. Verres had accumulated sufficient wealth to allow full exploitation of his father's expertise in political bribery and machination, and Cicero's allegations that Verres bribed his way into the praetorship may well have some substance.[18] Money may also have helped forge his aristocratic friendships. Cicero implies more than once that Hortensius' support was sustained by bribes, and he openly claims that Verres funded the electoral campaigns of the Metellan brothers in 70.[19] Political cooperation had further strengthened Verres' links with Hortensius. As praetor in 74 he had presided at the trial of Q. Opimius, who was charged with defying during his tribunate in 75 Sulla's limitations on the tribune's right of veto. Opimius was an outspoken dissident, and had deeply offended a number of leading nobles, notably Hortensius and Catulus. They were bent on an exemplary punishment, and Verres dispensed it, imposing a crushing fine after a cursory trial.[20] Such collaboration with the powerful was typical of Verres' political style, and this astute opportunism combined with effective use of his wealth had brought him a place of considerable prominence and influence in Roman politics. Cicero was facing a formidable adversary in his first prosecution.

3. The Trial

Verres' government of Sicily from 73-71 was marked by unusual cruelty and rapacity even by the standards of his time, and long before the end of his term complaints about the excesses of his administration were being made in Rome by prominent Sicilians. A concerted effort to bring him to justice followed quickly on his departure from office. All the Sicilian states, with the exception of Syracuse and Messana, joined in sending delegations to Rome to find a suitable *patronus* to handle their case.[21] Cicero was the obvious choice. He had served as quaestor in Sicily in 75 and had earned a high reputation for fairness and integrity among the Sicilians. Many of them had become his friends and clients and had strong claims on his support. He was, besides, among the most outstanding legal advocates in Rome in the late seventies after a decade of tireless and highly successful activity in the courts.[22]

He was easily persuaded to take the case. Like many politicians of his time he valued his provincial connections and was eager to cement them. The case also offered other benefits. Despite his success in the courts, and a promising beginning to his political career, which saw his election at the head of the poll to the quaestorship for 75, Cicero, as a new man (*novus homo*), faced an uphill struggle in his quest for the higher political offices in a society where the political system and political sentiment strongly favoured the highborn. He lacked the network of influential connections, clients, and longtime supporters inherited by most of his noble competitors. He also lacked the illustrious name, a powerful asset in a class-conscious society strongly partial to high birth and suspicious of those who sought to rise above their station. The new man had to prove his worth and win a name by his own achievements. The courts provided the readiest means of achieving recognition of talent and initiative in the world of the late Republic, and Cicero had used this route to distinction to good effect, but he had never conducted an *illustris accusatio*, the prosecution of a prominent politician, a time-honoured practice of younger politicians that was highly commended and had often brought quick fame to the politically obscure.[23]

The case of Verres provided Cicero with a particularly good opportunity to exploit the political benefits of such a prosecution at a critical point in his career. The trial was certain to arouse wide public interest. Verres was a well-known figure with famous friends; his corruption was notorious, and he was coming to trial at a time when the controversy over juries was focusing particular attention on the criminal courts. Cicero could move into the limelight as a concerned patriot seeking to preserve honest government in the provinces and an honest judicial system to deal with corrupt governors. The high rank and oratorical brilliance of his opponent, Q. Hortensius, would further increase the fruits of victory. It was a cause célèbre for varied reasons, ideally suited to serve the needs of a parvenu who was still striving to surmount the drawbacks of *novitas*.[24]

Cicero conducted the prosecution with energy and skill. He presented his request for permission to prosecute to the praetor of the extortion court, M'. Acilius Glabrio, in January of 70, a procedure known as *postulatio*, which by the post-Sullan era had become established as a necessary first step in a criminal prosecution. Another application to prosecute, presumably inspired by Verres in an attempt to get a collusive prosecutor, was lodged by Q. Caecilius Niger, who had served as Verres' quaestor in Sicily. This required the praetor to conduct a hearing (*divinatio*) before a jury, at which the rival applicants pressed their claims in set speeches and the jury determined which should be officially authorized to act as prosecutor. Cicero won this preliminary round, and proceeded to the next stage, the *nominis delatio*, which involved submitting a formal statement of the charge. After its acceptance (*nominis receptio*) he requested and received 110 days for the preparation of his case (*inquisitio*). He considered this the minimum time necessary, since he would have to travel to Sicily to procure witnesses and gather documents. It meant the case would be due to come to trial around the beginning of May.

At this stage Hortensius and Verres began manoeuvring to have the trial drag on into the following year, when conditions might be more favourable to Verres with a new president in the extortion court and with Hortensius most likely holding the consulship. Their first strategem was to initiate another prosecution for extortion against a former governor of Achaea. The prosecutor involved, whose name is unknown, asked for 108 days to conduct his *inquisitio*. This meant that his case came to court before that of Verres, delaying the latter, according to Cicero, for three months, during which attempts were made to discourage the witnesses from Sicily by circulating rumours that Cicero had agreed to a bribe to mismanage the prosecution. Finally, in the latter half of July, just before the consular elections, the proceedings in the Verrine trial commenced with the selection of the jury. Cicero was highly pleased with the jury that emerged. The selection by lot from the *decuria* assigned to the case and Cicero's careful challenging produced a panel of high distinction and integrity. Verres was temporarily dismayed, as the likelihood of acquittal by bribery receded, but soon his hopes were raised again with the election to the consulship of his friends, Q. Hortensius and Q. Metellus, and the appointment to the presidency of the extortion court for 69 of the praetor-elect, M. Metellus. Efforts to impede the prosecution and extend the trial into 69 were renewed. A campaign of bribery was launched to bring about Cicero's defeat at the aedilician elections, which followed soon after those for the consulship and praetorship. That failed utterly, as Cicero emerged at the top of the poll. The consul-elect, Q. Metellus, summoned the Sicilians and tried to intimidate them by reminding them of the increased influence of himself and his brothers and warning that numerous measures were being taken to insure Verres' acquittal. That too had little effect. But a strategy to prolong the trial into 69 held greater promise of success. The case was due to open on August 5th. Votive Games to celebrate Pompey's successful conclusion of the Sertorian war would begin on August 16th and extend through September 1. These would be followed by the *Ludi Romani*, which were held from September 4th to the 19th. Only the court dealing with crimes of political violence could sit during such public holidays. Hortensius expected that Cicero's presentation of the charges would take most of the time available before the beginning of the Votive Games and that he would be able to postpone his own reply until after September 19th. He then intended, by means of his own speech and by finding excuses for delay, to prolong the proceedings until the start of the Games of Victory on October 27th. These would be followed immediately by the Plebeian Games, lasting from November 4th to the 17th. After that there were very few days remaining in the year on which the courts could sit, and the extension of the trial into 69 would be unavoidable.

The benefits for Verres of such an extension had increased greatly since the elections. He would have a friend, M. Metellus, as president of the court, and could hope to have a friendlier jury as well. Eight members of the original panel were due to enter various offices in 69 and would have to be replaced. The selection of their substitutes by lot (*subsortitio*) would be conducted by Metellus. It would be easy to insure that well-disposed or manipulable replacements emerged.

Cicero was well aware of the strategy of the defence and of the implications of its success, and he was determined to defeat it. He decided to omit the customary long opening speech detailing all the charges (*accusatio perpetua*) and to proceed, after a short introductory address, to the hearing of witnesses and documents. This not only saved the time that would have been spent in presenting a detailed indictment, but also prevented the prosecution taking time to make a detailed rebuttal. The result was that Cicero was able to take the case through the first hearing (*actio prima*) to the compulsory adjournment (*comperendinatio*) before the Votive Games began on August 16th.[25]

The second hearing never took place. The speed of the trial and the mountain of evidence presented by Cicero convinced Verres that he had no hope of acquittal, and he withdrew into exile at Massilia, taking with him as much of his ill-gotten gains as he could. Cicero subsequently published the brief speech he had actually delivered to the jury, and he added to it five others, generally known as the Verrine Orations, which he would have delivered if Verres had not abandoned his defence. They comprised the *accusatio perpetua* that he had deliberately omitted at the first hearing, and their publication would demonstrate the thoroughness and oratorical skill that circumstances had prevented him exhibiting in full measure at the trial. Verres lived on at Massilia until 43, when he was proscribed by Mark Antony, reportedly for refusing to hand over his art treasures. And so he died around the same time and at the hands of the same man as Cicero.[26]

4. The Political Implications of the Trial

The prosecution of Verres is often linked to the political events of the late seventies and presented as promoting the cause of judicial reform by exposing the extreme corruption flourishing under senatorial rule, or as serving the interests of Pompey, who needed to protect his Sicilian clients and was eager to defeat the oligarchic coterie centred around the Metelli, who were befriending Verres and were bitter rivals of himself. Cicero is accordingly seen as an ally of the reformers or as a Pompeian partisan.[27]

There is little direct evidence to support such theories and much that would seem to contradict them. Verres had some friends among the *nobilitas*, but, as a Cinnan renegade of obscure and less than reputable parentage, he stood well apart from the Sullan oligarchy, and his misdeeds, however monstrous, could not readily be presented as typifying the behaviour or moral standards of the senate's leadership. Besides, many prominent members of the oligarchy came forth to testify against him. It was only his acquittal that could have aided the cause of those who were seeking a transfer of the courts, but in the event Verres was convicted, and in a manner that vindicated rather than impugned the integrity of senatorial juries.

The time at which the trial took place also militates against the notion that the case affected the course or resolution of the controversy over juries. By early August when the first hearing began, there can have been little controversy remaining. Cotta's bill was to appear within weeks and the elaborate compromise it offered, which was part of a wider process of constitutional adjustment in 70, and which passed into law without opposition from any segment and endured for the remainder of the Republic, must have involved careful deliberation and negotiation and have been worked out and agreed by various interests long before the revelations in the Verrine case began to be heard. Such a balanced and durable solution to a longterm dispute can hardly have sprung suddenly into being under the prompting of a criminal prosecution. The coincidence in time between its promulgation and the trial of Verres might suggest a link, but in fact makes unlikely a significant connection.[28]

As for the notion that the trial became an arena for a factional fight, the supporters and opponents of Verres do not readily divide into factional groupings. Among the most notable of those who testified for the prosecution were three members of the clan of the Claudii Marcelli; Cn. Cornelius Lentulus consul in 72 and censor in 70; M. Terentius Varro Lucullus and C. Cassius Longinus, consuls in 73; and L. Domitius Ahenobarbus, cousin of Catulus and brother-in-law of Cato, and future consul of 54.[29] They all had personal reasons for their involvement as friends or patrons of Verrine victims. They may all have also been friends of one another, but they formed no formal faction and certainly were not political foes of

Verres' main supporters, Hortensius and the Metellan brothers. Neither were they particular friends of Pompey, who, in any event, appears to have had only the most peripheral involvement in the case. Appeals were made to him as consul-elect and as consul by the Sicilians, but there is no evidence of a positive response or of supportive statements such as were submitted by other friends of the Sicilians.[30] Nor does Cicero claim him as an ally. His allusions to Pompey in the Verrines are few and fleeting, and none suggest even passive support for the prosecution. This sparing use of Pompey's name is highly significant in light of Cicero's usual care to exploit to the full in criminal cases the authority and popularity of powerful supporters.[31]

In summary, the prosecution of Verres was simply another in the long succession of extortion trials that mark the late Republic, differing, if at all, only in the unusual notoriety of the defendant and the unusual oratorical brilliance of the opposing advocates. Those who were involved on either side were motivated, as was usual, by the personal demands imposed by ties of friendship and patronage. Cicero, in taking the case, was coming to the help of valued clients and availing of an opportunity to boost his reputation and political prospects. He was not allying himself with any political movement or leader or faction. He presented himself as a concerned senator and patriotic citizen seeking to serve the state and justice. It was a predictable stance, calculated to conciliate a senatorial jury and impress the wider public. It had no deeper political significance.

5. The Transmission of the Text

The text of the Verrines is based on two families of manuscripts, one of which circulated in northern France and Germany, the other in Italy. The main manuscripts relevant to Verrines II.1 in the northern group are as follows: *Regius Parisinus* 7774A, known as R, which was written in the mid-ninth century. The surviving manuscript covers only Verrines II.4-5, but it seems likely that it once contained the whole of the Verrines and that derived from it is *Parisinus* 7775, known as S, which was written in the mid-twelfth century and contains Verrines II.1.90-111 as well as II.4-5. A careful copy of S, *Parisinus* 7823, known as D, was made in the fifteenth century, and provides a text of Verrines II.1 from the beginning up to section 111.

The most important manuscript in the Italian group is *Parisinus* 7776, known as p, which was written in the second half of the eleventh century and contains all the Verrine speeches. It has many corrections and interpolations, however, and is considered inferior to the main manuscripts of the northern family.

In addition, there survives a Vatican palimpsest, known as V, which contains parts of all five speeches of the *actio secunda* and dates from the third century. It is by far the earliest authority for the Verrines, and, though it seems to be based on a number of different recensions, it has considerable value.

I have used the text of Peterson, which represented a major advance over earlier editions, and I wish to convey my thanks to Oxford University Press for permission to use it. I have questioned a few of the readings, and have given the reasons in the relevant places in the commentary.

NOTES TO THE INTRODUCTION

1. The main examples are cited by Lintott (3), 165ff. and Gruen (1), 9ff.
2. Cf. Livy 43.2; *Per*. 47.
3. *Brut*. 106. *Off*. 2.75. *Verr*. 3.195; 4.56. Some scholars have argued the measure was designed to protect senators, but this directly contradicts the evidence of Cicero (cf. *In Caec*. 17-18) and assumes the ruling class were not concerned about the good name and good faith of Rome. Cf. *Off*. 2.27. Tacitus, *Ann*. 15.20. Gruen (1), 13ff. Ferguson, 86-100.
4. Acilius was also father of the praetor who presided at the trial of Verres (*Verr*. 1.51). We have references to another extortion law, a *Lex Junia*, passed before the *Lex Acilia*, but efforts to date it or identify its provisions have proved fruitless.
5. The tablet was part of a collection of Cardinal Bembo and is now in the Museo Nazionale in Naples. There has been much debate as to whether the law on the tablet is the *Lex Acilia*, but there is now substantial agreement that it is. Cf. Balsdon (1), 108ff. Lintott (3), 182ff.
6. The question continues to be debated. Cf. *Verr*. 1.38. Velleius 2.6. Tacitus, *Ann*. 12.60. Pliny, *NH* 33.34. Nicolet (1), 513ff. Badian (2), 65.
7. The conviction of the upright Rutilius Rufus by an equestrian jury in 92, in retaliation for his curtailment of the activities of *publicani* in Asia, showed the importance of controlling the criminal courts. Cf. *Brut*. 115. *De Or*. 1.230. *Pis*. 95.
8. For the judicial legislation between C. Gracchus and Sulla, cf. Griffin, 108-26.
9. *Brut*. 224. *Verr*. 2.1.26. Asconius 21, Clark.
10. The *praetor urbanus* held this responsibility after 70 (*Cluent*. 121) and most likely had assumed it after multiple permanent courts emerged.
11. Cf. *Verr*. 2.2.79. Greenidge (1), 438-39. It seems likely that each *decuria* contained senators of all grades. This

was certainly true for the Verrine jury. Cf. McDermott, 64-75.
12. *Verr.* 2.1.18; 2.2.77; 2.3.97; 2.5.114.
13. *Cluent.* 74. Cicero's statement in *Verr.* 1.30 that practically the entire Verrine jury would be changed after January 1st, when in fact only eight members would be replaced, is most likely a characteristic touch of hyperbole, and cannot be taken as precise evidence for the size of Sullan juries.
14. The *tribuni aerarii* were officials appointed by the censors to act as army paymasters. The money for army pay came from the property tax (*tributum*), and it is very likely that the task of collecting it was also a responsibility of the *tribuni*. Even after these functions ceased with the abolition of the *tributum* in 167 B.C., the *tribuni* clearly continued to be enrolled by the censors and to form an official, registered group. All indications are that they had always been well-to-do citizens, and it is very unlikely that they had a census-rating below that of the equestrian order. Cf. Varro, *LL* 5.181. Nicolet (2), 162ff. Wiseman (3), 71, 79.
15. Cf. *Pis.* 96. *Flacc.* 4. *Q.F.* 3.4.1. Asconius 28, Clark.
16. Cf. *Verr.* 2.1.35; 2.3.161.
17. *Verr.* 1.21, 26-28; 2.2.64, 110; 2.3.122, 153; 2.4.43, 79-81.
18. Cf. *Verr.* 1.22; 2.2.96-97, 102; 2.4.45.
19. Cf. *Verr.* 1.26; 2.2.192; 2.3.9.
20. *Verr.* 2.1.155-56. Ps. Asconius 255, Stangl.
21. *Verr.* 2.1.122; 2.2.83-118; 2.3.45, 204; 2.4.41, 136-37. *In Caec.* 14.
22. *In Caec.* 2-5, 11, 14. *Planc.* 64-66. *Brut.* 319.
23. Cf. *In Caec.* 66, 70-72. *Verr.* 2.2.117-18; 2.3.1-9.
24. Cicero describes the case as *maximum certamen* in *Brut.* 319. For his patriotic pose cf. *Verr.* 1.34ff.; 2.1.15ff.
25. Cf. *Verr.* 1.18-34; 2.1.16-20, 30-31.
26. Pliny, *NH* 34.6. Seneca, *Suas.* 6.24. Lactantius 2.4.37.
27. Cf. Stockton, 43ff. *Cambridge Ancient History*, 9.336ff. Badian (3), 278ff.
28. *Verr.* 5.177-78 indicates that Cotta's bill was promulgated soon after the first hearing. The question of its connection with the Verrine trial is more fully discussed in my book *Cicero: The Ascending Years*, 108-49.
29. *In Caec.* 13-14; *Verr.* 2.1.135, 139; 2.2.23; 2.3.97; 2.5.15.

30. Cf. *Verr.* 2.3.45, 204.
31. In his defence of Cornelius in 65 Cicero had gone out of his way to drag in the name and sing the praises of Pompey, an *amicus* of Cornelius. Cf. Quint. 4.3.13. For the impact of authoritative figures on juries cf. *De Or.* 2.196. *Mur.* 59. *Sulla* 10.

ABBREVIATIONS

AJP   *American Journal of Philology*

CP   *Classical Philology*

CQ   *Classical Quarterly*

CR   *Classical Review*

JRS   *Journal of Roman Studies*

PCPS   *Proceedings of the Cambridge Philological Society*

PBSR   *Papers of the British School at Rome*

RhM   *Rheinisches Museum für Philologie*

BIBLIOGRAPHY

Alexander, M.
(1) "Compensation in a Roman Criminal Law", *University of Illinois Law Review* (1984), 521-39.
(2) "*Praemia* in the *Quaestiones* of the Late Republic", *CP* 80 (1985), 20-32.
(3) "Repetition of Prosecution, and the Scope of Prosecutions, in the Standing Criminal Courts of the Late Republic", *Classical Antiquity* 1 (1982), 141-66.
(4) "Hortensius' Speech in Defense of Verres", *Phoenix* 30 (1976), 46-53.
Astin, A.E.   "Censorships in the Late Republic", *Historia* 34 (1985), 175-90.
Badian, E.
(1) "Manius Acilius Glabrio and the *audacissimi*", *AJP* 96 (1975), 67-75.
(2) *Publicans and Sinners*. Oxford, 1972.
(3) *Foreign Clientelae*. Oxford, 1958.
Balsdon, J.P.V.D.
(1) "History of the Extortion Court at Rome 123-70 B.C.", *PBSR* 14 (1938), 98-114.
(2) *Romans and Aliens*. London, 1979.
Broughton, T.R.S.
(1) *The Magistrates of the Roman Republic*. 2 vols. New York, 1951-52.
(2) *An Economic Survey of Ancient Rome*. Edited by T. Frank, Vol. IV. Baltimore, 1933.
Brunt, P.A.
(1) "*Nobilitas* and *Novitas*", *JRS* 72 (1982), 1-17.
(2) "*Amicitia* in the Late Roman Republic", *PCPS* 11 (1965), 1-20.
Carcopino, J.   *Autour des Gracques*. Paris, 1928.
Clarke, M.L.
(1) *The Roman Mind*. London, 1956.
(2) *Rhetoric at Rome*. London, 1953.
Crook, J.A.   *Law and Life of Rome*. London, 1967.
Ferguson, W.S.   "The *Lex Calpurnia* of 149 B.C.", *JRS* 11 (1921), 86-100.

Finley, M.I. *Ancient Slavery and Modern Ideology.* London, 1980.
Gotoff, H.C. *Cicero's Elegant Style. An Analysis of the Pro Archia.* Chicago, 1979.
Greenidge, A.H.J.
  (1) *The Legal Procedure of Cicero's Time.* Oxford, 1901.
  (2) *Roman Public Life.* London, 1911.
Griffin, M.T. "Pre-Sullan *leges iudiciariae*", *CQ* 67 (1973), 108-26.
Gruen, E.S.
  (1) *Roman Politics and the Criminal Courts, 149-78 B.C.* Harvard, 1968.
  (2) *The Last Generation of the Roman Republic.* Berkeley, 1974.
  (3) "The Dolabellae and Sulla", *AJP* 87 (1966), 215-33.
  (4) *The Hellenistic World and the Coming of Rome.* 2 vols. Berkeley, 1984.
Guite, H. "Cicero's Attitude Towards the Greeks", *Greece and Rome* 9 (1962), 142-59.
Harris, W.V. *War and Imperialism in Republican Rome.* Oxford, 1979.
Hassall, M., Crawford, M., and Reynolds, J. "Rome and the Eastern Provinces at the End of the Second Century B.C.", *JRS* 64 (1974), 195-220.
Hellegouarc'h, J. *Vocabulaire latin des relations et des partis politiques sous la république.* Paris, 1963.
Henderson, M.I.
  (1) "The Establishment of the *Equester Ordo*", *JRS* 53 (1963), 61-72.
  (2) "The Process *De Repetundis*", *JRS* 41 (1951), 71-88.
Jolowicz, H.F. and Nicholas, B. *Historical Introduction to the Study of Roman Law.* Cambridge, 1972.
Jones, A.H.M.
  (1) *The Criminal Courts of the Roman Republic and Principate.* Oxford, 1972.
  (2) *Cities of the Eastern Roman Provinces.* Oxford, 1971.
  (3) *Studies in Roman Government and Law.* Oxford, 1960.
Kennedy, G. *The Art of Rhetoric in the Roman World.* Princeton, 1972.
Kunkel, W. *An Introduction to Roman Legal and Constitutional History.* Trans. J.M. Kelly. Oxford, 1966.
Lacey, W.K. *The Family in Classical Greece.* Ithaca, 1968.
Laughton, E.
  (1) "Cicero and the Greek Orators", *AJP* 82 (1961), 27-49.
  (2) *The Participle in Cicero.* Oxford, 1964.

Lintott, A.W.
(1) *Violence in Republican Rome.* Oxford, 1968.
(2) "*Provocatio.* From the Struggle of the Orders to the Principate", *Aufstieg und Niedergang der römischen Welt.* 1.2, Berlin, 1972, 226-67.
(3) "The *leges de repetundis* and Associate Measures under the Republic", *Zeitschrift der Savigny-Stiftung für Rechtgeschichte* 98 (1981), 162-211.
Long, G. *M. Tullii Ciceronis Orationes.* Vol. I. London, 1862.
McDermott, W.C. "The Verrine Jury", *RhM* 120 (1977), 64-75.
Magie, D. *Roman Rule in Asia Minor.* 2 Vols. Princeton, 1950.
Mattingly, H.B.
(1) "The Character of the *Lex Acilia Glabrionis*", *Hermes* 107 (1979), 478-88.
(2) "The Two Republican Laws of the *Tabula Bembina*", *JRS* 59 (1969), 129-43.
Mitchell, T.N.
(1) *Cicero, the Ascending Years.* New Haven, 1979.
(2) "Cicero on the Moral Crisis of the Late Republic", *Hermathena* 86 (1984), 21-41.
Mommsen, Th., *Römisches Strafrecht.* Leipzig, 1899.
Nicolet, C.
(1) *L'Ordre équestre à l'époque républicaine.* (*312-43 av. J.-C.*) Paris, 1966.
(2) *The World of the Citizen in Republican Rome.* Trans. P.S. Falla. Berkeley, 1980.
Peterson, G. "Emendations of Cicero's Verrines", *CR* 17 (1903), 201.
Petrochilis, N. *Roman Attitudes to the Greeks.* Athens, 1974.
Pomeroy, S.B. *Goddesses, Whores, Wives and Slaves.* New York, 1975.
Rawson, E. *Intellectual Life in the Late Roman Republic.* London, 1985.
Schulz, F. *Classical Roman Law.* Oxford, 1951.
Seager, R. "Cicero and the Word *Popularis*", *CQ* 22 (1972), 328-38.
Shatzman, I.
(1) *Senatorial Wealth and Roman Politics.* Brussels, 1975.
(2) "The Roman General's Authority over Booty", *Historia* 21 (1972), 177-205.

Sherwin-White, A.N.
  (1) *"Poena Legis Repetundarum"*, PBSR 17 (1949), 5-25.
  (2) "The Extortion Procedure Again", JRS 42 (1952), 43-55.
  (3) *Roman Foreign Policy in the East.* London, 1984.
  (4) "Rome, Pamphylia and Cilicia", JRS 66 (1976), 1-14.
Smith, W.   *Dictionary of Greek and Roman Antiquities.* 2 Vols. London, 1890.
Stevenson, G.H.   *Roman Provincial Administration till the Age of the Antonines.* New York, 1939.
Stockton, D.   *Cicero. A Political Biography.* Oxford, 1971.
Taylor, L.R.
  (1) "Cicero's Aedileship", AJP 60 (1939), 194-202.
  (2) *Party Politics in the Age of Caesar.* Berkeley, 1949.
  (3) *Roman Voting Assemblies.* Ann Arbor, 1966.
Thompson, L.A.   "The Relationship between Provincial Quaestors and Their Commanders-in-Chief", *Historia* 11 (1962), 339-55.
Treggiari, S.   *Roman Freedmen during the Late Republic.* Oxford, 1969.
Watson, A.
  (1) *The Law of the Ancient Romans.* Dallas, 1970.
  (2) *Law Making in the Later Roman Republic.* Oxford, 1974.
  (3) *The Law of Succession in the Later Roman Republic.* Oxford, 1971.
  (4) *The Law of Persons in the Later Roman Republic.* Oxford, 1967.
  (5) *The Law of Property in the Later Roman Republic.* Oxford, 1968.
Wilkinson, L.P.   *Golden Latin Artistry.* Cambridge, 1966.
Wirszubski, W.   "*Audaces*: A Study in Political Phraseology", JRS 51 (1961), 12-22.
Wiseman, T.P.
  (1) "The Census in the First Century B.C.", JRS 59 (1969), 59-75.
  (2) *New Men in the Roman Senate 139 B.C. - 14 A.D.* Oxford, 1971.
  (3) "The Definition of *Eques Romanus* in the Late Republic and Early Empire", *Historia* 19 (1970), 67-83.
Woodcock, E.C.   *A New Latin Syntax.* Cambridge, Mass., 1959.
Yavetz, Z.   *Julius Caesar and His Public Image.* London, 1983.

SIGLA

S = Parisinus 7775, saecl. xiii, mutilus (ii. 1, §§ 90-111 *Dolabellae . . . istius singu*[*lari* continens)

D = Parisinus 7823, ineunte saecl. xv e cod. S nondum mutilato descriptus

G_2 = Guelferbytanus (41 Weissenburgensium) saecl. xv

L = Leidensis (Perizonianus 12) saecl. xv

K = Harleianus 4105, 'A.D. 1462' scriptus

Z = Harleianus 4852, saecl. xv

G_1 = Guelferbytanus (2652, Extravagantium) ad finem saecl. xv scriptus. Huius codicis gemellus est Parisinus 7822, scriptus anno 1471

s = codex S. Stephani

λ = codex Lambini

Hos omnes eiusdem esse familiae demonstravimus, cuius princeps est et parens mutilus cod. S (v. *Journal of Philology*, xxx. 161-207) : continent, praeter libros iv-v, priores orationes usque ad verba *istius singu*[*lari* ii. 1, § 111. Siglo G_3 consensum codicum G_1G_2L significaverunt editores. Nos omnium vel plurimorum in hoc genere codicum conspirationem nota Ψ indicavimus. Ipse cod. S et eius apographon D omnibus locis diserte citantur : $D\,al.$ = D aliique eiusdem familiae codices

V = fragmenta Palimpsesti Vaticani (Reginensis 2077) saecl. iii/iv. Continet ii. 1, §§ 105-114 docet hominem . . . usitata satis : §§ 119-130 videbantur quod . . . locavissent : §§ 137-139 Venit ad Ch. . . . esse deferre : §§ 142-148 bonis praedibus . . . existimationem con. : §§ 150-153 tabulae praedam . . . ut illorum : § 158 Q. Curtium . . . subsortiebatur. De hoc codice v. quae scripsimus *American Journal of Philology* (*Am.J.Ph.*), xxvi, pp. 409-436

p = Parisinus 7776, saecl. xi

q = Mediceus plut. xlviii, cod. 29, s. Lagomarsinianus 29, saecl. xv

r = Harleianus 2687, saecl. xv

π = consensus codicum pqr

b = cod. S. Marci 255, saecl. xv. Desinit in fine Actionis Secundae Lib. ii

δ = deteriores, e. g. Lagomarsiniani (*Lgg.*) et ceteri omnes e quibus initio constitutus est textus in libros impressos receptus

Citatur hic illic Parisinus 7786, saecl. xiv. Ad Cap. xvii Actionis Secundae Libri Primi commemoratur etiam fragmentum Palimpsesti Taurinensis

Asc. = Ps.-Asconius

M. TVLLI CICERONIS
ACTIONIS IN C. VERREM SECVNDAE

LIBER PRIMVS

DE PRAETVRA VRBANA

1 Neminem vestrum ignorare arbitror, iudices, hunc per hosce dies sermonem vulgi atque hanc opinionem populi Romani fuisse, C. Verrem altera actione responsurum non esse neque ad iudicium adfuturum. Quae fama non idcirco solum emanarat quod iste certe statuerat ac deliberaverat non adesse, verum etiam quod nemo quemquam tam audacem, tam amentem, tam impudentem fore arbitrabatur qui tam nefariis criminibus, tam multis testibus convictus ora iudicum aspicere aut os suum populo Romano ostendere auderet. **2** Est idem Verres qui fuit semper, ut ad audendum proiectus, sic paratus ad audiendum. Praesto est, respondet, defenditur; ne hoc quidem sibi reliqui facit ut, in rebus turpissimis cum manifesto teneatur, si reticeat et absit, tamen impudentiae suae pudentem exitum quaesisse videatur. Patior, iudices, et non moleste fero me laboris mei, vos virtutis vestrae fructum esse laturos. Nam si iste id fecisset quod prius statuerat, ut non adesset, minus aliquanto quam mihi opus esset cognosceretur quid ego in hac accusatione comparanda constituendaque elaborassem; vestra vero laus tenuis plane atque obscura, iudices,

---

8 testibus *prb Cuiac.* : iudicibus $D\Psi$ 10 est idem D *al. prb* : est enim idem q^1 *al.*   11 paratus *prō Schol. Gronov., Prisc.* : *om.* $D\Psi$
17 prius $D\Psi$: primus L : primo *prō*

THE SECOND SPEECH OF M.TULLIUS CICERO AGAINST VERRES

BOOK I: THE URBAN PRAETORSHIP

1   I. Gentlemen of the jury, I think none of you is unaware that in recent days it has been the common talk and the belief of the Roman people that C. Verres would not present himself for the second stage of the trial or attend the court. This rumour had not spread abroad merely because he had made a definite and deliberate decision not to attend, but also because nobody believed that anyone would be so brazen, demented, or shameless as to dare look on the faces of the jury or show his own face to the Roman people after being convicted of such wicked 2 crimes by so many witnesses. He is the same Verres as he ever was, as prepared to hear anything as he is prone to dare anything. He is here; he presents himself for trial; he offers a defence. He does not even leave open for himself the possibility that, though caught redhanded in the most disgraceful conduct, he might still seem, by remaining silent and staying away, to have looked for a decent ending to his indecencies. But I bear with it, gentlemen, and am in no way vexed that I shall reap the reward of my labour and you of your courage. For if he had carried out his initial decision not to attend, the amount of effort I expended in preparing and instituting this prosecution would be somewhat less well known than my needs require, while your praise, gentlemen, would be

3 esset. Neque hoc a vobis populus Romanus exspectat neque eo potest esse contentus, si condemnatus sit is qui adesse noluerit, et si fortes fueritis in eo quem nemo sit ausus defendere. Immo vero adsit, respondeat; summis opibus, summo studio potentissimorum hominum defendatur; certet mea diligentia cum illorum omnium cupiditate, vestra integritas cum illius pecunia, testium constantia cum illius patronorum minis atque potentia: tum demum illa omnia victa videbuntur cum in contentionem certamenque 4 venerint. Absens si esset iste damnatus, non tam sibi 2 consuluisse quam invidisse vestrae laudi videretur. Neque enim salus ulla rei publicae maior hoc tempore reperiri potest quam populum Romanum intellegere, diligenter reiectis ab accusatore iudicibus, socios, leges, rem publicam senatorio consilio maxime posse defendi; neque tanta fortunis omnium pernicies ulla potest accedere quam opinione populi Romani rationem veritatis, integritatis, fidei, re-
5 ligionis ab hoc ordine abiudicari. Itaque mihi videor [iudices] magnam et maxime aegram et prope depositam rei publicae partem suscepisse, neque in eo magis meae quam vestrae laudi existimationique servisse. Accessi enim ad invidiam iudiciorum levandam vituperationemque tollendam, ut, cum haec res pro voluntate populi Romani esset iudicata, aliqua ex parte mea diligentia constituta auctoritas iudiciorum videretur, *perperam si* esset hoc iudicatum, ut finis aliquando iudiciariae controversiae con-
6 stitueretur. Etenim sine dubio, iudices, in hac causa ea

1 neque *D*Ψ : neque enim *pr*δ 6 hominum *bG*₂ : nominum *p*₁ (*corr.* omnium) 7 istius *p Schol. Gronov.* δ 8 illa omnia *Dpr* : omnia illa *KZ al.* : omnia *om. b*δ 10 esset iste *D*Ψπ : iste esset *b*δ ipse sibi δ 12 enim *D al. pbr* : *om. G*₃ 16 ulla *pr Schol. Gronov.* : *om. D*Ψ*b* accedere *Dp rell.* : accidere *Manut.* (i § 39 : ii § 172 : iv § 2 : *Sest.* § 107 ; *cf. Cluent.* § 10) 18 abiudicari *pb* : -are *D*Ψ 19 iudices *Nonius, edd.* : *om. codd.* ac prope *Asc.* (i § 108) 25 perperam si *scripsi* (*Cl. Rev.* xvii. 201) : postremo ut *codd.* (utut *Muret.*, *Gulielm.*) : contra eam cum *Koch* : lacunam susp. *Iordan.*

3   slight indeed and dimly recognized. For this is not what the Roman people await from you, nor can they be content with it, that a man should be condemned who was not willing to appear, or that you should be resolute in the case of an individual whom no one dared defend. No, rather let him attend, let him present himself for trial, let him be defended with the greatest financial resources and with the most fervent support of very powerful men; let my diligence contend with the partisan zeal of all of them, your integrity with his money, the steadfastness of the witnesses with the threats and influence of his legal advocates: only then when all these recourses of theirs have been put to the test of a legal battle will they be
4   seen to have been worsted. Had Verres been condemned without appearing, he would seem not so much to have taken thought for his own interests as to have begrudged you your praise. II. For there is no greater source of safety for the state to be found at this time than a realisation on the part of the Roman people that, provided there is a careful challenging of jurors by the prosecutor, the allies, the laws, and the state can be protected to the greatest possible degree by a senatorial tribunal; nor can there come any greater source of destruction to the fortunes of all than a belief among the Roman people that the way of truth, integrity, good faith, and good conscience is being abolished by the judicial
5   verdicts of this order. I therefore think, gentlemen, that I have taken in hand an area of public affairs that is important and that is also very gravely ill and almost given up for lost, and that in doing this I have served your good name and reputation no less than my own. For I came to this case to reduce the ill-will against the courts and to abolish recrimination, seeking, if the matter was decided in accordance with the wishes of the Roman people, to have it appear that, to some extent at least, the authority of the courts had been set on a firm foundation by my diligence, and also seeking, however the case was finally decided, to bring an end at last to
6   the controversy surrounding the judiciary. For without a

res in discrimen adducitur. Reus est enim nocentissimus; qui si condemnatur, desinent homines dicere his iudiciis pecuniam plurimum posse; sin absolvitur, desinemus nos de iudiciis transferendis recusare.

Tametsi de absolutione istius neque ipse iam sperat nec 5 populus Romanus metuit: de impudentia singulari, quod adest, quod respondet, sunt qui mirentur. Mihi pro cetera eius audacia atque amentia ne hoc quidem mirandum videtur; multa enim et in deos et in homines impie nefarieque commisit, quorum scelerum poenis agitatur et 10
3
7 a mente consilioque deducitur. Agunt eum praecipitem poenae civium Romanorum, quos partim securi percussit, partim in vinculis necavit, partim implorantis iura libertatis et civitatis in crucem sustulit. Rapiunt eum ad supplicium di patrii, quod iste inventus est qui e complexu parentum 15 abreptos filios ad necem duceret, et parentis pretium pro sepultura liberum posceret. Religiones vero caerimoniaeque omnium sacrorum fanorumque violatae, simulacraque deorum, quae non modo ex suis templis ablata sunt sed etiam iacent in tenebris ab isto retrusa atque abdita, 20 consistere eius animum sine furore atque amentia non
8 sinunt. Neque iste mihi videtur se ad damnationem solum offerre, neque hoc avaritiae supplicio communi, qui se tot sceleribus obstrinxerit, contentus esse: singularem quandam poenam istius immanis atque importuna natura desiderat. 25 Non id solum quaeritur ut isto damnato bona restituantur iis quibus erepta sunt, sed et religiones deorum immortalium expiandae et civium Romanorum cruciatus multorumque
9 innocentium sanguis istius supplicio luendus est. Non

7 mirantur Z pro p^1 et pler.: propter s. l. p^2 et (om. cetera) $b\delta$
14 eum om. p 15 inventus est D rell. (iii § 21): unus inventus est Prisc. edd. e $D\Psi$: et e Garat. edd. (Act. Pr. § 39: iii § 175): ei π: ex Prisc. i. 306. 24, et a Prisc. ii. 264. 10 (v § 125) 17 liberum $Zp\delta$ Prisc. Non.: om. $G_{12}K$: add. in mg. D 26 non id solum quaeritur s. l. p^2 27 his pb

doubt, gentlemen, that issue is being brought to a resolution by this trial. For the accused is guilty in the extreme, and if he is condemned, people will stop saying that money rules supreme in these courts, but if he is acquitted, we will stop objecting to a transfer of judicial power.

Yet his acquittal is something he himself no longer hopes for, nor do the Roman people fear it, though his unparalleled impudence in attending the court and presenting himself for trial is a source of wonder to some. But to me, in view of his general reckless and mindless criminality, even this does not seem a cause for surprise. For he has committed many unholy and unspeakable acts against both gods and men, and the retribution owed for these crimes is tormenting him and depriving him of mind and reason. III. His punishments of Roman citizens, some of whom he beheaded, some killed in chains, some raised on a cross even while they invoked their rights as free men and citizens, are driving him headlong. The gods of his fatherland are hurrying him to his punishment, because he was the only man found ready to snatch sons from their parents' embrace and lead them to their death and to demand from the parents a price for the right to bury their children. Moreover, his violation of the sanctity and religious observances of all holy places and shrines, and the statues of the gods, which have not only been removed by him from their temples but have been cast out of sight and hidden away to lie in darkness, do not allow his mind to rest free of frenzy and insanity. And indeed he does not seem to me to be offering himself merely for condemnation nor, implicated as he is in so many crimes, to be content with the ordinary penalty for avarice; his savage and relentless nature longs for some unique punishment. And the goal being sought in this prosecution is not merely the restoration through this man's conviction of their property to those from whom it has been wrongfully taken; in addition, the offenses against the religion of the immortal gods must be expurgated and the sufferings of Roman citizens and the blood of many innocent people atoned for by his punishment. For we have brought

enim furem sed ereptorem, non adulterum sed expugna-
torem pudicitiae, non sacrilegum sed hostem sacrorum
religionumque, non sicarium sed crudelissimum carnificem
civium sociorumque in vestrum iudicium adduximus, ut
ego hunc unum eius modi reum post hominum memoriam 5
fuisse arbitrer cui damnari expediret.

4 Nam quis hoc non intellegit, istum absolutum dis
hominibusque invitis tamen ex manibus populi Romani
eripi nullo modo posse? Quis hoc non perspicit, praeclare
nobiscum actum iri si populus Romanus istius unius sup- 10
plicio contentus fuerit, ac non sic statuerit, non istum maius
in sese scelus concepisse,—cum fana spoliarit, cum tot
homines innocentis necarit, cum civis Romanos morte,
cruciatu, cruce adfecerit, cum praedonum duces accepta
pecunia dimiserit,—quam eos, si qui istum tot tantis tam 15
nefariis sceleribus coopertum iurati sententia sua liberarint?
10 Non est, non est in hoc homine cuiquam peccandi locus,
iudices; non is est reus, non id tempus, non id consilium,
(metuo ne quid adrogantius apud talis viros videar dicere),
ne actor quidem est is cui reus tam nocens, tam perditus, 20
tam convictus aut occulte subripi aut impune eripi possit.
His ego iudicibus non probabo C. Verrem contra leges
pecuniam cepisse? Sustinebunt tales viri se tot senatori-
bus, tot equitibus Romanis, tot civitatibus, tot hominibus
honestissimis ex tam inlustri provincia, tot populorum 25
privatorumque litteris non credidisse, tantae populi Romani
11 voluntati restitisse? Sustineant: reperiemus, si istum vivum
ad aliud iudicium perducere poterimus, quibus probemus
istum in quaestura pecuniam publicam Cn. Carboni consuli
datam avertisse, quibus persuadeamus istum alieno nomine 30

8 tamen *Naugerius* : eum *Dp et pler.* : tamen eum *Lgg* : *om. b*
14 cum praedonum . . . dimiserit π*b* : *om.* *D*Ψ   19 talis iudices *qr*
21 convictus *Halm* (ii, § 27) : victus *codd.*   24 equitibus ·r· *po* :
equitibus *D*Ψ   28 poterimus *D al. b* : potuerimus *p*δ

before your court not a thief but a plunderer, not an adulterer but a ravager of chastity, not a temple-robber but an enemy of sacred places and religious worship, not a murderer but a most cruel butcher of citizens and allies. He is such that I would consider him the one defendant in the history of man for whom condemnation would be a benefit.

IV. For who does not know that, even if he is acquitted against the wishes of gods and men, he still can in no way escape the hands of the Roman people? Who does not see that we will fare very well indeed if the Roman people are content with the punishment of this one individual and do not decide that he has committed no greater crime against them – though he has despoiled temples, killed so many innocent people, punished Roman citizens with death, torture, and crucifixion, released leaders of pirates for money – than those, if any there be, who, while under oath, set free by their vote a man buried deep in crimes so numerous, so enormous, and so unspeakable? There is not, there is not, I repeat, any scope for wrongdoing by anyone in relation to this man. This is not the defendant, not the time, not the tribunal, not even (here I fear I may seem to be speaking somewhat arrogantly before men such as you) the prosecutor to allow an accused man who is so guilty, so depraved, so clearly convicted to be spirited away unnoticed, or wrested away with impunity. With these men as judges shall I fail to prove that Verres took money illegally? Will such men have the gall not to believe so many senators, so many Roman knights, so many states, so many letters from communities and private individuals and to oppose so strong a wish of the Roman people? Suppose they do. We will find, if we can bring Verres alive before another court, jurors to whom we can prove that, in his quaestorship, he misappropriated public funds that had been assigned to the consul Cn. Carbo, and jurors whom we can persuade that he took money in another man's name from the urban quaestors, as you

a quaestoribus urbanis, quod priore actione didicistis, pecuniam abstulisse; erunt qui et in eo quoque audaciam eius reprehendant, quod aliquot nominibus de capite quantum commodum fuerit frumenti decumani detraxerit; erunt etiam fortasse, iudices, qui illum eius peculatum vel 5 acerrime vindicandum putent, quod iste M. Marcelli et P. Africani monumenta, quae nomine illorum, re vera populi Romani et erant et habebantur, ex fanis religiosissimis et ex urbibus sociorum atque amicorum non dubitarit auferre.

5
12 Emerserit ex peculatus etiam iudicio: meditetur de ducibus 10 hostium quos accepta pecunia liberavit, videat quid de illis respondeat quos in eorum locum subditos domi suae reservavit, quaerat non solum quem ad modum nostro crimini, verum etiam quo pacto suae confessioni possit mederi, meminerit se priore actione, clamore populi Romani 15 infesto atque inimico excitatum, confessum esse duces praedonum a se securi non esse percussos, se iam tum esse veritum ne sibi crimini daretur eos ab se pecunia liberatos; fateatur, id quod negari non potest, se privatum hominem praedonum duces vivos atque incolumis domi suae, postea- 20 quam Romam redierit, usque dum per me licuerit retinuisse. Hoc in illo maiestatis iudicio si licuisse sibi ostenderit, ego oportuisse concedam. Ex hoc quoque evaserit: proficiscar eo quo me iam pridem vocat populus
13 Romanus; de iure enim libertatis et civitatis suum putat 25 esse iudicium, et recte putat. Confringat iste sane vi sua consilia senatoria, quaestiones omnium perrumpat, evolet ex vestra severitate: mihi credite, artioribus apud populum Romanum laqueis tenebitur. Credet his equitibus Romanis populus Romanus qui ad vos ante producti testes ipsis 30

2 et *codd.* (*Div.* § 47) : *auct. Halm, Wesenberg, secl. Muell.* 9 dubitaverit δ   16–18 confessum . . . veritum *suppl. in mg. p*²   21 tenuisse *b*δ   24 me iam pridem *D al. p* : iam me pridem G_1 : me iam non pridem G_2 26 recte *Dp rell.* : ratione G_1 29 his *Dp* : iis *edd.*   30 antea *pb*δ

learned in the first stage of the trial. There will be people also to censure his criminal daring in deducting, by tampering with several entries, as much of the sum owing from the grain tithe as suited his purpose. Perhaps, gentlemen, there will even be those who will think that he should be punished most severely for his act of embezzlement in removing without scruple from the most sacred shrines and from the cities of allies and friends the monuments donated by M. Marcellus and P. Africanus, which in name were gifts of theirs, but in reality were gifts, and were considered to be gifts, of the Roman people. V. But suppose he escapes from the
12 embezzlement court also. Let him then think about the leaders of enemies of Rome that he set free for money; let him consider what to say about those he kept at his house as substitutes for these leaders; let him look for a means of counteracting not only our charge but also his own confession; let him recall that in the first stage of the trial, provoked by the angry and hostile outcries of the Roman people, he admitted that he had not beheaded leaders of the pirates and had been afraid at the time that he would be charged with having freed them for money; let him confess what cannot be denied, that as a private citizen he kept leaders of the pirates alive and well at his house, following his return to Rome, and did so for as long as I allowed him. If he shows in the treason court that he was entitled to do this, I will concede he was right to do it. Suppose he walks free from this court as well. I will then embark on the course
13 to which the Roman people have long been calling me. For they consider that, with regard to the right of freedom and citizenship, the judgement belongs to them, and they consider rightly. So let him break up with his violence the tribunals comprised of senators; let him force his way through courts comprised of any and all classes; let him escape your sternness; believe me he will be held with tighter bonds when he faces the Roman people. They will believe those Roman knights who were earlier brought

inspectantibus ab isto civem Romanum, qui cognitores homines honestos daret, sublatum esse in crucem dixerunt;
14 credent omnes v et xxx tribus homini gravissimo atque ornatissimo, M. Annio, qui se praesente civem Romanum securi percussum esse dixit; audietur a populo Romano vir 5 primarius, eques Romanus, L. Flavius, qui suum familiarem Herennium, negotiatorem ex Africa, cum eum Syracusis amplius centum cives Romani cognoscerent lacrimantesque defenderent, pro testimonio dixit securi esse percussum; probabit fidem et auctoritatem et religionem suam L. Suettius, 10 homo omnibus ornamentis praeditus, qui iuratus apud vos dixit multos civis Romanos in lautumiis istius imperio crudelissime per vim morte esse multatos. Hanc ego causam cum agam beneficio populi Romani de loco superiore, non vereor ne aut istum vis ulla ex populi Romani 15 suffragiis eripere, aut a me ullum munus aedilitatis amplius aut gratius populo Romano esse possit.

6
15 Quapropter omnes in hoc iudicio conentur omnia; nihil est iam quod in hac causa peccare quisquam, iudices, nisi vestro periculo possit. Mea quidem ratio cum in praeteritis 20 rebus est cognita, tum in reliquis explorata atque provisa est. Ego meum studium in rem publicam iam illo tempore ostendi cum longo intervallo veterem consuetudinem rettuli, et rogatu sociorum atque amicorum populi Romani, meorum autem necessariorum, nomen hominis audacissimi detuli. 25 Quod meum factum lectissimi viri atque ornatissimi, quo in numero e vobis complures fuerunt, ita probaverunt ut ei qui istius quaestor fuisset, et ab isto laesus inimicitias iustas persequeretur, non modo deferendi nominis, sed ne subscribendi 16 quidem, cum id postularet, facerent potestatem. In Siciliam 30

7 cum eum *pδ* : cum *D*Ψ : quem *Bake* (i, § 104)   10 Suettius *C. I. L.* iv. 1190 : Suetius *b* : Suectius *DpG*$_2$ (ii, § 31 ; v, § 147)   18 in hoc *D al. br* : hoc *pq, fort. recte* (i, § 63 ; ii, §§ 118, 133)   19 est enim *qr*   iudices quisquam *πb*   27 e numero *D al.*   probaverunt *Dp al.* : probarunt *δ* : comprobaverunt *qr*

14 before you as witnesses and testified that a Roman citizen had been raised on a cross by Verres before their eyes, though he was offering honourable men as guarantors of his identity. All thirty-five tribes will believe that most respected and distinguished gentleman, M. Annius, who said that a Roman citizen had been beheaded in his presence. The Roman people will listen to a leading citizen and Roman knight, L. Flavius, who said in evidence that his friend Herennius, a businessman from Africa, had been beheaded at Syracuse, although more than a hundred Roman citizens gave evidence of his identity and tearfully defended him. L. Suettius, a man who possesses every form of distinction and who testified before you under oath that many Roman citizens, on the orders of Verres, had been most cruelly punished by a violent death in the quarries, will convince his hearers of his good faith, reliability, and scrupulous integrity. When I plead this case from a loftier platform afforded me by favour of the Roman people, I have no fear that any form of violence can deliver this defendant from the judgement of the Roman people or that any public show provided by my aedileship can have more importance or be more pleasing to the Roman people.

15 VI. Therefore let anyone try anything he wishes in this court: there is no longer anything, gentlemen, that any of you can do amiss in this case except at your peril. My own line of action has become known from earlier events and has been carefully planned and preconsidered in relation to what remains to be done. I already showed my devotion to the state at the time when I restored an ancient practice after a long interval and, at the request of allies and friends of the Roman people, who were also intimate friends of my own, brought a charge against a most brazen criminal. My action met with such approval from the most outstanding and distinguished citizens, in whose number were many of you, that they refused a man who had been Verres' quaestor and was pursuing a just quarrel with him because of an injury he had suffered at his hands permission not only to bring the charge but to act as a subordinate accuser, though he was seeking
16 leave to do so. I set out for Sicily to gather evidence.

sum inquirendi causa profectus ; quo in negotio industriam
meam celeritas reditionis, diligentiam multitudo litterarum
et testium declaravit, pudorem vero ac religionem quod,
cum venissem senator ad socios populi Romani, qui in ea
provincia quaestor fuissem, ad hospites meos ac necessarios 5
causae communis defensor deverti potius quam ad eos qui
a me auxilium petivissent. Nemini meus adventus labori
aut sumptui neque publice neque privatim fuit: vim in
inquirendo tantam habui quantam mihi lex dabat, non
quantam habere poteram istorum studio quos iste vexarat. 10
17 Romam ut ex Sicilia redii, cum iste atque istius amici,
homines lauti et urbani, sermones eius modi dissipassent,
quo animos testium retardarent, me magna pecunia a vera
accusatione esse deductum, tametsi probabatur nemini,
quod et ex Sicilia testes erant ii qui quaestorem me in 15
provincia cognoverant, et hinc homines maxime inlustres,
qui, ut ipsi noti sunt, sic nostrum unum quemque optime
norunt, tamen usque eo timui ne quis de mea fide atque
integritate dubitaret donec ad reiciundos iudices venimus.
7 Sciebam in reiciundis iudicibus non nullos memoria 20
nostra pactionis suspicionem non vitasse, cum in ipsa
18 accusatione eorum industria ac diligentia probaretur. Ita
reieci iudices ut hoc constet, post hunc statum rei publicae
quo nunc utimur simili splendore et dignitate consilium
nullum fuisse. Quam iste laudem communem sibi ait 25
esse mecum ; qui cum P. Galbam iudicem reiecisset,
M. Lucretium retinuit, et cum eius patronus ex eo quaereret cur suos familiarissimos, Sex. Peducaeum, Q. Con-
sidium, Q. Iunium reici passus esset, respondit 'quod eos

9-10 non quantam ... vexarat p^2 in mg.   10 istorum Dp rell. :
illorum edd. : ipsorum Muell.   11 cum comites istius atque amici
Nonius   12 eius modi D al. π : huius modi b rell. (Div. § 38 ; ii, §§ 56,
60)   13 quo pbK : quos DG_1Z : per quos G_2 20 reiciendis p
21 ipsa in q 23 statum $\bar{p}.\bar{r}.\pi b$ 25 sibi ait esse $D\Psi\pi$: sibi esse
ait K : ait sibi esse $b\delta$

17 My energy in this task was shown by the speed of my return, my thoroughness by the multitude of documents and witnesses, and my restraint and scrupulous concern for right by the fact that, though I came as a senator to allies of the Roman people and had been a quaestor in the province, and though I was a defender of the public interest, I turned to my former hosts and intimates rather than to those who had sought my help. My arrival brought no trouble or expense, public or private, to anyone. I used as much authority in conducting my investigation as the law allowed me, but not as much as I could have as a result of the eager cooperation of those whom Verres had injured. When I returned to Rome from Sicily, Verres and his friends, men of respectability and refinement, in an effort to dampen the spirits of the witnesses, spread a rumour to the effect that I had been dissuaded from conducting a genuine prosecution by a large sum of money. Although no one believed it, both because the witnesses from Sicily were people who had known me when I was quaestor in the province and because those from here were especially distinguished and knew each of us as intimately as they were themselves known, I was nonetheless afraid right up to the time of challenging the jurors that someone might have doubts about my good faith and integrity.

VII. I was aware that some prosecutors within our memory had not escaped suspicion of collusion in relation to the challenging of jurors, though in the course of the prosecution itself their industry and diligence were 18 clearly proven. But I conducted the challenge in such a way that everyone agrees that, since the establishment of the present constitution of the state, there has not been a tribunal of equal distinction and prestige. Verres claims that he shares the praise for this with me; he who retained M. Lucretius as a juror while rejecting P. Galba and who told his defending counsel, when asked by him why he had allowed his very close friends Sex. Peducaeus, Q. Considius and M. Junius to be rejected,

in iudicando nimium sui iuris sententiaeque cognosset'.
19 Itaque iudicibus reiectis sperabam iam onus meum vobiscum esse commune; putabam non solum notis sed etiam ignotis probatam meam fidem esse et diligentiam. Quod me non fefellit; nam comitiis meis, cum iste infinita largitione contra me uteretur, populus Romanus iudicavit istius pecuniam, quae apud me contra fidem meam nihil potuisset, apud se contra honorem meum nihil posse debere. Quo quidem die primum, iudices, citati in hunc reum consedistis, quis tam iniquus huic ordini fuit, quis tam novarum rerum iudiciorum iudicumque cupidus qui 20 non aspectu consessuque vestro commoveretur? Cum in eo vestra dignitas mihi fructum diligentiae referret, id sum adsecutus, ut una hora qua coepi dicere reo audaci, pecunioso, profuso, perdito spem iudici corrumpendi praeciderem; ut primo die testium tanto numero citato populus Romanus iudicaret isto absoluto rem publicam stare non posse; ut alter dies amicis istius ac defensoribus non modo spem victoriae sed etiam voluntatem defensionis auferret, ut tertius dies sic hominem prosterneret ut morbo simulato non quid responderet, sed quem ad modum non responderet, deliberaret. Deinde reliquis diebus his criminibus, his testibus, et urbanis et provincialibus, sic obrutus atque oppressus est ut his ludorum diebus interpositis nemo istum comperendinatum, sed condemnatum iudicaret.

8
21 Quapropter ego quod ad me attinet, iudices, vici; non enim spolia C. Verris, sed existimationem populi Romani concupivi. Meum fuit cum causa accedere ad accusandum: quae causa fuit honestior, quam a tam inlustri provincia defensorem constitui et deligi? rei publicae consulere:

1 cognosset π: cognoscet D al. Schol. Gronov.: cognosceret rell. (i, § 97; ii, § 33)   4 esse meam fidem Zielinski p. 193   10 iniquus DΨ: inicus p: inimicus bδ (ii, § 167)   12 conspectu δ   consensuque pqD (sed hic corr. consessuque)   13 mihi dignitas δ   17 isto Zumpt edd.: ipso codd.   29 honestior DΨp: iustior δ: illustrior b

19 that he had discovered they were too independent and opinionated in judicial matters. In any event, when the challenging of jurors was over, I hoped that my burden was now shared with you, and I considered that my good faith and diligence had been proven not only to those who were known to me but also to those who were not. Nor was I mistaken in this judgement, for at my election, although Verres used limitless bribery against me, the Roman people decided that his money, which had had no influence with me to the detriment of my good faith, should have no influence with them to the detriment of my political advancement. Indeed on the day you were first summoned to sit in judgement on this defendant, who was there who was so ill-disposed towards this order, so eager for radical change in the courts and jury system, that he was not impressed by the sight of all of you

20 assembled together. And with your high standing repaying me in this fashion for my diligence, I managed within an hour of beginning my speech to cut short this brazen, wealthy, and wanton wastrel's hopes of corrupting the jury; I managed on the first day by the mass of witnesses I summoned to convince the Roman people that the state could not survive his acquittal; I managed on the second day to deprive his friends and defenders not only of the hope of victory but of the will to defend him; I managed on the third day to demolish the fellow to such an extent that, feigning illness, he began to consider not how to answer the charges but how to avoid answering them. Then during the remaining days he was so overwhelmed and crushed by the charges and by the witnesses from both the city and the provinces that, when the days of the festival intervened, everyone considered he had not achieved a postponement but was already convicted.

21 VIII. Therefore, gentlemen, so far as the case concerns me, I have won a victory. For I have been striving not for the despoilment of Verres but for the good opinion of the Roman people. My duty demanded that I have a valid reason for undertaking the prosecution. What reason was more honourable than my selection and appointment as its defender by so illustrious a province? My duty demanded

quid tam e re publica quam in tanta invidia iudiciorum adducere hominem cuius damnatione totus ordo cum populo Romano et in laude et in gratia posset esse? ostendere ac persuadere hominem nocentem adductum esse: quis est in populo Romano qui hoc non ex priore 5 actione abstulerit, omnium ante damnatorum scelera, furta, flagitia, si unum in locum conferantur, vix cum huius parva 22 parte aequari conferrique posse? Vos quod ad vestram famam existimationem salutemque communem pertinet, iudices, prospicite atque consulite: splendor vester facit ut 10 peccare sine summo rei publicae detrimento ac periculo non possitis. Non enim potest sperare populus Romanus esse alios in senatu qui recte possint iudicare, vos si non potueritis: necesse est, cum de toto ordine desperarit, aliud genus hominum atque aliam rationem iudiciorum requirat. 15 Hoc si vobis ideo levius videtur quod putatis onus esse grave et incommodum iudicare, intellegere debetis primum interesse utrum id onus vosmet ipsi reieceritis, an, quod probare populo Romano fidem vestram et religionem non potueritis, eo vobis iudicandi potestas erepta sit; deinde 20 etiam illud cogitare, quanto periculo venturi simus ad eos iudices quos propter odium nostri populus Romanus de 23 nobis voluerit iudicare. Verum vobis dicam id quod intellexi, iudices. Homines scitote esse quosdam quos tantum odium nostri ordinis teneat ut hoc palam iam dictitent, se 25 istum, quem sciant esse hominem improbissimum, hoc uno nomine absolvi velle ut ab senatu iudicia per ignominiam turpitudinemque auferantur. Haec me pluribus verbis,

1 quid tam e re publica *coni. Madvig.* : quid tamen re · p · honestius *D*Ψπ (tam *q* : iam *br*δ : in re pub. *Z*): Quid tandem *coni. Zumpt*: *an* Quid tamen (tandem?) in re publica honestius? 12 possitis *Kb* . possetis *D*Ψπ   potest sperare *Dp al.* : sperare potest *qr*   15 requirat iudiciorum *q*¹   18 reiceretis *p* : reiiceretis *q* : relegeritis *D*Ψ   23 Verū euobis *p* : Verum et vobis *qr*: verum ut vobis *Kayser* 28 Haec me res *D p rell.*   pluribus verbis iudices *D*Ψπ : plur. iud. verb. *b* : iud. plur. verb. δ

that I consult the interests of the state. What was so compatible with the public interest as the prosecution, at a time when the courts were experiencing such great unpopularity, of a man whose conviction could place the entire order in a position of esteem as well as favour with the Roman people? It was my duty to demonstrate persuasively that a guilty man had been brought to trial. Who was there among the Roman people who did not come away from the first stage of the trial with the knowledge that, if all the crimes, robberies, and shameful acts of all who had been previously convicted were gathered into one place, they could scarcely be likened or compared to a

22 tiny fraction of those of Verres? You, gentlemen, should give provident consideration to what affects your reputation and good name and the common safety. Your distinction makes it impossible for you to act wrongfully without the most serious harm and danger to the state. For the Roman people can have no hope that there are others in the senate capable of giving honest verdicts if you prove incapable, and it is inevitable, if they despair of the entire order, that they will seek another class of men and another judicial system. If this seems of less consequence to you because you consider your judicial duties a heavy and troublesome burden, you should first of all realize that there is a difference between you yourselves resigning this burden and having the power to act as jurors taken from you because you failed to convince the Roman people of your good faith and conscientiousness; you should then consider also how much danger will attend our appearance before those jurors whom the Roman people in their displeasure with us will have declared they wish to stand in judgement on

23 us. But I will tell you something that I have come to realize, gentlemen. You should know there are certain people who have such hatred for this order that they are now declaring openly that they want this man, whom they know to be a thorough scoundrel, to be acquitted for the single purpose that the courts may be transferred in circumstances of shame and dishonour from the control of the senate. These matters, gentlemen, I have felt compelled to discuss with you in rather many words, not

iudices, vobiscum agere coegit non timor meus de vestra fide, sed spes illorum nova, quae cum Verrem a porta subito ad iudicium retraxisset, non nulli suspicati sunt non sine causa illius consilium tam repente esse mutatum.

9 Nunc ne novo querimoniae genere uti possit Hortensius et ea dicere, opprimi reum de quo nihil dicat accusator, nihil esse tam periculosum fortunis innocentium quam tacere adversarios ; et ne aliter quam ego velim meum laudet ingenium, cum dicat me, si multa dixissem, sublevaturum fuisse eum quem contra dicerem, quia non dixerim, perdidisse : morem illi geram, utar oratione perpetua, non quo iam hoc sit necesse, verum ut experiar utrum ille ferat molestius me tunc tacuisse an nunc dicere. Hic tu fortasse eris diligens ne quam ego horam de meis legitimis horis remittam ; nisi omni tempore quod mihi lege concessum est abusus ero, querere, deum atque hominum fidem implorabis, circumveniri C. Verrem quod accusator nolit tam diu quam diu liceat dicere. Quod mihi lex mea causa dedit, eo mihi non uti non licebit ? Nam accusandi mihi tempus mea causa datum est, ut possem oratione mea crimina causamque explicare : hoc si non utor, non tibi iniuriam facio, sed de meo iure aliquid et commodo detraho. 'Causam enim', inquit, 'cognosci oportet' : ea re quidem quod aliter condemnari reus, quamvis sit nocens, non potest. Id igitur tu moleste tulisti, a me aliquid factum esse quo minus iste condemnari posset? nam causa cognita possunt multi absolvi, incognita quidem condemnari nemo potest. 'Adimo enim comperendinatum' : quod habet lex in se molestissimum, bis ut causa dicatur,—quod aut mea causa potius est constitutum quam tua, aut nihilo tua potius quam mea. Nam si bis dicere est commodum,

---

12 quo iam *Madv. edd.* : quoniam *codd.*   19 dedit *Asc., Muell.* : det *Dp rell.* (*prob. Stangl, Pseudoasconiana, p.* 121)   non uti licebit *D*Ψ   29 quod *codd.* : id *coni. Ernesti* : *fort.* id quidem

because of concern on my part about your good faith, but because of a fresh hope on the part of those I mention, which, after it had unexpectedly drawn Verres back from the gate to the court, led some to suspect his plan had not been changed so suddenly without good reason.

24 IX. Now, so that Hortensius may not be able to employ a novel form of complaint and make statements to the effect that an accused man about whom an accuser says nothing is a victim of oppression and that nothing so threatens the fortunes of the innocent as the silence of their adversaries, and that he may not praise my talent in ways other than I would wish by declaring that if I had spoken at length I would have lent support to the man I was speaking against, but because I did not speak I have ruined him, I will humour the gentleman and use a set speech, not because I have any longer a need to do so, but that I may find out whether he feels more 25 annoyed that I was earlier silent or that I now speak. At this point you will, no doubt, keep careful watch in case I should forego any of my legally allotted hours, and if I fail to use all the time permitted me by law, you will complain and call on heaven and earth to witness that Verres is being unjustly condemned because the prosecutor is unwilling to speak for the full period allowed him. Shall I not be permitted not to use what the law has given me for my benefit? And surely it was for my benefit that the period allotted for presenting the prosecution was given me, that I might have the right to set forth the charges and the case in my speech. If I fail to use this time I do you no injury but detract from my own rights and interests. "Yes," he says, "but the case should be heard." Indeed, and for the reason that a defendant, however guilty he may be, cannot otherwise be convicted. Is it this then that has upset you, that I have done something to make the conviction of Verres impossible? For while many may be acquitted when a case has been heard, certainly no one can be convicted when 26 it has not been heard. "But," you allege, "I am doing away with the process of adjournment"; a process that is a most troublesome feature in the law, providing that a case should be pleaded twice, but one established more for my benefit than for yours, or no more for yours than for mine. For if it is an advantage to plead twice, then of

certe utriusque commune est; si eum qui posterius dixit opus est redargui, accusatoris causa, ut bis ageretur, constitutum est. Verum, ut opinor, Glaucia primus tulit ut comperendinaretur reus; antea vel iudicari primo poterat vel amplius pronuntiari. Vtram igitur putas legem molliorem? 5 Opinor, illam veterem, qua vel cito absolvi vel tarde condemnari licebat. Ego tibi illam Aciliam legem restituo, qua lege multi semel accusati, semel dicta causa, semel auditis testibus condemnati sunt, nequaquam tam manifestis neque tantis criminibus quantis tu convinceris. Puta te 10 non hac tam atroci, sed illa lege mitissima causam dicere. Accusabo; respondebis; testibus editis ita mittam in consilium ut, etiamsi lex ampliandi faciat potestatem, tamen isti turpe sibi existiment non primo iudicare.

10
27 Verum si causam cognosci opus est, parumne cognita est? 15 Dissimulamus, Hortensi, quod saepe experti in dicendo sumus. Quis nos magnopere attendit umquam in hoc quidem genere causarum, ubi aliquid ereptum aut ablatum a quopiam dicitur? Nonne aut in tabulis aut in testibus omnis exspectatio iudicum est? Dixi prima actione me 20 planum esse facturum C. Verrem HS quadringentiens contra leges abstulisse. Quid? hoc planius egissem, si ita narrassem? 'Dio quidam fuit Halaesinus, qui, cum eius filio praetore C. Sacerdote hereditas a propinquo permagna venisset, nihil habuit tum neque negoti neque controversiae. 25 Verres simul ac tetigit provinciam, statim Messana litteras dedit, Dionem evocavit, calumniatores ex sinu suo adposuit qui illam hereditatem Veneri Erycinae commissam esse dic-

---

1 utriusque commune $D\Psi p$ (*Zielinski p.* 193): comm. utr. *qr*
dixit *codd. praeter q* (dixerit)   5 molliorem $DZqb$: moliorem *pr*:
meliorem G_3K 7 Ergo?   16-17 Hortensi ... sumus *suppl.* p^2
17 magnopere Dp *rell.* (*Act. Pr.* § 23; ii, § 28): magno opere *Iord.*
19 a quopiam $D\Psi pr$: cuipiam δ   22 leges pqG_2K: legem Zbδ: (lege D^1: legē D^1)   23 halaesinus p: halesinus D *rell.*   25 tum *om.* δ
26 Messanam Dp *et pler.*

course the advantage is common to both sides, but if it is essential that he who has spoken last be refuted, then the system of double pleading was set up for the benefit of the prosecutor. But, if I am not mistaken, it was Glaucia who first enacted that the accused should have an adjournment. Previously a verdict could be given on the first occasion or a further hearing could be announced. Which law then do you consider the more lenient? I think the latter, under which one could achieve a swift acquittal or could prolong conviction. I am restoring for you that law of Acilius, under which many, after a single arraignment, a single defence, a single hearing of witnesses, were condemned, and for crimes far less clearly proven and serious than those of which you, Verres, are being convicted. Consider yourself pleading not under a law as harsh as the present one, but under that earlier mildest of statutes. I will accuse, you will respond; after the witnesses have been produced I will send the jury to deliberate in such a manner that, even if the law does make provision for an adjournment, they will think it disgraceful for them not to give a verdict at the first sitting.

27 X. But if indeed the case must have its hearing, has it been insufficiently heard? We keep quiet, Hortensius, about something that we have often experienced in pleading. Who ever pays much attention to us advocates, especially in this type of case, where someone is alleged to have seized or stolen something? Is the expectant attention of the jurors not centred entirely on records and witnesses? I said in the first stage of the trial that I would plainly show that Verres took forty million sesterces in violation of the law. Well then, would I have shown this more plainly if I had provided a narrative as follows? "There was a man named Dio from Halaesa, who at the time his son received a large inheritance from a relative, when C. Sacerdos was governor, encountered no trouble or controversy. But as soon as Verres reached the island, he immediately despatched letters from Messana, summoned Dio, appointed lying witnesses from his own inner circle to say that the inheritance was forfeit to Venus Erycina, and indicated he would himself

28 erent; hac de re ostendit se ipsum cogniturum.' Possum deinceps totam rem explicare, deinde ad extremum id quod accidit dicere, Dionem HS deciens centena milia numerasse ut causam certissimam obtineret; praeterea greges equarum eius istum abigendos curasse, argenti, vestis stragulae quod 5 fuerit curasse auferendum. Haec neque cum ego dicerem neque cum tu negares, magni momenti nostra esset oratio. Quo tempore igitur auris iudex erigeret animumque attenderet? Cum Dio ipse prodiret, cum ceteri qui tum in Sicilia negotiis Dionis interfuissent, cum per eos ipsos dies 10 per quos causam Dio diceret reperiretur pecunias sumpsisse mutuas, nomina sua exegisse, praedia vendidisse; cum tabulae virorum bonorum proferrentur; cum qui pecuniam Dioni dederunt dicerent se iam tum audisse eos nummos sumi ut Verri darentur; cum amici, hospites, patroni Dionis, 15 homines honestissimi, haec eadem se audisse dicerent. 29 Opinor, cum haec fierent, tum vos audiretis, sicut audistis: tum causa agi vere videretur. Sic a me sunt acta omnia priore actione ut in criminibus omnibus nullum esset in quo quisquam vestrum perpetuam accusationem requireret. 20 Nego esse quicquam a testibus dictum quod aut vestrum cuipiam esset obscurum aut cuiusquam oratoris eloquentiam 11 quaereret. Etenim sic me ipsum egisse memoria tenetis ut in testibus interrogandis omnia crimina proponerem et explicarem, ut, cum rem totam in medio posuissem, tum denique 25 testem interrogarem. Itaque non modo vos, quibus est iudicandum, nostra crimina tenetis, sed etiam populus Romanus totam accusationem causamque cognovit.

Tametsi ita de meo facto loquor quasi ego illud mea

---

2 iudicare *qr*   4 equarum *Dpb* (*ut in cod. Clun.* ii, § 20) : equorum *K al. vulg.*   5 vestisque *bδ* : *in mg. p²* vestrisque stragulae quod fuerit   14 eos *Dp rell.* : eo *q*   16 hominis *Dp rell.* : *om.* G_2
19 omnibus *pb* : *om.* *DΨ*   22 cuipiam *Dp rell.* : cuiquam *Heindorf*, *Muell.* (ii, § 36)   24 et explicarem *in mg.* *D²*

28 conduct a hearing about the matter." I can go on to unravel the entire tale and conclude by telling what actually transpired, that Dio paid out one million sesterces to win a case about which there was not the slightest doubt, and that Verres in addition arranged to have his herds of horses driven off and such silver and tapestries as he possessed removed. Neither my speech narrating these events nor yours denying them would have any great impact. At what point then would the juror prick up his ears and give his attention? When Dio himself came forward, and the others who had been involved in Dio's business dealings in Sicily; when it was learned in the course of the days during which Dio was pleading his case that he had borrowed money, called in his debts, sold estates; when the accounts of honourable men were produced; when those who gave Dio money stated that they had even then heard that the cash was being borrowed to give to Verres; when friends, hosts, and patrons of Dio, men of the highest standing, declared

29 that they had heard the same thing. Then, I believe, when these events were happening, you would give your attention, as indeed you did. Then the case would seem to be proceeding in earnest. Now, in the first stage of the trial all matters were conducted by me in such a way that there was no aspect of any of the charges that would cause anyone to want a continuous exposition of the indictment. I maintain there was nothing said by the witnesses which any of you found obscure or which required the eloquence of any orator. XI. And indeed you recall that my own procedure in examining the witnesses was to set forth and explain all the charges, and to proceed to question a witness only after the entire matter had been placed in full view. So not only you, who must deliver a judgement, have a grasp of the charges we have brought, but the Roman people as well have come to know the entire case of the prosecution.

And yet, I am speaking about my action as if I took

30 voluntate potius quam vestra iniuria adductus fecerim. Interposuistis accusatorem qui, cum ego mihi C et X dies solos in Siciliam postulassem, C et VIII sibi in Achaiam postularet. Mensis mihi tris cum eripuissetis ad agendum maxime adpositos, reliquum omne tempus huius anni me vobis re- 5 missurum putastis, ut, cum horis nostris nos essemus usi, tu binis ludis interpositis quadragesimo post die responderes, deinde ita tempus duceretur ut a M'. Glabrione praetore et a magna parte horum iudicum ad praetorem alium iu-
31 dicesque alios veniremus. Hoc si ego non vidissem, si me 10 non omnes noti ignotique monuissent id agi, id cogitari, in eo elaborari ut res in illud tempus reiceretur, credo, si meis horis in accusando uti voluissem, vererer ne mihi crimina non suppeterent, ne oratio deesset, ne vox viresque deficerent, ne, quem nemo prima actione defendere ausus esset, eum 15 ego bis accusare non possem. Ego meum consilium cum iudicibus tum populo Romano probavi: nemo est qui alia ratione istorum iniuriae atque impudentiae potuisse obsisti arbitretur. Etenim qua stultitia fuissem, si, quam diem qui istum eripiendum redemerunt in cautione viderunt,—cum ita 20 caverent, ' si post Kalendas Ianuarias in consilium iretur ',—
32 in eam diem ego, cum potuissem vitare, incidissem? Nunc mihi temporis eius quod mihi ad dicendum datur, quoniam in animo est causam omnem exponere, habenda ratio est diligenter. 25
12 Itaque primum illum actum istius vitae turpissimum et flagitiosissimum praetermittam. Nihil a me de pueritiae suae flagitiis audiet, nihil ex illa impura adulescentia sua; quae qualis fuerit aut meministis, aut ex eo quem sui simillimum produxit recognoscere potestis. Omnia praeteribo quae 30

7 tu πb : tum DΨ 9 a pKZ et s. l. D : om. qr 11 in eo elaborari (lab. Zb) DΨp : id elab. qr: id lab. Lg. 42 (ii, § 124) 20 viderunt codd. : scripserunt Hugh E. P. Platt : fort. indixerunt 28 flagitiis DΨ : flagitiis peccatisque prδ

30 it led by my own wishes rather than the injustice of your tactics. For, when I had asked for a mere one hundred and ten days to go to Sicily, you put forward a prosecutor to thwart me by asking for one hundred and eight days for himself to go to Achaia. When you had deprived me of three months especially suitable for judicial proceedings, you thought I would give you free play with the time remaining in the year, so that, after we had used our allotted time you might, with the help of two intervening festivals, have your response take place forty days later, and might then drag out the time sufficiently to remove us from the court of this praetor, M'. Glabrio, and from a large part of these jurors, and
31 bring us before another praetor and other jurors. If I had not seen this, if everyone, friend and foe alike, had not warned me action was being taken, plans were being made, every effort was being strained to postpone the case to such a point, are we to suppose, if I had wanted to use my allotted time in presenting the prosecution, that I would have felt afraid to do so in case I had not sufficient charges, in case speech would fail me, in case my voice and strength would be inadequate, in case I would not be able to accuse twice a man whom no one dared defend at the first hearing? I have won approval for my plan from both the jurors and the Roman people. There is no one who thinks I could have resisted the injustice and effrontery of these people by any other means. How foolish I would have been, if I had stumbled into that day, when I could have avoided it, which those who had contracted to rescue Verres had kept before their eyes in inserting the proviso in which they stipulated the following: 'PROVIDED THE CASE GOES
32 BEFORE THE JURY AFTER JANUARY 1ST.' But now, since it is my intention to set forth the entire case, I must keep careful track of the time allotted me for my speech.

XII. I will therefore pass over that first most base and shameful stage of Verres' life. He will hear nothing from me about the disgraceful acts of his boyhood and nothing about those of his notoriously immoral youth, for either you remember what it was like or you can recall it by looking at the son he has brought forth, who is an exact replica of himself. I will pass over everything that I

mihi turpia dictu videbuntur, neque solum quid istum audire, verum etiam quid me deceat dicere considerabo. Vos, quaeso, date hoc et concedite pudori meo ut aliquam partem 33 de istius impudentia reticere possim. Omne illud tempus quod fuit antequam iste ad magistratus remque publicam accessit, habeat per me solutum ac liberum. Sileatur de nocturnis eius bacchationibus ac vigiliis; lenonum, aleatorum, perductorum nulla mentio fiat; damna, dedecora, quae res patris eius, aetas ipsius pertulit, praetereantur; lucretur indicia veteris infamiae; patiatur eius vita reliqua 34 me hanc tantam iacturam criminum facere. Quaestor Cn. Papirio consuli fuisti abhinc annos quattuordecim. Ex ea die ad hanc diem quae fecisti in iudicium voco: hora nulla vacua a furto, scelere, crudelitate, flagitio reperietur. Hi sunt anni consumpti in quaestura et legatione Asiatica et praetura urbana et praetura Siciliensi; quare haec eadem erit quadripertita distributio totius accusationis meae.

13 Quaestor ex senatus consulto provinciam sortitus es: obtigit tibi consularis, ut cum consule Cn. Carbone esses eamque provinciam obtineres. Erat tum dissensio civium, de qua nihil sum dicturus quid sentire debueris: unum hoc dico, in eius modi tempore ac sorte statuere te debuisse utrum malles sentire atque defendere. Carbo graviter ferebat sibi quaestorem obtigisse hominem singulari luxuria atque inertia; verum tamen ornabat eum beneficiis officiisque omnibus. Ne diutius teneam, pecunia attributa, numerata est: profectus est quaestor in provinciam: venit exspectatus in Galliam ad exercitum consularem cum pecunia. Simul ac primum ei occasio visa est,—cognoscite hominis principium magistratuum gerendorum et rei publicae ad-

1 dictu turpia *qr*: dictu *om. b* 8 perductorum *DΨpr*: perlectorum *q*: perditorum *L* 10 patietur *coni. Schuetz*: patitur *Orelli* 12 cōs. *D al. p*: consuli *G₂*, consule *G₁b* 17 quadripertita *D al. p*: quadripartita *Z al.* 25 ornabat *prb*: honorabat *DΨ* 27 in Galliam exsp. *bδ*

33 think it shameful to speak about and will bear in mind not only what it is proper for him to hear but for me to utter. You I would ask to allow me, as a concession to my sense of shame, to remain silent about a particular portion of this man's shamelessness. The entire period of his life before he took office and entered public affairs he can have clear and free, as far as I am concerned. Let nothing be said about his nocturnal revels and vigils, let there be no mention of pimps, gamblers, or panderers; let the financial losses and the shameful acts, which were inflicted on his father's property and his own young age, be passed over; let him have a present of the manifestations of his early disrepute; the remainder of his life will permit me to jettison even so large a catalogue of
34 crimes. You were quaestor to the consul Cn. Papirius fourteen years ago. I am bringing before the court all that you did from that day to this. We will find that not a single hour was free from robbery, criminality, cruelty, and wickedness. These years were spent by him as quaestor, as a legate in Asia, as urban praetor, and as governor of Sicily. I will, accordingly, arrange my entire presentation of the prosecution in a corresponding fourfold division.

XIII. As quaestor you cast lots in accordance with a decree of the senate to determine your sphere of duty. You received a consular assignment, to accompany the consul Cn. Carbo and have charge of the functions entailed in this. There was at the time a civil dispute. I am not going to say anything about what side you should have taken in it; I merely say this, that at such a time and with such an assignment you ought to have decided which side you preferred to take and defend. Carbo was unhappy that he had been allotted a quaestor who was exceptionally given to self-indulgence and laziness. Nevertheless, he honoured him with every kindness and courtesy. Not to detain you any longer, money was assigned and paid out. He set out as quaestor for his province. He arrived, eagerly awaited, in Gaul, at the army of the consul, bringing the money. But the moment the opportunity presented itself - observe the man's debut as a magistrate and public administrator - he, a

ministrandae,—aversa pecunia publica quaestor consulem,
35 exercitum, sortem, provinciamque deseruit. Video quid egerim : erigit se, sperat sibi auram posse aliquam adflari in hoc crimine voluntatis defensionisque eorum quibus Cn. Carbonis mortui nomen odio sit, quibus illam relictionem proditionemque consulis sui gratam sperat fore. Quasi vero id cupiditate defendendae nobilitatis aut studio partium fecerit, ac non apertissime consulem, exercitum, provinciamque compilarit et propter impudentissimum furtum aufugerit ! est enim obscurum et eius modi factum eius ut possit aliquis suspicari C. Verrem, quod ferre novos homines non potuerit, ad nobilitatem, hoc est ad suos, transisse, nihil
36 fecisse propter pecuniam ! Videamus rationes quem ad modum rettulerit : iam ipse ostendet quam ob rem Cn.
14 Carbonem reliquerit, iam se ipse indicabit. Primum brevitatem cognoscite: ACCEPI, inquit, VICIENS DVCENTA TRIGINTA QVINQVE MILIA QVADRINGENTOS DECEM ET SEPTEM NVMMOS. DEDI STIPENDIO, FRVMENTO, LEGATIS, PRO QVAESTORE, COHORTI PRAETORIAE HS MILLE SESCENTA TRIGINTA QVINQVE MILIA QVADRINGENTOS DECEM ET SEPTEM NVMMOS. RELIQVI ARIMINI HS SESCENTA MILIA. Hoc est rationes referre ? hoc modo aut ego aut tu, Hortensi, aut quisquam omnium rettulit ? Quid hoc est ? quae impudentia, quae audacia ? quod exemplum ex tot hominum rationibus relatis huiusce modi est ? Illa tamen HS sescenta milia, quae ne falso quidem potuit quibus data essent describere, quae se Arimini scribit reliquisse, quae ipsa HS sescenta milia reliqua facta sunt, neque

---

3 auram sibi posse *K*   afflare *coni. Zumpt, Cobet*   4 defensionisque *qr edd.* : dissensionisque *DΨpb* : adsensionisque *al.* An consensionisque ?   5 reiectionem *codd. et edd. ante Naugerium* (*cf.* § 22)   16 triginta *om. D al. pr*   17 decem sex *DΨp*   18–20 dedi stipendio . . . nummos *om.* G_1 18 pro quaestore *Asc.* : pro quaestoribus *Dp rell.*   19 milles quingenta quadraginta quinque *πb*   22 quispiam G_3K 24 relatis *pr edd.* : redditis DG_1KZ huius modi *pbδ* (*Zielinski p.* 193)   25 neque falso *DΨπ*   26 describere *Dp rell.* : discr. *Kays.* : perscr. *cod.* (?) *Vrs.*

35 quaestor, embezzled the state's money and deserted consul, army, his allotted duty, and his province. I see what I have done: he lifts his spirits, he hopes that, in relation to this charge, some breath of goodwill and justification can waft its way towards him from those to whom the name of Carbo, though he is dead, remains an abomination, and with whom he hopes his desertion and betrayal of his consul will find favour. As if indeed he acted out of a desire to defend the nobility or out of partisan zeal, and did not, after blatantly robbing consul, army, and province, take to his heels because of his most brazen thievery! Yes, his action to be sure, is one hard to fathom and such that one might infer that C. Verres, because he cannot stand new men, transferred his allegiance to the nobility, that is to his own class, 36 and was in no way influenced in his action by money! Let us see how he returned his accounts. He will soon show us himself why he abandoned Carbo, and will act as informer against himself. XIV. First observe the brevity of the accounts. 'I RECEIVED', he says, 'TWO MILLION, TWO HUNDRED AND THIRTY-FIVE THOUSAND, FOUR HUNDRED AND SEVENTEEN SESTERCES. I EXPENDED ON WAGES, GRAIN, PAYMENTS TO LEGATES, THE PROQUAESTOR, THE PRAETORIAN COHORT ONE MILLION, SIX HUNDRED AND THIRTY-FIVE THOUSAND FOUR HUNDRED AND SEVENTEEN SESTERCES. I LEFT SIX HUNDRED THOUSAND AT ARIMINUM.' Does this constitute returning accounts? Have I or you, Hortensius, or anyone at all, made returns in this manner? What is the meaning of this? What shamelessness! What effrontery! What precedent is there in the vast number of accounts that people have submitted for this type of return? In any event, that six hundred thousand, which he was unable, even by lying, to record as having been given to anyone, which he wrote he had left at Ariminum, and which six hundred thousand was the actual sum left over,

Carbo attigit neque Sulla vidit neque in aerarium relata sunt. Oppidum sibi elegit Ariminum, quod tum, cum iste rationes referebat, oppressum direptumque erat : non suspicabatur, id quod nunc sentiet, satis multos ex illa calamitate Ariminensium testis nobis in hanc rem reliquos esse. 37 Recita denuo. P. LENTVLO L. TRIARIO QVAESTORIBVS VRBANIS RES RATIONVM RELATARVM. Recita. EX SENATVS CONSVLTO. Vt hoc pacto rationem referre liceret, eo Sullanus repente factus est, non ut honos et dignitas nobilitati restitueretur.

Quodsi illinc inanis profugisses, tamen ista tua fuga nefaria proditio consulis tui conscelerata iudicaretur. 'Malus civis, improbus consul, seditiosus homo Cn. Carbo fuit.' Fuerit aliis : tibi quando esse coepit? posteaquam tibi pecuniam, rem frumentariam, rationes omnis suas exercitumque commisit. Nam si tibi antea displicuisset, idem fecisses quod anno post M. Piso. Quaestor cum L. Scipioni consuli obtigisset, non attigit pecuniam, non ad exercitum profectus est ; quod de re publica sensit, ita sensit ut nec fidem suam nec morem maiorum nec necessitudinem sortis laederet. Etenim si haec perturbare omnia ac permiscere volumus, totam vitam periculosam, invidiosam, infestamque reddemus,—si nullam religionem sors habebit, nullam societatem coniunctio secundae dubiaeque fortunae, nullam auctoritatem mores atque instituta maiorum. Omnium est communis inimicus qui fuit hostis suorum. Nemo umquam sapiens proditori credendum putavit. Ipse Sulla, cui adventus istius gratissimus esse debuit, ab se hominem atque ab exercitu suo removit: Beneventi esse iussit apud eos

3 direptumque *D al. b* : directumque *pr* : dirutumque *K Lg.* 42   6 G. Triar. *DZp* : Q. Triar. $G_{12}K$ 7 restaurationum relat. π   12 scelerata *Zδ*   14 tibi quando *pb* : tibi *iterum suppl. s. l. D* : tibi tibi quando *KZ* : quando tibi *qr*   17 legisses *DΨ* (*cf.* § 60 *infra*) Qui quaestor *malit Muell.*   22 invidiosam *Dp rell.* : insidiosam *Lamb. edd.*   25 institutaque *q*

37 Carbo did not touch, Sulla did not see, nor was it returned to the treasury. He chose Ariminum for his purposes, because at the time he was returning his accounts, it had been overrun and plundered. He did not suspect what he will now soon realize, that we have plenty of witnesses to this affair surviving from that calamity of the people of Ariminum. Read again the documents beginning: 'THE MATTER OF THE ACCOUNTS SUBMITTED TO THE URBAN QUAESTORS P. LENTULUS AND L. TRIARIUS.' Read the document beginning: 'IN ACCORDANCE WITH A DECREE OF THE SENATE.' It was to enable yourself to make returns in this fashion that you suddenly became a Sullan supporter, not to restore their rank and prestige to the nobility.

But if you had fled from there empty-handed, that vile act of desertion of yours would nonetheless be adjudged a criminal betrayal of your consul. "But Cn. Carbo was a disloyal citizen, an unprincipled consul, and a man given to sedition." I grant he did seem so to others, but when did he begin to seem so to you? After he entrusted to you his funds, his food supply, all his affairs, and his army. For if he had earned your disapproval before that, you would have taken the same action that M. Piso took the following year. When, as quaestor, he was assigned by lot to the consul, L. Scipio, he did not touch the funds and did not depart for the army. His political opinions he maintained in such a way as to avoid infringing his own good faith or the practice of our ancestors or the obligation imposed by the
38 lot. XV. For if we are willing to throw into disorder*and to confound all these principles, we will expose the whole of life to danger, hatred, and hostility – if the lot is going to have no religious force, an association in the ups and downs of fortune no power to forge friendship, the practices and institutions of our ancestors no authority. He who has proved an enemy to his own is the common enemy of all. No wise man ever thought a traitor should be trusted. Sulla himself, who had most reason to be pleased by Verres' arrival, kept him at a distance from his person and from his army. He ordered him to stay at Beneventum among those he knew to be the most

quos suis partibus amicissimos esse intellegebat, ubi iste summae rei causaeque nocere nihil posset. Ei postea praemia tamen liberaliter tribuit, bona quaedam proscriptorum in agro Beneventano diripienda concessit, habuit
39 honorem ut proditori, non ut amico fidem. Nunc quamvis sint homines qui mortuum Cn. Carbonem oderint, tamen hi debent non quid illi accidere voluerint, sed quid ipsis in tali re metuendum sit cogitare. Commune est hoc malum, communis metus, commune periculum. Nullae sunt occultiores insidiae quam eae quae latent in simulatione offici aut in aliquo necessitudinis nomine. Nam eum qui palam est adversarius facile cavendo vitare possis; hoc vero occultum intestinum ac domesticum malum non modo non exsistit, verum etiam opprimit antequam prospicere atque explorare
40 potueris. Itane vero? Tu cum quaestor ad exercitum missus sis, custos non solum pecuniae sed etiam consulis, particeps omnium rerum consiliorumque fueris, habitus sis in liberum loco, sicut mos maiorum ferebat, repente relinquas, deseras, ad adversarios transeas? O scelus, o portentum in ultimas terras exportandum! Non enim potest ea natura quae tantum facinus commiserit hoc uno scelere esse contenta: necesse est semper aliquid eius modi moliatur, necesse est in simili audacia perfidiaque versetur.
41 Itaque idem iste, quem Cn. Dolabella postea C. Malleolo occiso pro quaestore habuit, — haud scio an maior etiam haec necessitudo fuerit quam illa Carbonis, ac plus iudicium voluntatis valere quam sortis debeat,—idem in Cn. Dolabellam qui in Cn. Carbonem fuit. Nam quae in ipsum valebant crimina contulit in illum, causamque illius omnem ad inimicos accusatoresque detulit; ipse in eum cui legatus,

2 nil *Zielinski, p.* 178   7 accedere *D al. π* (i, § 4)   11 eum qui *DKZpbr*: qui *q*: cum G_2 13 non modo non *codd.*: non modo *Asc. edd.* (*Cl. Rev.* xx. 256)   15 Tu cum *pb*: tum cum *D al.*: cum G_2LK 28 in ipso *Asc. edd. vett.*

39 devoted to his party, and where Verres could do no harm to the general welfare or to the cause. Later, however, he did generously reward him, and allowed him to seize certain property of persons who had been proscribed in the territory of Beneventum, showing him the honour due a traitor, not the trust due a friend. Now, though there are people who hate Cn. Carbo even in death, they should nevertheless consider not what they wanted to happen to him but what they themselves have to fear in a similar situation. This is a common evil, a common fear, a common danger. No treachery is better hidden than that which lies concealed under a pretense of dutiful service, or under some title that implies an intimate connection. For one can easily avoid an open adversary by taking precautions. But the evil that is hidden, that is inside, in one's household, not only fails to show itself but
40 destroys before it can be foreseen and tracked down. So is this the true way of things? After you were sent as quaestor to the army and were the custodian not only of the funds but of the consul, and after you shared in all his affairs and deliberations and were treated as a son in accordance with the practice of our ancestors, were you then supposed suddenly to leave, desert, cross over to the enemy? What a scoundrel! What a monster of wickedness, deserving of banishment to the ends of the earth! For the nature that has committed so great an outrage cannot rest content with this one crime: it must needs always be engineering some scheme in this mould; it must needs be immersed in similar criminal brazenness and treachery.

41 And so this same Verres, when Cn. Dolabella later had him as a proquaestor, after C. Malleolus had been killed, (I am not sure that this was not a closer association than his connection with Cn. Carbo, and that a deliberate choice should not have stronger effects than the lot), behaved in the same manner towards Cn. Dolabella as he had towards Cn. Carbo. For charges that applied to himself he transferred to Dolabella and provided the information for the entire case against the latter to his enemies and prosecutors. And he personally gave highly damaging and unconscionable evidence against the man whom he had served as legate and as

cui pro quaestore fuerat, inimicissimum atque improbissimum
testimonium dixit.   Ille miser cum esset Cn. Dolabella,—
cum proditione istius nefaria, tum improbo ac falso eiusdem
testimonio,—tum multo ex maxima parte istius furtorum ac
flagitiorum invidia conflagravit. Quid hoc homine faciatis 5
aut ad quam spem tam perfidiosum, tam importunum animal
reservetis? qui in Cn. Carbone sortem, in Cn. Dolabella
voluntatem neglexerit ac violarit, eosque ambo non modo
deseruerit sed etiam prodiderit atque oppugnarit. Nolite,
quaeso, iudices, brevitate orationis meae potius quam rerum 10
ipsarum magnitudine crimina ponderare; mihi enim pro-
perandum necessario est, ut omnia vobis quae mihi constituta sunt possim exponere. Quam ob rem quaestura istius
demonstrata primique magistratus et furto et scelere
perspecto, reliqua attendite. In quibus illud tempus Sulla- 15
narum proscriptionum ac rapinarum praetermittam ; neque
ego istum sibi ex communi calamitate defensionem ullam
sinam sumere, suis eum certis propriisque criminibus accusabo. Quam ob rem hoc omni tempore Sullano ex accusatione circumscripto legationem eius praeclaram cognoscite. 20
    Posteaquam Cn. Dolabellae provincia Cilicia constituta
est, o di immortales, quanta iste cupiditate, quibus adlega-
tionibus illam sibi legationem expugnavit! id quod Cn.
Dolabellae principium maximae calamitatis fuit. Nam ut
est profectus, quacumque iter fecit, eius modi fuit, non ut 25
legatus populi Romani, sed ut quaedam calamitas perva-
dere videretur.   In Achaia—praetermittam minora omnia,

    2 Cn. Dolabella *del. Naugerius, Iord., Kays.* : *malim* Ille miser
(i, § 74) cum esset *conflictatus*, cum *etc.*   3 cum prodit *Dp et pler.* :
tum prodit $G_2 K\delta$ tum impr. *K al.* : cum impr. *Dp et pler.*   4 cum
multo G_2.   *Cf. Act. Pr.* § 34 ; i, §§ 65, 119 ; iii, § 188   5 de
hoc *qr*   7 Carbone . . . Dolabella *Manutius* : -em . . . -am *codd.*
8 ambo *D al.* π : ambos $bG_2 LKZ$ 22 dii *Dp*   25 est *Dp rell.* :
iste $G_1 \delta$: est iste *Kays., Muell. A verbo* quacunᵣque *usque ad* C.
Verrem i, § 45 *commemoratur fragmentum Palimpsesti Taurinensis,
mutilum ipsum* (*T.*)   26 persuadere *Tb*   27 Achaiam *T*

42 proquaestor. While it is true that Cn. Dolabella was in pitiable circumstances because of Verres' vile betrayal coupled with his unprincipled and lying testimony, by far the greatest part of the animosity that flared against him came from the thefts and crimes that were the work of Verres. XVI. What should you do with this man? What hopeful prospect is there for which you should preserve so treacherous and relentless an animal, who ignored and profaned the lot in the case of Cn. Carbo and his voluntary selection in the case of Cn. Dolabella, and not only deserted them both but betrayed and attacked them. Do not, I implore you, gentlemen, base your judgement of these charges on the brevity of my speech but on the gravity of the facts themselves, for I must of necessity hurry on, so that I may be able to set before you all the

43 matters I have determined to present. Therefore, now that his quaestorship has been described and the thievery and criminality of his first magistracy examined, look at the remainder of his career. I will omit from it the period of the proscriptions and pillagings under Sulla; I will not allow him to extract any defence from a general calamity, but will charge him with his own specific and special crimes. Therefore, with this entire Sullan era excluded from my indictment, observe his outstanding tenure as a legate.

44 XVII. After the province of Cilicia was assigned to Dolabella, good heavens! with* what covetous passion, with what missions of supplication he extorted that commission as legate! a commission that, for Cn. Dolabella, was the beginning of an extreme calamity. For the manner of his departure and of his journey was such that it appeared some form of natural disaster and not a legate of the Roman people was passing through. In Achaia (I will pass

quorum simile forsitan alius quoque aliquid aliquando fecerit; nihil dicam nisi singulare, nisi id quod, si in alium reum diceretur, incredibile videretur—magistratum Sicyonium nummos poposcit. Ne sit hoc crimen in Verrem: fecerunt alii. Cum ille non daret, animadvertit: improbum, 5
45 sed non inauditum. Genus animadversionis videte: quaeretis ex quo genere hominem istum iudicetis. Ignem ex lignis viridibus atque umidis in loco angusto fieri iussit: ibi hominem ingenuum, domi nobilem, populi Romani socium atque amicum, fumo excruciatum semivivum reli- 10 quit. Iam quae iste signa, quas tabulas pictas ex Achaia sustulerit, non dicam hoc loco: est mihi alius locus ad hanc eius cupiditatem demonstrandam separatus. Athenis audistis ex aede Minervae grande auri pondus ablatum; dictum est hoc in Cn. Dolabellae iudicio. Dictum? etiam 15 aestimatum. Huius consili non participem C. Verrem, sed principem fuisse reperietis.

46 Delum venit. Ibi ex fano Apollinis religiosissimo noctu clam sustulit signa pulcherrima atque antiquissima, eaque in onerariam navem suam conicienda curavit. Postridie 20 cum fanum spoliatum viderent ii qui Delum incolebant, graviter ferebant; est enim tanta apud eos eius fani religio atque antiquitas ut in eo loco ipsum Apollinem natum esse arbitrentur. Verbum tamen facere non audebant, ne forte
18 ea res ad Dolabellam ipsum pertineret. Tum subito tempe- 25 states coortae sunt maximae, iudices, ut non modo proficisci cum cuperet Dolabella non posset, sed vix in oppido consisteret: ita magni fluctus eiciebantur. Hic navis illa prae-

2 nisi singulare p^2 s. l.   nisi id T: nisi Dp rell.   4 poposcit πb: poscit D al.: possit G_2: petit K 7 hominem codd.: hominum Hotom. edd. (ii, § 17)   11 ista T 12 mihi alius T Asc.: alius mihi Dp rell.   13 istius $q\delta$ separatus $TD\Psi p$: servatus $p^2 rb\delta$ 15-16 dictum est... aestimatum $T\pi$: om. $D\Psi$ 15 est hoc Tb: hoc est π.   Cn. om. T (106. 19)   16 non part. T: non modo part. Dp rell.   Cf. i, § 106

over all minor offenses such as others may at some time and in some degree have also perpetrated; I will speak of nothing that is not unique and that would not, if alleged against another defendant, seem incredible) he demanded money from the magistrate of Sicyon. But let us not make this a charge against Verres; other have done it. When the magistrate failed to pay, he punished him, an improper action, but not unprecedented. Observe the manner of punishment: you will ask what manner of man you are to consider this fellow. He ordered a fire to be built in a confined space from green and sap-filled logs. There he left in agony and half-dead from the smoke a man who was free-born, who had the highest standing in his own country, and who was a friend and ally of the Roman people. The statues and paintings that he then carried off from Achaia I will not speak of here; I have reserved another place in which to show his greed in that regard. You have heard that at Athens a large mass of gold was taken from the temple of Minerva. The matter was raised at the trial of Cn. Dolabella. Did I say raised? In fact its value was even determined. You will discover that Verres was not a participant in this enterprise, but its leading figure.

He arrived at Delos. There he carried off secretly in the night from the most sacred temple of Apollo statues of great beauty and antiquity, and had them piled aboard his own transport-ship. The following day, when the inhabitants of Delos saw the plundered temple, they were deeply upset. This temple has such sanctity and antiquity in their eyes that they believe it is the birthplace of Apollo himself. Nevertheless, they did not dare to say anything in case Dolabella himself was involved in the affair. XVIII. Then suddenly, gentlemen, very severe storms arose, so that Dolabella was not only unable to set sail when he intended but was scarcely able to remain in the town, so great were the waves being driven ashore. At this point that brigand's ship, laden with the sacred donis istius, onusta signis religiosis, expulsa atque eiecta fluctu frangitur; in litore signa illa Apollinis reperiuntur; iussu Dolabellae reponuntur. Tempestas sedatur, Dolabella Delo proficiscitur.

47 Non dubito quin, tametsi nullus in te sensus humanitatis, nulla ratio umquam fuit religionis, nunc tamen in metu periculoque tuo tuorum tibi scelerum veniat in mentem. Potestne tibi ulla spes salutis commoda ostendi, cum recordaris in deos immortalis quam impius, quam sceleratus, quam nefarius fueris? Apollinemne tu Delium spoliare ausus es? Illine tu templo tam antiquo, tam sancto, tam religioso manus impias ac sacrilegas adferre conatus es? Si in pueritia non iis artibus ac disciplinis institutus eras ut ea quae litteris mandata sunt disceres atque cognosceres, ne postea quidem, cum in ea ipsa loca venisti, potuisti accipere id quod est proditum memoria 48 ac litteris, Latonam ex longo errore et fuga gravidam et iam ad pariendum temporibus exactis confugisse Delum atque ibi Apollinem Dianamque peperisse? qua ex opinione hominum illa insula eorum deorum sacra putatur, tantaque eius auctoritas religionis et est et semper fuit ut ne Persae quidem, cum bellum toti Graeciae, dis hominibusque, indixissent, et mille numero navium classem ad Delum adpulissent, quicquam conarentur aut violare aut attingere. Hoc tu fanum depopulari, homo improbissime atque amentissime, audebas? Fuit ulla cupiditas tanta quae tantam exstingueret religionem? Et si tum haec non cogitabas, ne nunc quidem recordaris nullum esse tantum malum quod non tibi pro sceleribus tuis iam diu debeatur?

2 illa $D\Psi r$: om. pqb Schol. Gronov.   7 venerit $q^1 r$ 11 illine D al. π : illi G_{12} 13 iis edd. recc. : his Dp rell.   16 memoriae $G_1 b\delta$ 18 ad pariendum vicinam $r\delta$ 19 ibi om. in lac. p 22 hominibusque pG_1 Asc. : hominibus $D\Psi$ 25 depopulari b : -are $D\Psi p$ al. : depeculari Lamb., Muell. (Act. Pr. § 14)   26 ulla G_1 al. : illa Dp et pler.   29 iam πb : tam $D\Psi$

statues, was tossed forth and cast upon the beach by a wave, and was broken asunder; the statues of Apollo were found on the shore. They were replaced by order of Dolabella. The storm abated and Dolabella set sail from Delos.

47 I have no doubt, though you have no spark of humanity in you and never had any religious convictions, that, nonetheless, in your present fear and danger, the thought of your crimes comes before your mind. Can any hope of deliverance seem opportune to you, when you recall how impious, how criminal, how vile has been your conduct towards the immortal gods? Did you dare despoil Apollo of Delos? Did you attempt to lay impious and sacrilegious hands on a temple so ancient, so sacred, so revered? If in your childhood you received no training in those arts and studies that would have given you a thorough knowledge of the contents of literature, even later on, after you arrived in these very places, did you fail to learn the story that has been handed down in
48 tradition and literature, how Latona, after long wanderings in flight, heavy with child and with the time of delivery already at hand, took refuge in Delos and there gave birth to Apollo and Diana. Because of this popular belief, that island is considered sacred to these deities, and so great is the religious reverence it inspires and always has inspired, that not even the Persians, though they had declared war on the whole of Greece, gods and men alike, and had brought a fleet of a thousand ships to Delos, attempted to defile or lay a finger on anything. Was it this shrine you dared despoil, you most unprincipled and demented creature? Did there exist a greed so great as to destroy so great a centre of religion? And if you did not think about such things, do you not even now realize that there is no evil so great that it is not long owing to you for your crimes.

19 In Asiam vero postquam venit, quid ego adventus istius
49 prandia, cenas, equos muneraque commemorem? Nihil
cum Verre de cotidianis criminibus acturus sum: Chio per
vim signa pulcherrima dico abstulisse, item Erythris et
Halicarnasso. Tenedo—praetereo pecuniam quam eripuit 5
—Tenem ipsum, qui apud Tenedios sanctissimus deus
habetur, qui urbem illam dicitur condidisse, cuius ex nomine
Tenedus nominatur, hunc ipsum, inquam, Tenem pulcherrime factum, quem quondam in comitio vidistis, abstulit
50 magno cum gemitu civitatis. Illa vero expugnatio fani anti- 10
quissimi et nobilissimi Iunonis Samiae quam luctuosa Samiis
fuit, quam acerba toti Asiae, quam clara apud omnis, quam
nemini vestrum inaudita! de qua expugnatione cum legati
ad C. Neronem in Asiam Samo venissent, responsum
tulerunt eius modi querimonias, quae ad legatos populi 15
Romani pertinerent, non ad praetorem sed Romam deferri
oportere. Quas iste tabulas illinc, quae signa sustulit! quae
cognovi egomet apud istum in aedibus nuper, cum obsi-
51 gnandi gratia venissem. Quae signa nunc, Verres, ubi sunt?
illa quaero quae apud te nuper ad omnis columnas, omnibus 20
etiam intercolumniis, in silva denique disposita sub divo vidimus. Cur ea, quam diu alium praetorem cum iis iudicibus
quos in horum locum subsortitus esses de te in consilium
iturum putasti, tam diu domi fuerunt: posteaquam nostris
testibus nos quam horis tuis uti malle vidisti, nullum signum 25
domi reliquisti praeter duo quae in mediis aedibus sunt,
quae ipsa Samo sublata sunt? Non putasti me tuis fami-

1 adv. istius, prandia : *sic distinxit Madvigius, et ita est in p* 2
muneraque *Dp rell.* : munera *Asc., edd. vett.* commemorarem *p et
primo D* 10 vero *om. p* expilatio *Koch, Muell. (et* 13) : iii,
§§ 6, 23 12 apud deos δ (*ex* apud ōs, *credo, ortum*) 15 legatos
DΨp: -um *rb* 17 illinc *D al.* πb : istinc *s* : istinc illinc $G_{12}K$ 20
in omnibus *Klotz, Muell.* 21 in intercol. *Halm, Kays.* 23 subsortitus πb (*Act. Pr.* § 30): sortitus *DΨ* (i, § 158) esses *Zumpt*:
es *codd.* subsortiturus eras *coni. Hotom.* 25 tuis *Dp rell.* : *om.
Asc., cod.* (?) *Vrs.* tuis horis *b*

49 XIX. Furthermore, after he reached Asia – I see no reason to recount the lunches, dinners, horses, and presents that attended his arrival, for I do not intend to accuse Verres of any ordinary offenses – but I do assert that he carried off by force from Chios statues of the highest excellence, and did the same thing from Erythrae and Halicarnassus. From Tenedos (I disregard the money he seized) he carried off Tenes himself, who is regarded by the people of Tenedos as their most sacred divinity, who is said to have founded the city, and after whose name it is called Tenedos – this same Tenes, I repeat, a most beautifully sculptured work, which you once saw in the *Comitium*, he carried off amid the loud lamentations of

50 the entire community. Furthermore, that onslaught of his on the very ancient and most celebrated temple of Samian Juno, what grief it caused the people of Samos, what bitterness it caused in all of Asia, how notorious it became everywhere, how unavoidably it was forced on the attention of every one of us! When envoys from Samos came to C. Nero in Asia in connection with this assault on the temple, they received the reply that complaints of this sort, which related to a legate of the Roman people, should be reported, not to a praetor, but to Rome. What a wealth of paintings and statues he took from Samos! I recently got firsthand knowledge of them at his house,

51 when I went there to seal evidence. Where are those statues now, Verres? I am asking about those I recently saw at your house, set out by every column, and even in all the spaces between the columns, and indeed in the shrubbery under the open air. Why were they kept at your house for as long as you thought a different praetor and jurors, which you have allotted to replace this present panel, would decide your case? After you saw that we preferred to use our witnesses rather than abide by your timetable, you left no statue in the house except two that stood in the middle of it, and even they were taken from Samos. Did you not expect that I would

liarissimis in hanc rem testimonia denuntiaturum, qui tuae
domi semper fuissent, ex quibus quaererem, signa scirentne
fuisse quae non essent? Quid tum hos de te iudicaturos
arbitratus es, cum viderent te iam non contra accusatorem
tuum, sed contra quaestorem sectoremque pugnare? Qua
de re Charidemum Chium testimonium priore actione
dicere audistis, sese, cum esset trierarchus et Verrem ex Asia
decedentem prosequeretur iussu Dolabellae, fuisse una cum
isto Sami, seseque tum scire spoliatum esse fanum Iunonis
et oppidum Samum; posteaque se causam apud Chios
civis suos Samiis accusantibus publice dixisse, eoque se
esse absolutum quod planum fecisset ea quae legati Samiorum
dicerent ad Verrem, non ad se pertinere.

53   Aspendum vetus oppidum et nobile in Pamphylia scitis
esse, plenissimum signorum optimorum. Non dicam illinc
hoc signum ablatum esse et illud: hoc dico, nullum te
Aspendi signum, Verres, reliquisse, omnia ex fanis, ex locis
publicis, palam, spectantibus omnibus, plaustris evecta exportataque esse.   Atque etiam illum Aspendium citharistam,
de quo saepe audistis id quod est Graecis hominibus in
proverbio, quem omnia 'intus canere' dicebant, sustulit et
in intimis suis aedibus posuit, ut etiam illum ipsum suo
54 artificio superasse videatur. Pergae fanum antiquissimum
et sanctissimum Dianae scimus esse: id quoque a te nudatum, ac spoliatum esse, ex ipsa Diana quod habebat auri
detractum atque ablatum esse dico.

Quae, malum, est ista tanta audacia atque amentia! Quas
enim sociorum atque amicorum urbis adisti legationis iure
et nomine, si in eas vi cum exercitu imperioque invasisses,

2 semper $D\Psi$: saepe prb Bake, Kays. (Zielinski p. 159)   3 ibi fuisse quae nunc non essent   6 chium $D\Psi b$: cophium pq^1 18 plostris Dp al.   20 gregis p 21 intus om. pq^1 22 suo art. $D\Psi$: art. suo $pbr\delta$: suo om. Asc., Schol. Gronov.   29 si in eas π D^2 vulg. : quin ea D^1, quin eas Ψ (quam eas L) : cum in eas Klotz, Kays., Muell.

52 require your very close friends, who had been constant visitors at your house, to give evidence about this matter and would ask them if they know about the existence of these statues that have now become non-existent? XX. What did you think they would then conclude about you when they saw that you were now battling not the prosecutor but the quaestor and public bidder? In relation to this affair you heard Charidemus of Chios state in evidence at the first hearing that, while serving as commander of a trireme and acting, on orders from Dolabella, as escort for Verres on the latter's departure from Asia, he had been present with him at Samos and was then aware that the temple of Juno and the town of Samos had been plundered. You also heard that later he had publicly defended himself before his fellow-citizens of Chios against accusations of the Samians and had been acquitted because he had plainly shown that the charges which the Samian envoys were making against Verres had nothing to do with him.

53 You are aware that Aspendus is an old and famous town in Pamphylia, full of the finest statuary. I am not going to say this or that statue was removed from there; this is what I say, that you, Verres, left not a single statue in Aspendus, that all of them, from temples and from public places, were openly and before the eyes of all carried off on wagons and shipped out. Even that lyre-player of Aspendus, about whom you have often heard the expression that has become proverbial among the Greeks, of whom they used to say "he played all his music inside," he carried away and placed deep inside his house, so that he might seem to have surpassed the lyre 54 player himself at his craft. We know there is a very ancient and sacred temple of Diana at Perga; this too I assert was stripped bare by your pillaging, and from Diana herself any gold the statue contained was torn off and carried away.

You scoundrel, what is the meaning of this monstrous effrontery and mindless folly? For even if, instead of visiting those cities of friends and allies with the authority and title of a legate, you had forcefully invaded them with an army and full military authority,

tamen, opinor, quae signa atque ornamenta ex iis urbibus sustulisses, haec non in tuam domum neque in suburbana amicorum, sed Romam in publicum deportasses. Quid ego de M. Marcello loquar, qui Syracusas, urbem ornatissimam, cepit? quid de L. Scipione, qui bellum in Asia gessit Antiochumque, regem potentissimum, vicit? quid de Flaminino, qui regem Philippum et Macedoniam subegit? quid de L. Paulo, qui regem Persen vi ac virtute superavit? quid de L. Mummio, qui urbem pulcherrimam atque ornatissimam, Corinthum, plenissimam rerum omnium, sustulit, urbisque Achaiae Boeotiaeque multas sub imperium populi Romani dicionemque subiunxit? Quorum domus, cum honore ac virtute florerent, signis et tabulis pictis erant vacuae; at vero urbem totam templaque deorum omnisque Italiae partis illorum donis ac monumentis exornatas videmus. Vereor ne haec forte cuipiam nimis antiqua et iam obsoleta videantur; ita enim tum aequabiliter omnes erant eius modi ut haec laus eximiae virtutis et innocentiae non solum hominum, verum etiam temporum illorum esse videatur. P. Servilius, vir clarissimus, maximis rebus gestis, adest de te sententiam laturus: Olympum vi, copiis, consilio, virtute cepit, urbem antiquam et omnibus rebus auctam et ornatam. Recens exemplum fortissimi viri profero; nam postea Servilius imperator populi Romani Olympum urbem hostium cepit quam tu in isdem illis locis legatus quaestorius oppida pacata sociorum atque amicorum diripienda ac vexanda curasti. Tu quae ex fanis religiosissimis per scelus et latrocinium abstulisti, ea nos videre nisi in tuis amicorumque tuorum tectis non possumus: P. Servilius quae signa

1 atque *pr al.* : et que *D*, et quae Ψ (quae *K*, et *G₁*) iis *Zumpt* (is *ed. Rom.*): his *Dp al.* : istis *G₂* 8 Paulo *codd.*: Paullo *Iord., Klotz, Kays.* 14 templa *Kδ* 16 forte *om. G₁ Prisc.* 18 huius modi πbδ (*Div.* § 38; i, §§ 17, 151): vel huius modi *G₂KZ* (vel *s. l. D²*) 21 laturus est *prδ* Olinthium *D* : Olinphum *p*. Olynthum *rell.* virtute consilio *q* 24 Olinthum *Dp*

you should still, in my opinion, not have conveyed to your house or to the suburban villas of your friends any statues or works of art that you had removed from these cities, but should have brought them to Rome as the property of the nation. XXI. What need is there to speak of M. Marcellus, who captured Syracuse, a city of the most lavish magnificence? or of L. Scipio, who conducted a war in Asia and defeated Antiochus, a king of the most formidable power? or of Flamininus, who subdued King Philip and Macedonia? or of L. Paulus, who overcame King Perses with armed might and manly spirit? or of L. Mummius, who destroyed the most beautiful and splendidly adorned city of Corinth, abounding in riches of every kind, and brought under the authority and dominion of Rome many cities of Achaia and Boeotia? The houses of these men, though they shone with distinction and virtue, were empty of statues and paintings, but we see the entire city and the temples of the gods and all regions of Italy adorned with their gifts and monuments. But I fear these examples may perhaps seem excessively old to some and by now out of date; for then all were so uniformly in this mould that the praise for their outstanding virtue and cleanhandedness seems to belong not only to the individuals but to their times. P. Servilius, a man of the highest eminence and achievement, is here to give his verdict in your case. He, by force of arms and by wise judgement and courage, captured Olympus, an ancient city containing every form of wealth and splendour. I am putting forward a recent example of a very valiant man; for Servilius, as a general of the Roman people, captured Olympus, a hostile city, in the period since you, as a legate holding the position of proquaestor, caused peaceful towns of allies and friends in these same regions to be plundered and devastated. The treasures you carried off in acts of criminal brigandage from shrines of the highest sanctity we cannot see except in your own house or in the houses of your friends: the statues and

atque ornamenta ex urbe hostium vi et virtute capta belli lege atque imperatorio iure sustulit, ea populo Romano adportavit, per triumphum vexit, in tabula publica ad aerarium perscribenda curavit. Cognoscite ex litteris publicis hominis amplissimi diligentiam. Recita. RATIONES RE- 5 LATAE P. SERVILI. Non solum numerum signorum, sed etiam unius cuiusque magnitudinem, figuram, statum litteris definiri vides. Certe maior est virtutis victoriaeque iucunditas quam ista voluptas quae percipitur ex libidine et cupiditate. Multo diligentius habere dico Servilium praedam 10 populi Romani quam te tua furta notata atque perscripta.

22
58 Dices tua quoque signa et tabulas pictas ornamento urbi foroque populi Romani fuisse. Memini; vidi simul cum populo Romano forum comitiumque adornatum ad speciem magnifico ornatu, ad sensum cogitationemque acerbo et 15 lugubri; vidi conlucere omnia furtis tuis, praeda provinciarum, spoliis sociorum atque amicorum. Quo quidem tempore, iudices, iste spem maximam reliquorum quoque peccatorum nactus est; vidit enim eos qui iudiciorum se 59 dominos dici volebant harum cupiditatum esse servos. Socii 20 vero nationesque exterae spem omnem tum primum abiecerunt rerum ac fortunarum suarum, propterea quod casu legati ex Asia atque Achaia plurimi Romae tunc fuerunt, qui deorum simulacra ex suis fanis sublata in foro venerabantur, itemque cetera signa et ornamenta cum cognoscerent, 25 alia alio in loco lacrimantes intuebantur. Quorum omnium hunc sermonem tum esse audiebamus, nihil esse quod quisquam dubitaret de exitio sociorum atque amicorum, cum quidem viderent in foro populi Romani, quo in loco

---

1 vi *s. l. r* : *om. Dp rell.* (per virtutem *K*) 3 tabula pub. *pq* (v, § 103) : tabulas publicas *rell. praeter Cuiac. in quo fuisse dicitur* tabulis publicis: *secl. Muell.*   5 Recita . . . Servili *prb* : *om. D*Ψ 19 iudic se *Dp rell.* : se iudic. *Asc., Schol. Gronov.*   21 omnem *L* : omnium *Dp rell.*   24 fanis suis *qr*   25 itemque *p al.* : item qui *D*Ψ

works of art that P. Servilius, in accordance with the rules of war and his rights as a general, removed from a hostile city captured by military might and valour, he conveyed to the Roman people, paraded in his triumph, and had recorded in detail in an official record for lodgment in the treasury. You can see from his official papers the thoroughness of this most eminent man. Read them out. 'THE REGISTERED ACCOUNTS OF P. SERVILIUS.' You see that not only the number of statues but the size, form, and posture of each one is specified in the document. It is clear that the enjoyment deriving from virtue and victory is greater than the pleasure experienced from lustfulness and greed; for I affirm that Servilius has labelled and recorded the public spoils of the Roman people far more carefully than have you your private pillagings.

58 XXII. You will say that your statues and paintings have also adorned the city and forum of the Roman people. I recall the occasion, for I, together with the Roman people, saw the forum and *Comitium* resplendent with a display magnificent to the eye, but painful and distressing to the heart and mind. I saw everything around me gleaming with the products of your thievery, with plunder from provinces, with spoils of allies and friends. Indeed on this occasion, gentlemen, Verres acquired his strongest hope of committing further misdeeds in the future, for he saw that those who wanted to be called masters of the courts were servants of this 59 type of greed. But the allies and foreign nations then for the first time abandoned all hope for their property and possessions, because, as it happened, there was then present in Rome a very large number of envoys from Asia and Achaia, and they kept paying worship in the forum to images of gods taken from their own temples and, in similar vein, when they recognised other statues and works of art, they kept gazing at them in their different locations with tears in their eyes. We heard reports that the immediate comment of all of them was to the effect that there was no longer any reason to doubt that the destruction of the allies and friends of Rome was inevitable, when they actually saw openly arrayed in the forum of the Roman people – the very place where

antea qui sociis iniurias fecerant accusari et condemnari solebant, ibi esse palam posita ea quae ab sociis per scelus ablata ereptaque essent.

60 Hic ego non arbitror illum negaturum signa se plurima, tabulas pictas innumerabilis habere; sed, ut opinor, solet 5 haec quae rapuit et furatus est non numquam dicere se emisse, quoniam quidem in Achaiam, Asiam, Pamphyliam sumptu publico et legationis nomine mercator signorum 23 tabularumque pictarum missus est. Et istius et patris eius accepi tabulas omnis, quas diligentissime legi atque digessi, 10 patris, quoad vixit, tuas, quoad ais te confecisse. Nam in isto, iudices, hoc novum reperietis. Audimus aliquem tabulas numquam confecisse; quae est opinio hominum de Antonio falsa, nam fecit diligentissime; verum sit hoc genus aliquod, minime probandum. Audimus alium non ab initio 15 fecisse, sed ex tempore aliquo confecisse; est aliqua etiam huiusce rei ratio. Hoc vero novum et ridiculum est, quod hic nobis respondit cum ab eo tabulas postularemus, usque ad M. Terentium et C. Cassium consules confecisse, postea 61 destitisse. Alio loco hoc cuius modi sit considerabimus; 20 nunc nihil ad me attinet; horum enim temporum in quibus nunc versor habeo tabulas et tuas et patris. Plurima signa pulcherrima, plurimas tabulas optimas deportasse te negare non potes. Atque utinam neges! Vnum ostende in tabulis aut tuis aut patris tui emptum esse: vicisti. Ne haec 25 quidem duo signa pulcherrima quae nunc ad impluvium tuum stant, quae multos annos ante valvas Iunonis Samiae

7 Asiam Db : *om. pq* : *ante* Achaiam K 9 Habeo et istius Dp *al.* (ipsius) *Asc.* : ab eo istius b *al.* : *num* At vero *s.* Age vero istius ? *Cl. Rev.* xvii. 202   10 accepti Dp *rell.* : accepti *Asc.* (accepti et expensi ?) : *secl. edd.*   12, 15 Audivimus G_2 13 numquam tab. qr 14 Antonio Dp *rell.* : M. Antonio *Asc. edd.* (*Div.* § 22)   fecit p *al.* : leḡ DZ, legis $G_{12}K$, legit s 17 huiusce pb *Asc.* (i, § 56) : eiusce $D\Psi$ 18 ab *om.* Dp 19 et Dp *rell.* : *om. Asc.* (v, § 34)   23 optimas Dpq : *om.* $G_2K\delta$ 26 impluvium qrb (impluium p) : pluium *s.* pluvium $D\Psi$ 27 ad valvas δ

previously those who had wronged the allies were commonly brought to trial and condemned - property that had been criminally stolen and seized from the allies.

60 I do not think that Verres will at this point deny that he has in his possession a very large number of statues and countless paintings, but, if I am not mistaken, he has a tendency to assert on occasion that these, though in fact seized and stolen, were purchased by him, since he was, of course, sent to Achaia, Asia, and Pamphylia at public expense and with the title of legate to traffic in statues and paintings. XXIII. I have acquired all the accounts both of Verres and his father and have most carefully read them and put them in order, the father's for as long as he lived, yours for as long as you say you kept accounts. For in dealing with Verres, gentlemen, you will discover this new way of doing things. We have heard that certain people never kept accounts. This is the common belief about Antonius, though it is false, since he kept the most careful records. But let us accept that this particular situation does exist, though it is in no way to be commended. We have heard that others did not keep accounts from the beginning but from a certain period. There is a certain reasonableness even in this practice. But here is a new and absurd notion, which Verres related to us when we asked him for his accounts, namely that he kept records up to the consulship of M. Terentius and C. Cassius, but

61 stopped doing so after that. We will consider what kind of behaviour this is at another time. It does not concern me at the moment, for I have the accounts of both yourself and your father for the period with which I am now dealing. You cannot deny that you brought back a very large number of the finest statues and a very large number of excellent paintings. I wish you would deny it! Show me from your own or from your father's accounts that a single one of them was purchased, and you have won the day. Even the two very beautiful statues that now stand by the pool in your atrium, which stood for many years before the doors of the temple of Samian

24

steterunt, habes quo modo emeris, haec, inquam, duo quae in aedibus tuis sola iam sunt, quae sectorem exspectant, relicta ac destituta a ceteris signis.

62 At, credo, in hisce solis rebus indomitas cupiditates atque effrenatas habebat: ceterae libidines eius ratione aliqua aut modo continebantur. Quam multis istum ingenuis, quam multis matribus familias in illa taetra atque impura legatione vim attulisse existimatis? Ecquo in oppido pedem posuit ubi non plura stuprorum flagitiorumque suorum quam adventus sui vestigia reliquerit? Sed ego omnia quae negari poterunt praetermittam; etiam haec quae certissima sunt et clarissima relinquam; unum aliquod de nefariis istius factis eligam, quo facilius ad Siciliam possim aliquando, quae mihi hoc oneris negotique imposuit, pervenire.

63 Oppidum est in Hellesponto Lampsacum, iudices, in primis Asiae provinciae clarum et nobile; homines autem ipsi Lampsaceni cum summe in omnis civis Romanos officiosi, tum praeterea maxime sedati et quieti, prope praeter ceteros ad summum Graecorum otium potius quam ad ullam vim aut tumultum adcommodati. Accidit, cum iste a Cn. Dolabella efflagitasset ut se ad regem Nicomedem regemque Sadalam mitteret, cumque iter hoc sibi magis ad quaestum suum quam ad rei publicae tempus adcommodatum depoposcisset, ut illo itinere veniret Lampsacum cum magna calamitate et prope pernicie civitatis. Deducitur iste ad Ianitorem quendam hospitem, comitesque eius item apud ceteros hospites conlocantur. Vt mos erat istius, atque ut eum suae libidines flagitiosae facere admonebant, statim negotium dat illis suis comitibus, nequissimis turpissimisque

---

1 habes dicere *Lamb.*, *Kays.* 8 ecquo *D* : hecquo *p* : et quo *δ* 9 quam *om.* *D al. p* : stupr. flag. suor. quam *del.* *Kays.* 10 ego relinquam *qr* 16 autem *DΨbr*: *om.* *pq* 17 ipsi *om.* *K* Lampsaceni *secl. Bake*, *Kays.* 19 Graecorum *D rell. Non.* : *om. pq*[1] : *secl. Kays.* 24 in illo *Lg.* 42 *Kays* (i, § 15) 28 flagitiose *Dp rell.* admonebant *DΨpr*: commonebant *K* : monebant *q*

Juno, you cannot show were bought – I mean these two which now stand alone in your house and await the public bidder, left abandoned by the other statues.

XXIV. But I suppose we are to believe it was only in relation to these matters that his desires were untamed and unbridled, and that his other passions were restrained by some degree of rationality and moderation! How many women of free birth, how many mothers of families do you think he sexually assaulted during his foul and depraved tenure as a legate? In what town did he set foot where the imprints left by his shameful lecheries did not outnumber the physical imprints of his arrival? But I will pass over all matters to which he could offer a denial. I will disregard even those events that are indisputable and very well known, and will select one particular instance of his abominable behaviour that I may more easily come at last to Sicily, which has laid this burdensome task upon me.

There is a town named Lampsacum in the Hellespont, gentlemen, which is among the most famous and distinguished in the province of Asia. The people of Lampsacum, moreover, are particularly conscious of their duty to all Roman citizens, and are furthermore extremely tranquil and peace-loving, adapted, almost to a greater extent than the rest of their race, to the highly relaxed way of life of the Greeks rather than to any form of violence or disruption. It so happened, after Verres had insistently pressed Dolabella to send him to King Nicomedes and King Sedala, demanding for himself a journey better suited to serve his personal profit than the needs of the state, that he arrived, in the course of that journey, at Lampsacum, bringing with him a major calamity and the near destruction of the community. He was taken to the house of a host named Janitor, and his aides were similarly quartered with other hosts. As was his custom, and in accordance with the usual urgings of his shameful lusts, he immediately gave those aides of his, men of the most depraved and loathsome character,

hominibus, uti videant et investigent ecqua virgo sit aut
mulier digna quam ob rem ipse Lampsaci diutius commo-
25 raretur. Erat comes eius Rubrius quidam, homo factus ad
64 istius libidines, qui miro artificio, quocumque venerat, haec
investigare omnia solebat. Is ad eum rem istam defert, 5
Philodamum esse quendam, genere, honore, copiis, existimatione facile principem Lampsacenorum ; eius esse filiam,
quae cum patre habitaret propterea quod virum non haberet,
mulierem eximia pulchritudine ; sed eam summa integritate
pudicitiaque existimari. Homo, ut haec audivit, sic exarsit 10
ad id quod non modo ipse numquam viderat, sed ne audierat
quidem ab eo qui ipse vidisset, ut statim ad Philodamum
migrare se diceret velle. Hospes Ianitor, qui nihil suspi-
caretur, veritus ne quid in ipso se offenderetur, hominem
summa vi retinere coepit. Iste, qui hospitis relinquendi 15
causam reperire non posset, alia sibi ratione viam munire ad
stuprum coepit ; Rubrium, delicias suas, in omnibus eius
modi rebus adiutorem suum et conscium, parum laute
65 deversari dicit ; ad Philodamum deduci iubet. Quod ubi
est Philodamo nuntiatum, tametsi erat ignarus quantum 20
sibi ac liberis suis iam tum mali constitueretur, tamen
ad istum venit ; ostendit munus illud suum non esse ; se,
cum suae partes essent hospitum recipiendorum, tum ipsos
tamen praetores et consules, non legatorum adseculas,
recipere solere. Iste, qui una cupiditate raperetur, totum 25
illius postulatum causamque neglexit ; per vim ad eum,
26 qui recipere non debebat, Rubrium deduci imperavit. Hic
Philodamus, posteaquam ius suum obtinere non potuit, ut

1 ut π*b*   hecquae *p*, ecquae *s* : qua *DG*$_1$: si qua *KG*$_2$ 2
commoretur *Ern. auct. Klotz, Kays.*   5 · istam *Dp rell.* : ita *Pluyg.,
Madv.. Muell.*   13 Ianitor *secl. Bake, Kays., Muell.*   20 erat *tres
Lgg., Non.* : non erat *D*Ψ*prb* : erat non *q al.*   21 mali π*b* : *om. D*Ψ
22 munus illud suum *DZ*π*b* : illud munus suum *G*$_2$*K* : munus suum
illud *G*$_1$ 23 ipsos tantum *Lg.* 42   24 adseculas (ass.) *D*π :
asseclas *rell.*

64 the task of observing and investigating whether there was any unmarried or married woman on whose account it would be worth his while staying longer at Lampsacum. XXV. Among his aides was a certain Rubrius, an ideal instrument of Verres' lusts, who was in the habit, wherever they went, of investigating all these matters with wondrous skill. He brought him the news that there was a man named Philodamus, who was easily the foremost of the people of Lampsacum in birth, standing, wealth, and reputation, and that he had a daughter who lived with her father because she had no husband, a woman of outstanding beauty, but with a reputation for the highest integrity and purity. This fellow, when he heard this, developed such a passion for something he had not only never personally seen, but had not even heard about from someone who had, that he declared he wanted to move immediately to the house of Philodamus. His host Janitor, who suspected nothing and was afraid that Verres was in some way displeased with himself, began to oppose his going with all his might. Since he could not find a reason for abandoning his host, Verres began to build his route to debauchery by another means. He declared that Rubrius, his precious favourite, and his helper and confidant in all matters of this sort, did not have sufficiently comfortable lodgings, and he ordered

65 him to be taken to the house of Philodamus. When Philodamus was informed of this, though he had no idea how great a misfortune was even then being set in motion for himself and for his children, he nonetheless came to see Verres. He pointed out that he had no obligation in this matter; that even when it was his turn to accept guests, it was still just praetors and consuls he was in the habit of receiving, not attendants of legates. Verres, swept along by his one driving passion, ignored Philodamus' entire petition and argument. He ordered that Rubrius should be forcefully billeted with a man who had no obligation to receive him. XXVI. At this point Philodamus, having failed to secure his rights, worked

humanitatem consuetudinemque suam retineret laborabat. Homo, qui semper hospitalissimus amicissimusque nostrorum hominum existimatus esset, noluit videri ipsum illum Rubrium invitus domum suam recepisse; magnifice et ornate, ut erat in primis inter suos copiosus, convivium 5 comparat; rogat Rubrium ut quos ei commodum sit invitet, locum sibi soli, si videatur, relinquat; etiam filium suum, lectissimum adulescentem, foras ad propinquum suum 66 quendam mittit ad cenam. Rubrius istius comites invitat; eos omnis Verres certiores facit quid opus esset. Mature 10 veniunt, discumbitur. Fit sermo inter eos, et invitatio ut Graeco more biberetur; hortatur hospes, poscunt maioribus poculis, celebratur omnium sermone laetitiaque convivium. Posteaquam satis calere res Rubrio visa est, ' Quaeso,' inquit, ' Philodame, cur ad nos filiam tuam non 15 intro vocari iubes?' Homo, qui et summa gravitate et iam id aetatis et parens esset, obstipuit hominis improbi dicto. Instare Rubrius. Tum ille, ut aliquid responderet, negavit moris esse Graecorum ut in convivio virorum accumberent mulieres. Hic tum alius ex alia parte, ' Enim vero ferendum 20 hoc quidem non est; vocetur mulier!' Et simul servis suis Rubrius ut ianuam clauderent et ipsi ad foris adsisterent 67 imperat. Quod ubi ille intellexit, id agi atque id parari ut filiae suae vis adferretur, servos suos ad se vocat; his imperat ut se ipsum neglegant, filiam defendant; excurrat 25 aliquis qui hoc tantum domestici mali filio nuntiet. Clamor interea fit tota domo; inter servos Rubri atque hospitis iactatur domi suae vir primarius et homo honestissimus; pro se quisque manus adfert; aqua denique ferventi a Rubrio ipso Philodamus perfunditur. Haec ubi filio nuntiata sunt, 30

6 comparat *Dp rell. Non.* (*Zielinski p.* 193) : apparat *q¹ Muell.*
17 obstipuit (ops. *p*) *fq*λ : obstupuit *Dr rell.*   18 ille *πb* : om. *D*Ψ
27 pugna inter *contra codd. Rufinianus*   28 primarius *Non. edd.* :
primus *codd.* : (optimus *s et ed. Iunt.*)   homo *πb Non.* : om. *D*Ψ

hard to maintain his graciousness and normal mode of behaviour. As a man who had always been considered most hospitable and friendly towards our people, he did not wish it to appear that he had taken even a man like Rubrius into his house against his will. He prepared a magnificent and elegant banquet, as might be expected from someone who was among the wealthiest of his community; he asked Rubrius to invite whom he pleased and to reserve a place, if he so wished, only for him; even his son, a most exceptional young man, he sent
66 away to have dinner with one of his relatives. Rubrius invited Verres' aides, and Verres instructed them all in what was required of them. They arrived early and took their places. Conversation began, and they were invited to drink in the traditional Greek style: the host urged them on, they called for toasts with larger cups, the banquet was filled with talk and merriment arising from every guest. When it seemed to Rubrius that the atmosphere had heated up sufficiently, he said, "Tell me, Philodamus, why not ask your daughter to be summoned to join us?" As a man of the strictest principles and of already advanced years, and also as a parent, Philodamus was rendered speechless by the scoundrel's suggestion. Rubrius began to insist. Then Philodamus, wishing to make some response, said it was not a practice of the Greeks to have women recline at table at a dinner-party of men. At this point someone else spoke up from another part of the room, "Really, this is intolerable, let the woman be summoned." At the same time, Rubrius ordered his slaves to close the door of the house and to take
67 positions alongside the entrance. When Philodamus came to realise that the purpose behind these actions and preparations was a sexual attack on his daughter, he summoned his slaves and told them to take no action on his behalf, but to defend his daughter; and someone was to hurry to tell his son of this terrible trouble at his house. Meanwhile there was uproar all over the house. In the midst of the slaves of Rubrius and those of his host a man of the highest importance and repute was being knocked about in his own house; everyone was joining in the fight to the extent that he was able; finally, Philodamus had boiling water poured all over him by Rubrius. When the son was informed of these events, he

statim exanimatus ad aedis contendit, ut et vitae patris et pudicitiae sororis succurreret; omnes eodem animo Lampsaceni, simul ut hoc audierunt, quod eos cum Philodami dignitas tum iniuriae magnitudo movebat, ad aedis noctu convenerunt. Hic lictor istius Cornelius, qui cum eius 5 servis erat a Rubrio quasi in praesidio ad auferendam mulierem conlocatus, occiditur; servi non nulli vulnerantur; ipse Rubrius in turba sauciatur. Iste, qui sua cupiditate tantos tumultus concitatos videret, cupere aliqua evolare, si posset. Postridie homines mane in contionem conveniunt; 10 quaerunt quid optimum factu sit; pro se quisque, ut in quoque erat auctoritatis plurimum, ad populum loquebatur; inventus est nemo cuius non haec et sententia esset et oratio, non esse metuendum, si istius nefarium scelus Lampsaceni ulti vi manuque essent, ne senatus populusque Romanus in 15 eam civitatem animadvertendum putaret; quodsi hoc iure legati populi Romani in socios nationesque exteras uterentur, ut pudicitiam liberorum servare ab eorum libidine tutam non liceret, quidvis esse perpeti satius quam in tanta vi atque acerbitate versari. Haec cum omnes sentirent, et 20 cum in eam rationem pro suo quisque sensu ac dolore loqueretur, omnes ad eam domum in qua iste deversabatur profecti sunt; caedere ianuam saxis, instare ferro, ligna et sarmenta circumdare ignemque subicere coeperunt. Tunc cives Romani, qui Lampsaci negotiabantur, concurrunt; 25 orant Lampsacenos ut gravius apud eos nomen legationis quam iniuria legati putaretur; sese intellegere hominem illum esse impurum ac nefarium, sed quoniam nec perfecisset quod conatus esset, neque futurus esset Lampsaci

3 cum *Dpq* : tum Ψδ   9 aliqua *Dpr* : aliq̄. *KZ* : aliquo *L*   10 mane homines *prb*   11 factu *D al. p Asc.* : factum *G₁qr*   13 oratio *pb* : ratio *DΨr*   22 devers. *D* : divers. *pr Schol. Gronov.*   24 subiicere *Dpr*: circum *add. in mg. D²*, *et ita* Ψ   Tunc *DΨ* : tum *pb*

immediately rushed home, faint with fear, to help protect his father's life and his sister's chastity. All the people of Lampsacum, as soon as they heard the news, assembled with similar intent at the house in the night, roused to action both by the high standing of Philodamus and the magnitude of the injury. At this point, Verres' lictor Cornelius, who had been posted with his slaves by Rubrius in a protected position, as it were, for the abduction of the woman, was killed. Some of the slaves were wounded, and Rubrius himself was injured in the throng. Verres, realizing the enormous commotion provoked by his lecherous passions, was eager to escape by any means he could. XXVII. The following morning the people gathered at a meeting and considered what the best course of action might be. The most authoritative citizens addressed the people in order, each to the best of his ability. Not one speaker emerged whose thoughts and words deviated from the view that there must be no fear that if the people of Lampsacum avenged with physical force the vile crime of Verres, the senate and people of Rome would think their community deserving of punishment; they argued that, if legates of the Roman people used their authority over allies and foreign peoples in such a way that they were not allowed to safeguard their children's chastity against their lust, it was preferable to suffer any consequence than to be subject to such violence and cruelty. When all were agreed about this, and each speaker was giving voice to this reasoning as his own emotions and sense of outrage dictated, they all set out for the house where Verres was staying. They began to break down the door with stones and to attack it with swords and to surround it with logs and brushwood, which they proceeded to set on fire. Then the Roman citizens, who were engaged in business at Lampsacum, quickly gathered and pleaded with the people of the town to give greater weight to the title of legate than to the injury done by a legate; they realized the man was dissolute and evil, but since he had not succeeded in his wicked endeavour and would not return

postea, levius eorum peccatum fore si homini scelerato pepercissent quam si legato non pepercissent.

70 Sic iste multo sceleratior et nequior quam ille Hadrianus aliquanto etiam felicior fuit. Ille, quod eius avaritiam cives Romani ferre non potuerunt, Vticae domi suae vivus exustus est, idque ita illi merito accidisse existimatum est ut laetarentur omnes neque ulla animadversio constitueretur : hic sociorum ambustus incendio tamen ex illa flamma periculoque evolavit, neque adhuc causam ullam excogitare potuit quam ob rem commiserit, aut quid evenerit, ut in tantum periculum veniret. Non enim potest dicere, 'cum seditionem sedare vellem, cum frumentum imperarem, cum stipendium cogerem, cum aliquid denique rei publicae causa gererem, quod acrius imperavi, quod animadverti, quod minatus sum.' Quae si diceret, tamen ignosci non oporteret, si nimis atrociter imperando sociis in tantum adductus

28
71 periculum videretur. Nunc cum ipse causam illius tumultus neque veram dicere neque falsam confingere audeat, homo autem ordinis sui frugalissimus, qui tum accensus Ċ. Neroni fuit, P. Tettius, haec eadem se Lampsaci cognosse dixerit, vir omnibus rebus ornatissimus, C. Varro, qui tum in Asia militum tribunus fuit, haec eadem ipse se ex Philodamo audisse dicat, potestis dubitare quin istum fortuna non tam ex illo periculo eripere voluerit quam ad vestrum iudicium reservare? Nisi vero illud dicet, quod et in Tetti testimonio priore actione interpellavit Hortensius—quo tempore quidem signi satis dedit, si quid esset quod posset dicere, se tacere non posse, ut, quam diu tacuit in ceteris testibus, scire omnes possemus nihil habuisse quod diceret : hoc tum dixit, Philodamum et filium eius a C. Nerone esse damnatos.

5 potuerant δ   6 ita πb : om. DΨ   19 tunc D al.   20 Tettius δ : Pettius DKp : Pectius qr   22 mil. trib. DΨ : trib. mil. p (*errant Zumpt, Iord.*) br   ipse *coni. Benecke* : ipsa *codd.* : ipso *Haase, Kays.*   26 quo tempore quidem Dp *rell.* (*praeter* G₂K quo temp. ipse qu.) : quo quidem temp. *Siesbye, Muell.*

again to Lampsacum, the people would be guilty of a lesser fault if they spared a criminal than if they failed to spare a legate.

70 And so Verres, though a much more heinous and depraved scoundrel than the notorious Hadrianus, was still considerably more fortunate. For Hadrianus was burned alive in his home in Utica because the Roman citizens could not endure his avarice, and he was considered to have so richly deserved his fate that everyone was glad of it and no punishment was decreed; but Verres, though scorched by the fire lit by allies, escaped that perilous blaze. He has failed, however, to this day to devise any explanation to show what act of his or what event brought him to a situation of such danger. For he cannot say, "It happened when I was seeking to calm unrest, when I was requisitioning grain, when I was exacting the tribute, when I was, in short, conducting business on behalf of the state, because my demands, my punishments, my threats were too severe." Even if he were saying such things, he would still not deserve to be exonerated, if it appeared he had been landed in such serious danger because of excessively
71 harsh impositions on the allies. XXVIII. But now, when he does not dare mention the true cause of that disturbance or invent a false one; when, moreover, a most reputable member of his own order, P. Tettius, who was then an aide to C. Nero, has said that he learned this same story at Lampsacum; when a man most distinguished in every way, C. Varro, who was then a military tribune in Asia, personally tells us that he heard the self-same version from Philodamus, can you doubt that fortune wished not so much to rescue him from that danger as to reserve him for your verdict? Unless indeed he makes the same assertion that Hortensius interjected during the testimony of Tettius at the first hearing (at which time, incidentally, he provided a sufficiently strong indication that he could not keep silent, if he had any point that could be made, to let us all feel sure when he did keep quiet during the evidence of the rest of the witnesses that he had no argument to offer) - in any case this is what he stated then, that Philodamus and his
72 son had been condemned by C. Nero. To avoid a long

72 De quo ne multa disseram tantum dico, secutum id esse Neronem et eius consilium : quod Cornelium lictorem occisum esse constaret, putasse non oportere esse cuiquam ne in ulciscenda quidem iniuria hominis occidendi potestatem. In quo video Neronis iudicio non te absolutum esse improbitatis, sed illos damnatos esse caedis.

Verum ista damnatio tamen cuius modi fuit ? Audite, quaeso, iudices, et aliquando miseremini sociorum et osten-
29 dite aliquid iis in vestra fide praesidi esse oportere. Quod toti Asiae iure occisus videbatur istius ille verbo lictor, re vera minister improbissimae cupiditatis, pertimuit iste ne Philodamus Neronis iudicio liberaretur ; rogat et orat Dolabellam ut de sua provincia decedat, ad Neronem proficiscatur ; se demonstrat incolumem esse non posse, si Philodamo vivere atque aliquando Romam venire licuisset.
73 Commotus est Dolabella : fecit id quod multi reprehenderunt, ut exercitum, provinciam, bellum relinqueret, et in Asiam hominis nequissimi causa in alienam provinciam proficisceretur. Posteaquam ad Neronem venit, contendit ab eo ut Philodami causam cognosceret. Venerat ipse qui esset in consilio et primus sententiam diceret ; adduxerat etiam praefectos et tribunos militaris suos, quos Nero omnis in consilium vocavit ; erat in consilio etiam aequissimus iudex ipse Verres ; erant non nulli togati creditores Graecorum, quibus ad exigendas pecunias improbissimi cuiusque
74 legati plurimum prodest gratia. Ille miser defensorem reperire neminem poterat ; quis enim esset aut togatus, qui Dolabellae gratia, aut Graecus, qui eiusdem vi et imperio non moveretur ? Accusator autem adponitur civis Romanus de creditoribus Lampsacenorum ; qui si dixisset quod iste

1 multa π : multum D Ψ   5 Neronis iudicio *del. Bake*   7 fuerit audite *qr edd. recc.*   9 his *codd*   17 in Asiam *auct. Iord. secl. Kays.*   26 rep. nem. pot. πbδ, *Zielinski p.* 193 : nem. rep. pot. D Ψ
30 quod iste iussisset *s. l. p²*

discussion of this point, I merely say that Nero and his tribunal followed the principle that, since there was agreement that the lictor Cornelius had been killed, they were not entitled to suppose that anyone had the right to kill a man, even in avenging an injury. This judgement of Nero does not signify to me that you were acquitted of wrongdoing, but that they were convicted of murder.

But, laying all that aside, what kind of conviction was it? Listen to the story, I beseech you, gentlemen, and at last have pity on the allies and show that your good faith insures some measure of protection for them. XXIX. Because the victim, who was in name the lictor of Verres, but in reality the servant of his most wanton licentiousness, seemed to all of Asia to have been justly killed, Verres was terrified that Philodamus would be acquitted by Nero's court. He asked and begged Dolabella to leave his province and head for Nero. He pointed out that he could not be safe if Philodamus were allowed to
73 live and at any time come to Rome. Dolabella was swayed by his appeal, and took an action that has been censured by many, leaving his army, his province, and a war, and heading for Asia and another man's province in the interests of a totally worthless man. After he reached Nero, he urgently pressed him to hear the case of Philodamus. He had come personally so that he could serve on the tribunal and be the first to give a judgement. He had also brought with him prefects and military tribunes, all of whom Nero summoned to serve on the tribunal. Even Verres himself, most impartial of judges, was on the tribunal, as were some Roman creditors of the Greeks, for whom the goodwill of every unscrupulous legate is of the greatest benefit in
74 extracting their money. The wretched Philodamus could find no one to defend him, for what Roman was there who was not influenced by the thought of Dolabella's influence, or what Greek by the thought of his military might and authority? Moreover, a Roman citizen from among the creditors of the people of Lampsacum was appointed prosecutor, and was told that, if he said what

iussisset, per eiusdem istius lictores a populo pecuniam posset exigere. Cum haec omnia tanta contentione, tantis copiis agerentur ; cum illum miserum multi accusarent, nemo defenderet ; cumque Dolabella cum suis praefectis pugnaret in consilio, Verres fortunas agi suas diceret, idem testimonium diceret, idem esset in consilio, idem accusatorem parasset,—haec cum omnia fierent, et cum hominem constaret occisum, tamen tanta vis istius iniuriae, tanta in isto improbitas putabatur ut de Philodamo AMPLIVS pronuntiaretur. Quid ego nunc in altera actione Cn. Dolabellae spiritus, quid huius lacrimas et concursationes proferam, quid C. Neronis, viri optimi atque innocentissimi, non nullis in rebus animum nimium timidum atque demissum ? qui in illa re quid facere *oporteret* non habebat, nisi forte, id quod omnes tum desiderabant, ut ageret eam rem sine Verre et sine Dolabella. Quicquid esset sine his actum, omnes probarent ; tum vero quod pronuntiatum est non per Neronem iudicatum, sed per Dolabellam ereptum existimabatur. Condemnatur enim perpaucis sententiis Philodamus et eius filius. Adest, instat, urget Dolabella ut quam primum securi feriantur, quo quam minime multi ex illis de istius nefario scelere audire possent. Constituitur in foro Laodiceae spectaculum acerbum et miserum et grave toti Asiae provinciae, grandis natu parens adductus ad supplicium, ex altera parte filius, ille quod pudicitiam liberorum, hic quod vitam patris famamque sororis defenderat. Flebat uterque non de suo supplicio, sed pater de fili morte, de patris filius. Quid lacrimarum ipsum Neronem putatis profudisse? quem fletum totius Asiae fuisse, quem luctum et gemitum Lampsacenorum ? securi esse percussos homines innocentis nobilis, socios populi Romani atque amicos,

14 oporteret *scripsi* : potuerit *Dp rell.* (i, § 103 ; iii, § 113 : *Cl. Rev.* xvii. 202) 21 quod quam *prG*$_{12}$δ : quod quoniam *DZs* 23 laodiceē *b* : laodicie *D* : laodiciae πλs 29 luctum et *om. G*$_2$*K*

Verres ordered, he could extract his money with the help of Verres' lictors. But despite the fact that all these matters were being conducted with such great haste and with the backing of such great resources; that many were accusing the unfortunate Philodamus and no one was defending him; that Dolabella, supported by his prefects, was fighting for a conviction in the tribunal; that Verres was declaring his own future was at stake, and was also acting as a witness, was serving on the tribunal, and was the man who had primed the prosecutor; – despite all this and the further fact that it was agreed a man had been killed, still, the impact of the injury done by Verres was so overwhelming and the villainy of his nature was considered so immense that a further hearing for Philodamus was announced.

75   XXX. What need is there to bring up at this juncture the aggressiveness of Dolabella at the second hearing, or the tears and scurryings of Verres, or the character of that excellent and blameless man, C. Nero, which in certain situations was excessively timid and submissive? In this affair there was nothing he could have done, except perhaps what everyone then wanted him to do, namely conduct the proceedings without Verres and Dolabella. Any action taken in the absence of these men would have everyone's approval, but the verdict then announced was viewed, not as a judgement made by Nero, but as one extorted by Dolabella. For Philodamus and his son were condemned by a very few votes. Dolabella was at hand, urging and insisting that they be executed as quickly as possible, so that as few as possible might hear from them
76   about Verres' vile crime. In the forum of Laodicea there was enacted a cruel and pitiable scene that was a source of grief to the entire province of Asia: an elderly parent was led forth to his punishment and from another side was led the son, the former because he had defended the chastity of his children, the latter because he had defended the life of his father and the reputation of his sister. Each wept, not for his own punishment, but the father for the death of his son, the son for the death of his father. You can imagine the tears shed by Nero himself, the weeping throughout all of Asia, the grief and lamentation of the people of Lampsacum. To think that innocent men of the highest rank, allies and friends of

propter hominis flagitiosissimi singularem nequitiam atque improbissimam cupiditatem !

77 Iam iam, Dolabella, neque me tui neque tuorum liberorum, quos tu miseros in egestate atque in solitudine reliquisti, misereri potest. Verresne tibi tanti fuit ut eius libidinem hominum innocentium sanguine lui velles ? Idcircone exercitum atque hostem relinquebas ut tua vi et crudelitate istius hominis improbissimi pericula sublevares ? Quod enim eum tibi quaestoris in loco constitueras, idcirco tibi amicum in perpetuum fore putasti ? nesciebas ab eo Cn. Carbonem consulem, cuius re vera quaestor fuerat, non modo relictum sed etiam spoliatum auxiliis, pecunia, nefarie oppugnatum et proditum ? Expertus igitur es istius perfidiam tum cum ipse se ad inimicos tuos contulit, cum in te homo ipse nocens acerrimum testimonium dixit, cum rationes ad aerarium nisi damnato te referre noluit.

31
78 Tantaene tuae, Verres, libidines erunt ut eas capere ac sustinere non provinciae populi Romani, non nationes exterae possint ? Tune quod videris, quod audieris, quod concupieris, quod cogitaris, nisi id ad nutum tuum praesto fuerit, nisi libidini tuae cupiditatique paruerit, immittentur homines, expugnabuntur domus, civitates non modo pacatae, verum etiam sociorum atque amicorum ad vim atque ad arma confugient, ut ab se atque a liberis suis legati populi Romani scelus ac libidinem propulsare possint ? Nam quaero abs te circumsessusne sis Lampsaci, coeperitne domum in qua deversabare illa multitudo incendere, voluerintne legatum populi Romani comburere vivum Lampsaceni ? Negare non potes ; habeo enim testimonium tuum quod apud Neronem dixisti, habeo quas ad eundem litteras

3 me *Dp al.* : *om. Lgg. praeter q* Quint. *Asc. cdd*   6 innocentum G_1Z
10 sperasti *L*   24 a liberis *om. pq*¹
liberorum $D\Psi\pi b$: liberum elui *Bake* (sanguines lui *p*)
29 tuum *Dp rell* : publicum tuum *Asc*, *Klotz*

the Roman people, were beheaded because of the unparalleled depravity and most wanton licentiousness of an utterly shameless reprobate!

77 No longer, Dolabella, can I pity you or your children, whom you have left wretched, and destitute, and alone. Was Verres so important to you that you were willing to expiate his licentiousness with the blood of innocent men? Was it for this you turned your back on your army and the enemy, that you might lessen by force and cruelty the dangers confronting that unprincipled villain? Because you had appointed him to replace your quaestor did you think he would therefore be your friend forever? Did you not know that the consul Cn. Carbo, whose real quaestor he had been, was not only deserted, but was also robbed of his supplies and funds and then foully attacked and betrayed by this man? Well then, you experienced his treachery when he betook himself to your enemies and, guilty though he was himself, gave the most hostile evidence against you, and proved unwilling to return his accounts to the treasury until after your conviction.

78 XXXI. Are your passions, Verres, to become so extreme that the provinces of the Roman people and foreign peoples cannot contain or endure them? If everything you see, hear, crave, and conceive is not available at your nod and obedient to your passions and appetites, are men to be dispatched, houses stormed, states that are not only at peace, but included among our allies and friends, to take refuge in armed force as a means of repelling from themselves and their children the wickedness and licentiousness of a legate of the Roman people? Well then, I ask you if you were besieged at Lampsacum, if the crowd mentioned earlier started to set fire to the house in which you were quartered, if the people of Lampsacum wanted to burn alive a legate of the Roman people? You cannot deny these facts, for I have the evidence that you yourself gave before Nero, and I have the letters that

79 misisti. Recita hunc ipsum locum de testimonio. TESTI-
MONIVM C. VERRIS IN ARTEMIDORVM. NON MVLTO POST
IN DOMVM —. Bellumne populo Romano Lampsacena
civitas facere conabatur? deficere ab imperio ac nomine
nostro volebat? Video enim et ex iis quae legi et audivi 5
intellego, in qua civitate non modo legatus populi Romani
circumsessus, non modo igni, ferro, manu, copiis oppugnatus,
sed aliqua ex parte violatus sit, nisi publice satis factum sit,
80 ei civitati bellum indici atque inferri solere. Quae fuit
igitur causa cur cuncta civitas Lampsacenorum de contione, 10
quem ad modum tute scribis, domum tuam concurreret? Tu
enim neque in litteris quas Neroni mittis, neque in testimonio causam tanti tumultus ostendis ullam. Obsessum te
dicis, ignem adlatum, sarmenta circumdata, lictorem tuum
occisum esse dicis, prodeundi tibi in publicum potestatem 15
factam negas : causam huius tanti terroris occultas. Nam
si quam Rubrius iniuriam suo nomine ac non impulsu tuo
et tua cupiditate fecisset, de tui comitis iniuria questum ad
te potius quam te oppugnatum venirent. Cum igitur quae
causa illius tumultus fuerit testes a nobis producti dixerint, 20
ipse celarit, nonne causam hanc quam nos proposuimus cum
illorum testimonia tum istius taciturnitas perpetua confirmat?

32
81   Huic homini parcetis igitur, iudices, cuius tanta peccata
sunt ut ii quibus iniurias fecerit neque legitimum tempus 25
exspectare ad ulciscendum neque vim tantam doloris in
posterum differre potuerint? Circumsessus es. A quibus?
A Lampsacenis. Barbaris hominibus, credo, aut iis qui
populi Romani nomen contemnerent. Immo vero ab
hominibus et natura et consuetudine et disciplina lenissi- 30

1-3 Recita ... domum *in mg. pr* (ipsum hunc *b*) : *om. D*Ψ   3
lampsaceni civ. fac. conabatur *p* : lampsaceni fac. conabantur δ   11
tuam *pr* : *om. D*Ψ   concurreret *b Lg.* 42 : -erit *Dp rell.*   22
perpetua confirmat *Dp rell.* : conf. perp. *qr* (*Zielinski, p.* 193) 26
ad ulcisc. exsp. q^1

79 you sent that same official. Read the relevant section from the evidence beginning: 'THE TESTIMONY OF C. VERRES AGAINST ARTEMIDORUS. NOT LONG AFTERWARDS ...' Was the state of Lampsacum attempting to make war on the Roman people? Did they wish to defect from the empire and name of Rome? For I see from my observations and know both from what I have read and heard that it is the practice, unless public reparation has been made, to declare and make war on any state in which a legate of the Roman people has been insulted in any respect, not to mention besieged and attacked by fire
80 and the sword and violent throngs. What then caused the entire community of Lampsacum to rush from a meeting to your house, as you yourself describe in writing? For neither in the letters you sent Nero nor in your testimony do you produce any explanation for such a serious disturbance. You say you were besieged, that a fire was set, that brushwood was piled around, that your lictor was killed, that you were denied the opportunity of appearing in public, but the cause of this situation of such great terror you keep a secret. For if Rubrius had done any wrong on his own account and not as a result of your instigation and your lust, they would have come to you to complain about the injury done by your aide rather than to attack you. Since, therefore, the witnesses produced by us have told what the cause of that disturbance was and he has concealed it, is not the cause as we have set it before you confirmed both by the evidence of those witnesses and by his continued silence?

81   XXXII. Will you then spare this man, gentlemen, whose misdeeds are so enormous that those whom he has wronged could not await the legally appointed hour of vengeance or defer till later so overwhelming a rush of grief? You were besieged. By whom? By the people of Lampsacum. An uncivilised people, I suppose, or the sort who despise the name of the Roman state. On the contrary, a people who are by nature, custom, and training gentle in the extreme, and who are, moreover,

mis, porro autem populi Romani condicione sociis, fortuna
servis, voluntate supplicibus: ut perspicuum sit omnibus,
nisi tanta acerbitas iniuriae, tanta vis sceleris fuisset ut
Lampsaceni moriendum sibi potius quam perpetiendum pu-
tarent, numquam illos in eum locum progressuros fuisse ut 5
vehementius odio libidinis tuae quam legationis metu move-
82 rentur. Nolite, per deos immortalis, cogere socios atque
exteras nationes hoc uti perfugio, quo, nisi vos vindicatis,
utentur necessario! Lampsacenos in istum numquam ulla
res mitigasset nisi eum poenas Romae daturum credi- 10
dissent: etsi talem acceperant iniuriam, quam nulla lege
satis digne persequi possent, tamen incommoda sua nostris
committere legibus et iudiciis quam dolori suo permittere
maluerunt. Tu mihi, cum circumsessus a tam inlustri civitate sis propter tuum scelus atque flagitium, cum coegeris 15
homines miseros et calamitosos quasi desperatis nostris legibus et iudiciis ad vim, ad manus, ad arma confugere, cum te
in oppidis et civitatibus amicorum non legatum populi
Romani, sed tyrannum libidinosum crudelemque praebueris,
cum apud exteras nationes imperi nominisque nostri famam 20
tuis probris flagitiisque violaris, cum te ex ferro amicorum
populi Romani eripueris atque ex flamma sociorum evolaris,
hic tibi perfugium speras futurum? Erras: ut huc inci-
deres, non ut hic conquiesceres, illi te vivum exire passi
sunt. 25

33
83   Et ais iudicium esse factum te iniuria circumsessum esse
Lampsaci, quod Philodamus cum filio condemnatus sit.
Quid, si doceo, si planum facio teste homine nequam, verum
ad hanc rem tamen idoneo—te ipso, inquam, teste docebo
te huius circumsessionis tuae causam et culpam in alios 30
transtulisse, neque in eos, quos tu insimularas, esse animad-

    4 moriendum sibi potius *Dp rell.* : mor. potius sibi G_2 : sibi mor.
pot. *K*   8 quod *codd*   26 At ais *Muell.*   31 contulisse *Asc.*
insimularas *Dp rell., praeter* G_{12} (insimulares) *Lg.* 42 (-abas) : insimu-
laris *edd.* (*Cl. Rev.* xvii. 202)

by legal agreement allies of the Roman state, by fortune its subjects, by inclination its suppliants. It should therefore be clear to everyone that, if the pain of their injury had not been so great and the impact of the crime against them so intolerable that the people of Lampsacum considered they should die rather than endure it, they would never have reached the point where they were more powerfully influenced by loathing for your licentiousness than by the awe in which they held the office of legate.

82 Do not, in the name of the immortal gods, force allies and foreign nations to use this means of protection, which they will inevitably use if you fail to protect them. Nothing would ever have assuaged the feelings of the people of Lampsacum towards Verres except the belief that he would pay the penalty at Rome. Though they had suffered the kind of injury for which no truly fitting retribution could be sought under any law, nevertheless they prferred to entrust their misfortunes to your laws and courts than to allow their grief to deal with them. And do you, though you were placed under siege by such a distinguished community because of your shameful crime; though you forced its poor unfortunate people, in virtual despair of our laws and courts, to take refuge in violence and armed force; though you behaved in the towns and states of our friends not as a legate of the Roman people but as a lecherous and savage tyrant; though you sullied the reputation of our empire and our name among foreign nations by your shameful misconduct; though you escaped from the swords of friends of the Roman people and from a fire lit by allies, do you have hopes that you will find a refuge here? You are mistaken. Those people allowed you to depart alive so that you might fall into our power in Rome, not find peace in it.

83   XXXIII. You also assert that, because Philodamus and his son were condemned, a judgement of the courts has affirmed that you were unjustly besieged at Lampsacum. What if I show, if I make clear on the evidence of a man who is indeed a scoundrel, but nonetheless an appropriate witness in this case – what I mean is, that, using you yourself as a witness, I will show that you have put the reason and the blame for this blockade you experienced on other shoulders and that they were not punished whom

versum. Iam nihil te iudicium Neronis adiuvat. Recita quas ad Neronem litteras misit. EPISTVLA C. VERRIS AD NERONEM. THEMISTAGORAS ET THESSALVS —. Themistagoram et Thessalum scribis populum concitasse. Quem populum? Qui te circumsedit, qui te vivum comburere conatus est. Vbi hos persequeris, ubi accusas, ubi defendis ius nomenque legati? in Philodami iudicio dices id actum? 84 Cedo mihi ipsius Verris testimonium : videamus quid idem iste iuratus dixerit. Recita. AB ACCVSATORE ROGATVS RESPONDIT IN HOC IVDICIO NON PERSEQVI : SIBI IN ANIMO ESSE ALIO TEMPORE PERSEQVI. Quid igitur te iuvat Neronis iudicium, quid Philodami damnatio? Legatus cum esses circumsessus, cumque, quem ad modum tute ad Neronem scripsisti, populo Romano communique causae legatorum facta esset insignis iniuria, non es persecutus : dicis tibi in animo esse alio tempore persequi. Quod fuit id tempus? quando es persecutus? Cur imminuisti ius legationis, cur causam populi Romani deseruisti ac prodidisti, cur iniurias tuas coniunctas cum publicis reliquisti? Non te ad senatum causam deferre, non de tam atrocibus iniuriis conqueri, non eos homines qui populum concitarant con-
85 sulum litteris evocandos curare oportuit? Nuper M. Aurelio Scauro postulante, quod is Ephesi se quaestorem vi prohibitum esse dicebat quo minus e fano Dianae servum suum, qui in illud asylum confugisset, abduceret, Pericles Ephesius, homo nobilissimus, Romam evocatus est, quod auctor illius iniuriae fuisse arguebatur : tu, si te legatum ita Lampsaci tractatum esse senatum docuisses ut tui comites vulnerarentur, lictor occideretur, ipse circumsessus paene incenderere, eius autem rei duces et auctores principes fuisse,

1-3 Recita ... Thessalus *prb* (i, § 79) : *om. D*Ψ   9 Recita *prb* : *om.* D *rell.*   10 sibi π*b* : in hoc sibi *D*Ψ (in *om. G*₁)   19 Nonne te *r Lgg. praeter q*   21 concitarent *G*₂*qr*   27 argueretur *bδ* (*Zielinski p.* 193)   30 actores π   et princ. *Lamb. edd.*

84 you had alleged were responsible. The verdict of Nero is no longer any help to you. Read the letter he sent to Nero beginning: 'THE LETTER OF C. VERRES TO NERO. THEMISTAGORAS AND THESSALUS ...' You write that Themistagoras and Thessalus stirred up the people. What people? Those who placed you under siege, who wanted to burn you alive. Where then are you taking legal action against these men, where are you charging them, where are you vindicating the authority and name of a legate? Will you maintain this was done at the trial of Philodamus? Let us have the evidence of Verres himself, let us see what the man said under oath. Read the section beginning: 'WHEN ASKED BY THE PROSECUTOR HE REPLIED THAT HE WAS NOT PROCEEDING AGAINST THEM AT THIS TRIAL; IT WAS HIS INTENTION TO DO SO ON ANOTHER OCCASION.' How then does the judgement of Nero, how does the condemnation of Philodamus help you? Though you, a legate, were subjected to a siege, though, as you yourself wrote to Nero, a signal injury was done to the Roman people and to the common cause of legates, you took no legal action. You say you intended to do so on another occasion. What occasion was that? When have you taken that legal action? Why have you diminished the authority of the office of legate, why have you abandoned and betrayed the cause of the Roman people, why have you disregarded personal injuries that also involved injuries to the state? Was it not your duty to refer the matter to the senate, to lodge a complaint about such outrageous wrongs, to see to it that the men who had stirred up the people were summoned by

85 dispatches from the consuls? Recently, on the demand of M. Aurelius Scaurus and as a result of his statement that, when quaestor, he was forcefully prevented at Ephesus from removing from the temple of Diana a slave of his who had fled there for refuge, there was summoned to Rome a man of the highest distinction named Pericles of Ephesus as the person accused of being the author of that outrage. If you had informed the senate that, when holding the office of legate, you were so badly treated at Lampsacum that your aides were wounded, your lictor killed, you yourself besieged and almost burned to death, and that, further, the leaders and prime authors in the affair were the men you mention

quos scribis, Themistagoram et Thessalum, quis non commoveretur, quis non ex iniuria quae tibi esset facta sibi provideret, quis non in ea re causam tuam, periculum commune agi arbitraretur? Etenim nomen legati eius modi esse debet quod non modo inter sociorum iura, sed etiam 5 inter hostium tela incolume versetur.

34 Magnum hoc Lampsacenum crimen est libidinis atque
86 improbissimae cupiditatis: accipite nunc avaritiae prope modum in suo genere non levius. Milesios navem poposcit, quae eum praesidi causa Myndum prosequeretur: 10 illi statim myoparonem egregium de sua classe ornatum atque armatum dederunt. Hoc praesidio Myndum profectus est. Nam quid a Milesiis lanae publice abstulerit, item de sumptu in adventum, de contumeliis et iniuriis in magistratum Milesium tametsi dici cum vere tum graviter et vehementer 15 potest, tamen dicere praetermittam eaque omnia testibus integra reservabo: illud, quod neque taceri ullo modo neque
87 dici pro dignitate potest, cognoscite. Milites remigesque Miletum Myndo pedibus reverti iubet: ipse myoparonem pulcherrimum de decem Milesiorum navibus electum L. 20 Magio et L. Fannio, qui Myndi habitabant, vendidit. Hi sunt homines quos nuper senatus in hostium numero habendos censuit: hoc illi navigio ad omnis populi Romani hostis usque ab Dianio [quod in Hispania est] ad Sinopam [quae in Ponto est] navigaverunt. 25

O, di immortales, incredibilem avaritiam singularemque audaciam! Navem tu de classe populi Romani, quam tibi Milesia civitas ut te prosequeretur dedisset, ausus es vendere? Si te magnitudo malefici, si hominum existimatio non

8 nunc Dp $al.$: vero G_3K (D in $mg.$ ' $al.$ $vero$ ') 13 a πK: $om.$ DZ $al.$ (milesios p). $Cf.$ ii, § 26 lanae publice p : lane publice D $al.$: -ae -ae $vulg.$ 17 taceri $om.$ pq^1 21 Mario DG_{12} Fannio $Asc.$ $edd.$: Fabio Dp $rell.$, $praeter$ $br\delta$ (Rabio) 24 ab pq $al.$: a $s.$ ad $rell.$ $Verba$ $seclusa$ $om.$ $Asc.$: $mance$ p usque ab dianopam quae in ponto est nav.

in your letter, Themistagoras and Thessalus, who would not have been stirred by this, who would not have taken precautions to safeguard themselves as a result of the injury done to you, who would not have considered that it was not a personal cause of yours but a danger common to all that was at issue in this affair? For the name of legate should have a status that would insure safe movement not only in the law-abiding states of our allies, but amidst the weapons of our enemies.

86   XXXIV. This crime of lust and wanton passion at Lampsacum is serious indeed, but listen now to a crime of avarice which is, in its own way, almost equally grave. He asked the Milesians for a ship to accompany him as a protective escort to Myndus. They immediately gave him a splendid galley from their fleet, fully equipped and armed. With this escort he set out for Myndus. Now, though one could speak not just with truth but with vehemence and passion about the wool he took from the Milesians in the name of the state, and likewise about the expense caused by his arrival and the insults and injuries heaped on the Milesian magistrate, I will nonetheless forego discussion of all these matters and will leave them untouched for the witnesses. But I want you to learn the facts of the following affair, which cannot, under any circumstances, be passed over in silence nor yet dealt
87 with as it deserves. He ordered the marines and oarsmen to return to Miletus from Myndus on foot; he himself sold the galley, which had been selected as the finest of the ten Milesian ships, to L. Magius and L. Fannius, who were living at Myndus. These are the men the senate lately decreed should be numbered among the enemies of the state. With this ship they have made voyages to every enemy of the Roman people from Dianium in Spain to Sinope in Pontus.

    Good heavens! What incredible greed and unparalleled brazenness! Did you dare sell a ship from the fleet of the Roman people, which the state of Miletus had given you as an escort? If the magnitude of the crime, if considerations of public opinion did not influence

movebat, ne illud quidem cogitabas, huius improbissimi furti
sive adeo nefariae praedae tam inlustrem ac tam nobilem
88 civitatem testem futuram? An quia tum Cn. Dolabella in
eum qui ei myoparoni praefuerat, Milesiisque rem gestam
renuntiarat, animadvertere tuo rogatu conatus est, renuntia-
tionemque eius, quae erat in publicas litteras relata illorum
legibus, tolli iusserat, idcirco te ex hoc crimine elapsum
35 esse arbitrabare? Multum te ista fefellit opinio, et quidem
multis in locis. Semper enim existimasti, et maxime in
Sicilia, satis cautum tibi ad defensionem fore, si aut referri
aliquid in litteras publicas vetuisses, aut quod relatum esset
tolli coegisses. Hoc quam nihil sit, tametsi ex multis
Siciliae civitatibus priore actione didicisti, tamen etiam in
hac ipsa civitate cognosce. Sunt illi quidem dicto audientes,
quam diu adsunt ii qui imperant: simul ac discesserunt, non
solum illud perscribunt quod tum prohibiti sunt, sed etiam
causam adscribunt cur non tum in litteras relatum sit.
89 Manent istae litterae Mileti, manent, et dum erit illa civitas
manebunt. Decem enim navis iussu L. Murenae populus
Milesius ex pecunia vectigali populo Romano fecerat, sicut
pro sua quaeque parte Asiae ceterae civitates. Quam ob
rem unam ex decem, non praedonum repentino adventu sed
legati latrocinio, non vi tempestatis sed hac horribili tem-
pestate sociorum amissam in litteras publicas rettulerunt.
90 Sunt Romae legati Milesii, homines nobilissimi ac principes
civitatis, qui tametsi mensem Februarium et consulum
designatorum nomen exspectant, tamen hoc tantum facinus
non modo negare interrogati, sed ne producti quidem
reticere poterunt: dicent, inquam, et religione adducti et
domesticarum legum metu, quid illo myoparone factum sit,
ostendent C. Verrem, in ea classe quae contra piratas aedi-
ficata sit, piratam ipsum consceleratum fuisse.

17 causam *om. pG*$_1$ (*s. l. p*^{2}) : causas *qr Dr*) *D al. p* : quoque *G*$_3$*K*   21 quaeque (queque

you, did you not even consider that this community, of such high distinction, and renown, would bear witness to this most unscrupulous theft, or rather foul act of plunder? Or did you think that you had wriggled out of this charge because Cn. Dolabella at the time attempted, at your request, to take action against the man who had commanded the galley and had reported the incident to the Milesians, and because he had further ordered the man's report, which, in accordance with the laws of the Milesians, had been entered in the public record, to be expunged? XXXV. That expectation has led you very much astray, and indeed has done so on many occasions. For you always considered, and especially during your tenure in Sicily, that it would be a sufficient provision for your defence if you forbade a particular matter to be entered in the public record, or forced something that had been entered to be removed. Though you learned from many Sicilian communities at the first hearing how useless that strategy was, nonetheless, learn the lesson again in relation to this particular community. They did indeed comply with the order as long as those giving it were present, but as soon as they departed, they not only wrote out in full what they were forbidden to record, but added the reason why it was not entered at the time in the public record. Those documents survive at Miletus; they survive and will survive as long as that community exists. For the people of Miletus, on the orders of L. Murena, had built ten ships with the money raised in taxes for the Roman people. The other Asian states had done the same in proportion to their resources. They have recorded in their public documents the reason why one of the ten ships was lost, a reason due not to a sudden attack by pirates but to the brigandage of a legate, not to the force of a storm but to this terrible human tempest sweeping through the allies. There are Milesian envoys at Rome, men of the highest rank who hold leading positions in their state. Though they are nervously contemplating the month of February and the names of the consuls-elect, still they will prove unable not only to deny so serious a crime as this if questioned as witnesses but to keep silent about it even if they are not brought into court. They will tell us, I assure you, directed by their sense of right and their regard for the laws of their own state, what happened to that galley, and they will show that C. Verres acted himself like the vilest of pirates in his dealings with a fleet that was built to fight the pirates.

36 C. Malleolo, quaestore Cn. Dolabellae, occiso duas sibi hereditates venisse arbitratus est, unam quaestoriae procurationis, nam a Dolabella statim pro quaestore iussus est esse; alteram tutelae, nam cum pupilli Malleoli tutor esset, 91 in bona eius impetum fecit. Nam Malleolus in provinciam 5 sic copiose profectus erat ut domi prorsus nihil relinqueret; praeterea pecunias occuparat apud populos et syngraphas fecerat, argenti optimi caelati grande pondus secum tulerat, nam ille quoque sodalis istius erat in hoc morbo et cupiditate; grande pondus argenti, familiam magnam, multos artifices, 10 multos formosos homines reliquit. Iste quod argenti placuit invasit; quae mancipia voluit abduxit; vina ceteraque quae in Asia facillime comparantur, quae ille reliquerat, asportavit; 92 reliqua vendidit, pecuniam exegit. Cum ad HS viciens quinquiens redegisse constaret, ut Romam rediit, nullam 15 litteram pupillo, nullam matri eius, nullam tutoribus reddidit; servos artifices pupilli cum haberet domi, circum pedes autem homines formosos et litteratos, suos esse dicebat, se emisse. Cum saepius mater et avia pueri postularent uti, si non redderet pecuniam nec rationem daret, diceret saltem 20 quantum pecuniae Malleoli deportasset, a multis efflagitatus aliquando dixit HS deciens; deinde in codicis extrema cera nomen infimum in flagitiosa litura fecit; expensa Chrysogono servo HS sescenta milia, accepta pupillo Malleolo rettulit. Quo modo ex deciens HS sescenta sint facta, quo modo 25 DC eodem modo quadrarint ut illa de Cn. Carbonis pecunia reliqua HS sescenta facta sint, quo modo Chrysogono

1 dolobellae occiso : *in his verbis incipit codex S, mutilus* 6 ·copiose· *p, secl. Ern. Kays.*; *cf. Act. Pr.* § 33   nil *Zielinski, p.* 178   9 sodalis istius *prb* : sodalicius $SD\Psi$ (sodalius G_1)   13 facillime SD *al. p* : facile *qr* (*Serv. ad Verg. Ecl.* v. 36)   14 et pec. G_1 HS $\overline{\text{XX}}$ $\bar{\text{D}}$ quinquies p ($\overline{\text{XX}}$·D SD : XX·D· G_2KZr)   18 homines formosos $DZpb$: form. hom. G_2K *et* (*cum signis transp.*) S (i, § 105) 20 pec. non redd. G_1 23 in (*post* infimum) *om.* $G_{12}K$ 25 sint facta SDp : facta sint G_3 26 de eodem SD : in eodem p 27 facta sint SDp : facta sunt b : '*al. fort. recte.*' *Muell.*

XXXVI. When C. Malleolus, the quaestor of Cn. Dolabella, was killed, Verres considered that two legacies had come his way, one consisting in the functions of quaestor, for Dolabella immediately appointed him proquaestor, the other consisting in a guardianship, for, while acting as guardian to the young Malleolus, he launched an attack against his property. Now, Malleolus had set out for his province so abundantly supplied that he left absolutely nothing at home. In addition, he had loaned money to the communities and had taken promissory notes from them and had brought with him a large amount of beautifully wrought silver, for he was also a comrade of Verres in that diseased fraternity of the avaricious. He left behind at his death a large quantity of silver and a large body of slaves, many skilled craftsmen and many handsome fellows among them. Verres seized as much of the silver as he pleased, and took what slaves he wanted. The wines and other products that Malleolus had left behind and that are easily obtainable in Asia he carried off. Everything else he sold, and he made sure to secure payment. Though it was agreed that he had realized up to two and a half million sesterces, he sent no record of it on his return to Rome to his ward or to his ward's mother or guardians, and though he kept skilled slaves belonging to his ward at his house and had others, who were handsome and highly educated, all around him, he declared they were his own and that he had bought them. When the boy's mother and grandmother repeatedly demanded that he should at least tell how much of Malleolus' money he had brought back with him, even if he was not going to return it or give an accounting of it, he finally stated, under pressure from many sources, a figure of one million. But then, on the last leaf of the account book he made an entry at the bottom over a disgraceful erasure, recording that six hundred thousand sesterces, received on behalf of his ward Malleolus, had been paid to the slave Chrysogonus. You will decide for yourselves how the one million was turned into six hundred thousand, how the figure worked out to match exactly the sum of six hundred thousand into which the balance of the funds belonging to Cn. Carbo had been converted, how it came to be recorded as paid to

101

expensa lata sint, cur id nomen infimum in lituraque sit,
93 vos existimabitis. Tamen HS sescenta milia cum accepta
rettulisset, HS quinquaginta milia soluta non sunt ; homines,
posteaquam reus factus est, redditi *alii,* alii etiam nunc reti-
37 nentur ; peculia omnium vicariique retinentur. Haec est 5
istius praeclara tutela. En cui tuos liberos committas, en
memoriam mortui sodalis, en metum vivorum existimationis !
Cum tibi se tota Asia spoliandam ac vexandam praebuisset,
cum tibi exposita esset omnis ad praedandum Pamphylia,
contentus his tam opimis rebus non fuisti ? manus a tutela, 10
manus a pupillo, manus a sodalis filio abstinere non potuisti ?
Iam te non Siculi, non aratores, ut dictitas, circumveniunt,
non hi qui decretis edictisque tuis in te concitati infestique
sunt : Malleolus a me productus est et mater eius atque
avia, quae miserae flentes eversum a te puerum patriis bonis 15
94 esse dixerunt. Quid exspectas ? an dum ab inferis ipse
Malleolus exsistat, atque abs te officia tutelae sodalitatis
familiaritatisque flagitet ? Ipsum putato adesse. Homo
avarissime et spurcissime, redde bona sodalis filio, si non
quae abstulisti, at quae confessus es ! Cur cogis sodalis 20
filium hanc primam in foro vocem cum dolore et querimonia
emittere ? cur sodalis uxorem, sodalis socrum, domum denique totam sodalis mortui contra te testimonium dicere ? cur
pudentissimas lectissimasque feminas in tantum virorum
conventum insolitas invitasque prodire cogis ? Recita 25
omnium testimonia. Testimonivm matris et aviae.
38
95 Pro quaestore vero quo modo iste commune Milyadum
vexarit, quo modo Lyciam, Pamphyliam, Pisidiam Phry-

4 redditi alii alii etiam *scripsi* : redditi alii etiam *SDp rell. praeter r.*
aliis (= alii sunt ?) redditi alii etiam. *Vulg.* alii redditi alii etiam
5 omnium *SDZ*: omnia π   vicariique] *habet in mg. p* (*m. pr.*)
'*servi in loco manumissorum suppositi*'   7 memoria G_2Kb 9
tibi *om.* G_1 10 optimis *codd*.   13 hi *codd.* : ii *Iord*.   15
miserę *Sp* : misere *D al. r*   patris $G_2\delta$ 17 abs te *om. SD al.*
18 puta G_1 20 at *prb* : *om. SD*Ψ   22 amittere *codd*.   27
                              i
Myliadum *SD*   28 vexarit *b* : vexaret *Spq* : vexaret *D*

Chrysogonus, and why that entry is the last in the book and imposed over an erasure. In any event, though he had recorded that he received six hundred thousand, fifty thousand sesterces of it was not paid. As for the slaves, some were returned after he was indicted, but others are even now being kept in his possession, as are the personal funds and under-slaves of all of them. XXXVII. Such was his glorious guardianship. Behold a man to whom you should entrust your children, behold his remembrance of his dead fraternal comrade, behold his regard for the opinion of the living! Though the whole of Asia had been made yours to despoil and pillage, and all Pamphylia had been made available to you as plunder, were you not content with possessions of such richness? Could you not keep your hands off a boy who was under your protection, who was your ward, who was the son of a fraternal comrade? No longer is it the Sicilians or the farmers, as you keep saying, who beset you, or those whose hatred has been aroused against you by your decrees and edicts. It is Malleolus I have brought before the court, and his mother and grandmother who, in sorrow and in tears, testified that the boy has been deprived by you of the property of his father. What are you waiting for? Is it for Malleolus himself to come forth from the dead and demand from you the obligations that belong to guardianship, fraternity, and friendship? Imagine him present. You most greedy and revolting of men, give back his property to the son of a fraternal comrade, if not what you have actually taken, at least what you have admitted to taking. Why do you compel the son of this comrade to utter these his first words in the forum in tones of grief and plaintive lamentation? Why do you compel the wife of this comrade, the mother-in-law of this comrade, in short, the entire household of this dead comrade to give evidence against you? Why do you compel these exceptional and exceedingly modest women to appear, against their wishes and their practice, before so large a gathering of men? Read the evidence of all these witnesses beginning: 'THE EVIDENCE OF MOTHER AND GRANDMOTHER.'

XXXVIII. There is no need to describe how he further ravaged, as proquaestor, the commune of the Milyades, how he oppressed the whole of Lycia, Pamphylia, Pisidia,

giamque totam frumento imperando, aestimando, hac sua,
quam tum primum excogitavit, Siciliensi aestimatione
adflixerit, non est necesse demonstrare verbis : hoc scitote,
[his nominibus—quae res per hunc gestae sunt] cum iste
civitatibus frumentum, coria, cilicia, saccos imperaret, neque 5
ea sumeret proque iis rebus pecuniam exigeret—his nominibus solis Cn. Dolabellae HS ad triciens litem esse aesti-
matam. Quae omnia, etiamsi voluntate Dolabellae fiebant,
96 per istum tamen omnia gerebantur. Consistam in uno
nomine; multa enim sunt ex eodem genere. Recita. DE 10
LITIBVS AESTIMATIS CN. DOLABELLAE PR. PECVNIAE RE-
DACTAE. QVOD A COMMVNI MILYADVM —. Te haec
coegisse, te aestimasse, tibi pecuniam numeratam esse dico,
eademque vi et iniuria, cum pecunias maximas cogeres,
per omnis partis provinciae te tamquam aliquam calamitosam 15
97 tempestatem pestemque pervasisse demonstro. Itaque M.
Scaurus, qui Cn. Dolabellam accusavit, istum in sua potestate
ac dicione tenuit. Homo adulescens cum istius in inquirendo
multa furta ac flagitia cognosset, fecit perite et callide; volu-
men eius rerum gestarum maximum isti ostendit ; ab homine 20
quae voluit in Dolabellam abstulit ; istum testem produxit ;
dixit iste quae velle accusatorem putavit. Quo ex genere
mihi testium qui cum isto furati sunt, si uti voluissem,
magna copia fuisset ; qui ut se periculo litium, coniunctione
criminum liberarent, quo ego vellem descensuros pollice- 25
98 bantur. Eorum ego voluntatem omnium repudiavi ; non
modo proditori, sed ne perfugae quidem locus in meis
castris cuiquam fuit. Forsitan meliores illi accusatores

4 his nom. . . . sunt *secl. Bake, Kays., Muell.* per ipsum *L* 6
iis] his *SDp* 11 P·R· pecuniam redactae *p* (redacta e *SDG₂* : redacta
est *D²G₁Z*) 15 aliquam calam. *SD al. p* : cal. aliq. *G₂* 16
pestem *s. l. p²* : pestem tempestatemque *qr* 19 cognosset *SDp rell.*
praeter G₁b (cognosceret) *et K* (cognoscet) : i, § 18 21 produxit
D : protulit produxit *SG₁₂* (*sed in S linea ducta sub* protulit) 25
descensuros *pbr* : discessuros *SDΨ*

and Phrygia by requisitioning grain in accordance with this system of assessment of his that he employed in Sicily but first conceived at this time; this however, you should know, that under these headings – I refer to the abuses perpetrated by Verres, when he requisitioned grain, hides, blankets, sacks, and then, instead of taking them, extorted money in their place – under these headings alone, the damages assessed against Cn. Dolabella came to three million sesterces. All of these activities, though they were done with the consent of

96 Dolabella, were nonetheless carried out by Verres. I will concentrate on one category, since many of them are similar in nature. Read the section beginning: 'THE DAMAGES ASSESSED AGAINST THE PRAETOR CN. DOLABELLA IN RELATION TO MONEY PAID HIM. INASMUCH AS FROM THE COMMUNE OF THE MILYADES.' I say it was you collected this money, you made the estimates, it was to you the money was paid, and I am making the point that, while collecting huge sums of money, you swept, with similar violence and injustice, through all parts of the province like a ravaging storm or

97 pestilence. As a result, M. Scaurus, who prosecuted Cn. Dolabella, had Verres in his power and at his beck and call. When, in the course of his investigation, the young prosecutor learned of Verres' numerous thefts and infamies, he acted with skill and cunning. He showed him an enormous dossier containing his exploits; he got from him the information he wanted against Dolabella. He produced him as a witness; he said what he thought the prosecutor wanted. If I had wanted to use them, I could have had an abundant supply of witnesses of this variety, men who had shared in Verres' pillaging and who were pledging to demean themselves in any way I wanted to get free of the risk of prosecution and of involvement

98 in his crimes. I rejected the willing cooperation of all of them; there was no place in my camp even for refugees, not to mention traitors. Perhaps those who have resorted to all these methods should be considered better

habendi sint, qui haec omnia fecerunt. Ita est; sed ego defensorem in mea persona, non accusatorem maxime laudari volo. Rationes ad aerarium, antequam Dolabella condemnatus est, non audet referre; impetrat a senatu ut dies sibi prorogaretur, quod tabulas suas ab accusatoribus Dolabellae obsignatas diceret, proinde quasi exscribendi potestatem non haberet. Solus est hic qui numquam rationes ad aerarium referat.

39 Audistis quaestoriam rationem, tribus versiculis relatam; legationis, non nisi condemnato et eiecto eo qui posset reprehendere; nunc denique praeturae, quam ex senatus consulto statim referre debuit, usque ad hoc tempus non rettulit. Quaestorem se in senatu exspectare dixit, proinde quasi non, ut quaestor sine praetore possit rationem referre, —ut tu, Hortensi, ut omnes—eodem modo sine quaestore praetor. Dixit idem Dolabellam impetrasse. Omen magis patribus conscriptis quam causa placuit: probaverunt. Verum quaestores quoque iam pridem venerunt: cur non rettulisti? Illarum rationum ex ea faece legationis quaestoriaeque tuae procurationis illa sunt nomina, quae Dolabellae necessario sunt aestimata. EX LITIBVS AESTIMATIS DOLABELLAE PR. ET PRO PR.: Quod minus Dolabella Verri acceptum rettulit quam Verres illi expensum tulerit, HS quingenta triginta quinque milia, et quod plus fecit Dolabella Verrem accepisse quam iste in suis tabulis habuit, HS ducenta triginta duo milia, et quod plus frumenti fecit accepisse istum, HS deciens et octingenta milia, quod tu homo castissimus aliud in tabulis habebas. Hinc illae extraordinariae pecuniae, quas nullo duce tamen aliqua ex

1 Ita est *codd.* (ista est G_2): *om. b*: *secl. Muell.*   5 prorogarentur *codd.*   6 proinde *codd. praeter Lg.* 48 *et* δ (perinde)   8 ad aerar. rationes G_1 11 quam $SD\Sigma p$: *om.* G_2LK 13 quaestorem se SDp: quaestores sese *ex Asc.* (quaestor esse se) *edd.*   deinde quasi SDp *al.*   14 et quaestor *codd.*   posset δ   27 octing. duo milia G_2LK 28 callidissimus G_1 aliis *coni. Wyttenb.*

prosecutors, and this is indeed the case, but my wish is to bring special praise to the role of defender, rather than to the role of prosecutor. He did not dare to return his accounts to the treasury before Dolabella was condemned; he succeeded in getting an extension of the deadline from the senate on the basis of his assertion that his accounts had been sealed by Dolabella's accusers, as if he did not have the right to make copies. He is the only person who can never manage to submit his accounts to the treasury.

XXXIX. You have heard of his accounts · from his quaestorship, submitted in three short lines; those from his tenure as legate werế submitted only after the man who was in a position to dispute them had been condemned and banished; lastly, those of his praetorship, which, by decree of the senate, he was bound to submit immediately, he has not submitted to this day. He said in the senate he was waiting for his quaestor to return, as if a praetor is not entitled to submit accounts independently of his quaestor in the same way a quaestor can submit them independently of his praetor – as you did, Hortensius, and everyone else. He said that Dolabella had been granted a similar postponement. It was what that parallel portended rather than the merits of the case that appealed to the senators and brought their approval. But the quaestors have returned long ago; why then have you not submitted your accounts? In the accounts from that cesspool of iniquity to which he reduced his commission as legate and his administration of the duties of quaestor occur the following items, which had to be reckoned in the assessments against Dolabella. 'EXTRACT FROM THE DAMAGES ASSESSED AGAINST THE PRAETOR AND PROPRAETOR DOLABELLA.' Because Dolabella recorded he received less from Verres than the latter recorded he paid, five hundred and thirty-five thousand sesterces were assessed; because Dolabella made it seem Verres had received more than he had entered in his accounts, two hundred and thirty-two thousand sesterces were assessed; because he made it seem Verres had received too large an amount of grain, one million eight hundred thousand sesterces were assessed, a judgement based on the fact that you, spotless paragon that you are, had a different figure in your accounts. This is the source from which this abundance of unrecorded sums has come, which, though without anyone

particula investigamus, redundarunt, hinc ratio cum Q. et Cn. Postumis Curtiis multis nominibus, quorum in tabulis iste habet nullum ; hinc HS quater deciens P. Tadio numeratum Athenis testibus planum faciam ; hinc empta apertissime praetura, nisi forte id etiam dubium est, quo modo iste praetor factus sit. Homo scilicet aut industria aut opera probata aut frugalitatis existimatione praeclara aut denique, id quod levissimum est, adsiduitate, qui ante quaesturam cum meretricibus lenonibusque vixisset, quaesturam ita gessisset quem ad modum cognovistis, Romae post quaesturam illam nefariam vix triduum constitisset, absens non in oblivione iacuisset sed in adsidua commemoratione omnibus omnium flagitiorum fuisset, is repente, ut Romam venit, gratiis praetor factus est. Alia porro pecunia ne accusaretur data. Cui sit data, nihil ad me, nihil ad rem pertinere arbitror : datam quidem esse tum inter omnis recenti negotio facile constabat. Homo stultissime et amentissime, tabulas cum conficeres et cum extraordinariae pecuniae crimen subterfugere velles, satis te elapsurum omni suspicione arbitrabare si, quibus pecuniam credebas, iis expensum non ferres, neque in tuas tabulas ullum nomen referres, cum tot tibi nominibus acceptum Curtii referrent? Quid proderat tibi te expensum illis non tulisse? an tuis solis tabulis te causam dicturum existimasti?

Verum ad illam iam veniamus praeclaram praeturam, criminaque ea quae notiora sunt his qui adsunt quam nobis qui meditati ad dicendum paratique venimus ; in quibus non dubito quin offensionem neglegentiae vitare

1 ratio . Q̄ . Q̄. postumus curtus SDp al.   4 numerata *codd.* : *corr.* Gronov. (ii, §§ 20, 50)   15 nil *Asc.*   18 cum (*ante* confic.) *om.* SD   20 arbitrare pG_1 21 his SDp al.   22 nomen ullum qr nominis SD   24 solius? *Muell.*   26 *habet p in mg.* hinc incipit de praetura urbana : D^2 admissa in praetura urbana, tertia pars divisionis   29 quin pr: quid in SD al.

101 to guide us, we are nonetheless tracking down to some small extent. This is the source of the account with Quintus and Cn. Postumus Curtius, an account with multiple entries, none of which appear in Verres' records; this is the source of the payment of fourteen hundred thousand sesterces to P. Tadius of Athens, as I will plainly show by the evidence of witnesses; this is the source of the money for his most blatant purchase of the praetorship, unless perhaps there is still some doubt as to how he won election as praetor. He was a man, I suppose, who had shown industry, or had praiseworthy activity to his credit, or had a high reputation for sobriety, or finally, to mention the most trivial of virtues, had shown diligence in canvassing the electorate – despite the fact that, before his quaestorship, he had lived with prostitutes and pimps, had administered his quaestorship in the manner you well know, had, after that scandalous quaestorship, stayed scarcely three days in Rome, had, though absent, not languished in oblivion but had lived in the constant recounting of all his crimes by everyone – such a man, I suppose, was suddenly, on his return to Rome, elected praetor free of charge. Additional money was paid to prevent his prosecution. To whom it was paid I consider of no concern to me and of no relevance to the matter at hand, but that it was indeed paid was readily agreed by all at the time, while

102 the affair was fresh. You utterly senseless fool, when you were completing your accounts and were seeking to avoid the charge of unrecorded funds, did you think that you would sufficiently escape all suspicion if you failed to record payments to those to whom you gave money, and made no entry in your account books, when the Curtii were recording payments from you in multiple entries? What good did it do you not to record your payments to them? Or did you think you would plead your case on the basis of your own accounts alone?

103 XL. But now let us come to that illustrious praetorship and to charges that are better known to this audience than to us who have rehearsed them and have come prepared to speak about them. In dealing with them I am afraid I cannot avoid or escape resentment on grounds of

atque effugere non possim. Multi enim ita dicent, ' De illo nihil dixit in quo ego interfui ; illam iniuriam non attigit quae mihi aut quae amico meo facta est, quibus ego in rebus interfui '. His omnibus qui istius iniurias norunt, hoc est populo Romano universo, me vehementer excusatum 5 volo non neglegentia mea fore ut multa praeteream, sed quod alia testibus integra reservari velim, multa autem propter rationem brevitatis ac temporis praetermittenda existimem. Fatebor etiam illud invitus, me prorsus, cum iste punctum temporis nullum vacuum peccato praeterire 10 passus sit, omnia quae ab isto commissa sint non potuisse cognoscere. Quapropter ita me de praeturae criminibus auditote ut ex utroque genere, et iuris dicendi et sartorum tectorum exigendorum, ea postuletis quae maxime digna sint eo reo cui parvum ac mediocre obici nihil oporteat. 15
104 Nam ut praetor factus est, qui auspicato a Chelidone surrexisset, sortem nactus est urbanae provinciae magis ex sua Chelidonisque quam ex populi Romani voluntate. Qui principio qualis in edicto constituendo fuerit cognoscite.
41 P. Annius Asellus mortuus est C. Sacerdote praetore. 20 Is cum haberet unicam filiam neque census esset, quod eum natura hortabatur, lex nulla prohibebat, fecit ut filiam bonis suis heredem institueret. Heres erat filia. Faciebant omnia cum pupilla, legis aequitas, voluntas patris, edicta praetorum, consuetudo iuris eius quod erat tum cum 25
105 Asellus est mortuus. Iste praetor designatus — utrum admonitus an temptatus an, qua est ipse sagacitate in his rebus, sine duce ullo, sine indice pervenerit ad hanc impro-

3 aut *om. LK*   in *om. $G_1 K$*   4 iis *SD*   8 brev. rat. G_1
13 ex *p Asc. Prisc.* δ : *om. SD*Ψ   dicendi *SDp Prisc.* : dicundi δ
15 aut *Prisc.*   nihil oporteat *DpZS²*: nihilo poterat S^1 (i, § 75)
20 C. Annius *codd.* : *corr. Naugerius* (i, § 107 : ii, § 21)   . pR . *D corr., Zr*: p^{i}r *p* : . p . R . *SD primo*   22 eum *SDKZpr*: cum *q* : *om. b edd.*   23 omnia faciebant *qr*   24 puella *Prisc.*   legis *SDp* : leges *Prisc.*   26 mortuus est *Kr*   27 an temptatus *p* : atemptatus (att.) *SD*Ψ   ipse *SD*Ψ*p* : iste *b*δ

110

negligence. For many will say: "he has said nothing about the issue in which I was myself involved; he has not touched upon the injustice done to me or on that done to my friend, matters in which I was myself involved." To all those who have experienced Verres' injustices - and that means the entire Roman people - I want to say emphatically in my defence that my many omissions will not be due to negligence on my part, but to a desire to leave some matters untouched for the witnesses, and also to my belief that many things must be omitted for reasons of brevity and economy of time. I will also reluctantly confess that, since Verres allowed no moment to pass without using it for some form of wrongdoing, I was simply unable to learn the facts of all the crimes committed by him. I ask you therefore to listen to me as I speak about the crimes of his praetorship, expecting only to hear instances of wrongdoing from two categories of crime arising from his administration of justice and the maintenance of public buildings, and only those that are especially worthy of this defendant, who does not deserve

104 to be charged with any small or medium offence. Well then, when he became praetor, and when he had risen with favourable omens from the arms of Chelidon, he obtained by lot the office of urban praetor, which pleased him and Chelidon more than it did the Roman people. Observe the kind of man he showed himself to be at the very beginning, in the formulation of his edict.

XLI. P. Annius Asellus died when C. Sacerdos was praetor. Since he had an only daughter and he was not on the census rolls, he was moved by the promptings of nature and the absence of any legal bar to make his daughter heir to his property. The daughter became the heir. Everything worked in favour of the young girl, the fairness of the law, the wishes of her father, the edicts of praetors, the legal usage prevailing at the time of

105 Asellus' death. Verres, while praetor-elect - whether he was urged or incited to such villainy, or was brought to it by some keen instinct of his own in such matters without

bitatem, nescio : vos tantum hominis audaciam amentiamque cognoscite—appellat heredem L. Annium, qui erat institutus secundum filiam (non enim mihi persuadetur istum ab illo prius appellatum) ; dicit se posse ei condonare edicto hereditatem ; docet hominem quid possit fieri. Illi bona res, 5 huic vendibilis videbatur. Iste, tametsi singulari est audacia, tamen ad pupillae matrem submittebat ; malebat pecuniam accipere, ne quid novi ediceret, quam ut hoc edictum tam 106 improbum et tam inhumanum interponeret. Tutores pecuniam praetori si pupillae nomine dedissent, grandem 10 praesertim, quem ad modum in rationem inducerent, quem ad modum sine periculo suo dare possent, non videbant ; simul et istum fore tam improbum non arbitrabantur ; saepe appellati pernegaverunt. Iste ad arbitrium eius cui condonabat hereditatem ereptam a liberis quam aequum 15 edictum conscripserit, quaeso, cognoscite. CVM INTELLEGAM LEGEM VOCONIAM —. Quis umquam crederet mulierum adversarium Verrem futurum ? an ideo aliquid contra mulieres fecit ne totum edictum ad Chelidonis arbitrium scriptum videretur ? Cupiditati hominum ait se obviam ire. 20 Quis potius non modo his temporibus, sed etiam apud maiores nostros ? quis tam remotus fuit a cupiditate ? Dic, quaeso, cetera ; delectat enim me hominis gravitas, scientia iuris *praetorii*, auctoritas. Recita. QVI AB A. POSTVMIO

1 audaciam amentiamque *pbrK* : am. aud. *ZG¹λ et SD* (*sed hi cum signis transp.* § 2)   5 possit *SDΨp* : posset *V Prisc.*   6 singulari *pKZ et corr. SD* : -aris *Vb al., et pr. SD* : *fort.* singularis audaciae ?   8 diceret *Vb*   9 tam *V* : *om. SDZpbr* : tam *K Harl.* 5428   13 et *om. Vb* (*Am. J. Ph.* xxvi. 411)   15 condonabat *VSDp rell.* : -averat *Prisc.* : -arat δ   a *SDp rell.* : *om. Vb Prisc.*   aecum *Vp* : aequum *SDb* : et cum *qr* (qua maecum *p₁ corr.*)   16 Cum . . . Voconiam *om. V*   17 Verr. mul. advers. *bδ*   19 fecit *SDp rell.* : scripsit *V* (i, § 110 : *Am. J. Ph. l.c.*)   21 etiam *om. V* (*Am. J. Ph. ibid.* 412 : *cf.* i, § 45)   22 fuit *om. G₂*   24 praetorii (i, § 114) *add. Koch, V secutus in quo est* P · R · (iii, § 17) : praetoris auctoritas *Klotz*   Recita *V* : *om. SDp rell.* (*cf.* dic . . . recita i. § 143)   ab *om. V*

benefit of leader or guide, I know not, but just observe his effrontery and mindless folly – he approached the man who had been appointed heir in the will next to the daughter and whose name was L. Annius (for I refuse to believe it was Verres who first was approached by him), and told him that he could, by means of his edict, present him with the inheritance. He explained to him what could be done. The idea seemed attractive to Annius, and to Verres likely to fetch a price. The latter, though his brazenness knew no bounds, nonetheless made secret overtures to the girl's mother; he preferred to get his money for not making any novel proclamations than to receive it for inserting such an unprincipled and heartless clause in his edict. The guardians did not see, if they gave the praetor the money in the girl's name, especially a large sum, how they could record it in the accounts or how they could pay it without risk to themselves. They thought as well that Verres would not prove so unscrupulous, and so they continued to refuse his repeated demands. I ask you to observe what an equitable edict he composed to suit the wishes of the man to whom he had presented an inheritance snatched from the testator's offspring. 'SINCE I UNDERSTAND THAT THE VOCONIAN LAW ...' Who would have believed that Verres would become an adversary of women? Or did he make a gesture of hostility towards them so it would not appear his entire edict had been written in accordance with the wishes of Chelidon? He declares that he is taking measures to block the greed of man. Who better to do so, not only in these times, but even among our ancestors? Who has been so far removed from greed? Please let me hear the rest of the edict. The man's sternness and knowledge of praetorian law and his authoritativeness delights me. Read the section beginning: 'ANYONE WHO,

Q. FVLVIO CENSORIBVS POSTVE EA — — FECIT FECERIT.
107 'Fecit fecerit'? quis umquam edixit isto modo? quis umquam eius rei fraudem aut periculum proposuit edicto, quae neque post edictum reprehendi neque ante edictum provideri
42 potuit? Iure, legibus, auctoritate omnium qui consulebantur, testamentum P. Annius fecerat non improbum, non inofficiosum, non inhumanum: quodsi ita fecisset, tamen post illius mortem nihil de testamento illius novi iuris constitui oporteret. Voconia lex te videlicet delectabat. Imitatus esses ipsum illum C. Voconium, qui lege sua hereditatem ademit nulli neque virgini neque mulieri: sanxit in posterum, qui post eos censores census esset, ne quis
108 heredem virginem neve mulierem faceret. In lege Voconia non est 'FECIT FECERIT', neque in ulla praeteritum tempus reprehenditur nisi eius rei quae sua sponte tam scelerata et nefaria est ut, etiamsi lex non esset, magnopere vitanda fuerit. Atque in his ipsis rebus multa videmus ita sancta esse legibus ut ante facta in iudicium non vocentur; Cornelia testamentaria, nummaria, ceterae complures, in quibus non ius aliquod novum populo constituitur, sed sancitur ut, quod semper malum facinus fuerit, eius quaestio ad populum
109 pertineat ex certo tempore. De iure vero civili si quis novi quid instituit, is non omnia quae ante acta sunt rata esse patietur? Cedo mihi leges Atinias, Furias, Fusias, ipsam, ut dixi, Voconiam, omnis praeterea de iure civili: hoc reperies in omnibus statui ius quo post eam legem populus utatur. Qui plurimum tribuunt edicto, praetoris edictum legem annuam dicunt esse: tu edicto plus amplecteris quam

3 eius rei *SD* : ei rei *V*   4 reprehendi *V sol.* (*Am. J. Ph.* xxvi. 410)   6 P. Annius *VSD* (*in mg.* D ' *al. C* ') 10 ipsum illum *VSDpr*: illum ipsum *Kδ Prisc.*   C *SDp al.* : *om.* V (*Div.* § 22 : § 111 *infra*)   15 tam *V*: *om. SDp rell.*   et *codd.*: ac *Asc.* (§ 5 *supra*) 16 magnopere *VSD* (*Act. Pr.* § 22): magno opere *Iord.*   17 his *V* : is π : *om. SDΨ*   22 ex *Vp*: *om. SDΨ* : (a certo *Asc.*)   23 instituerit *Prisc. contra codd.*   non *Vs Prisc.* : non *SD* : *om. G₂Lq et in lac. p*   24 patietur *V Asc.* : patitur *SDp al.*   Fusias *SDp al.* : nufias *V*   28 amplecteris *VSD* : compl. *bδ*

107 SINCE THE CENSORSHIP OF A. POSTUMIUS AND Q. FULVIUS OR IN THE FUTURE, HAS DONE OR SHALL DO ...' "Has done or shall do?" Who ever composed an edict in these terms? Who ever gave notice in an edict of an offense or liability arising from an action that could not be faulted after the edict nor safeguarded against illegality before the edict. XLII. On grounds of justice, the law, the opinions of all who were consulted, P. Annius made a will that was lacking neither in moral integrity, nor in duty to family, nor in humanity. But even if he had made a will lacking in these respects, it would nonetheless be improper to institute any new legal provision in regard to his will after his death. I can see that you were charmed by the Voconian law. You should then have imitated Voconius himself, who did not deprive by his law any woman, either unmarried or married, of her inheritance. He imposed a regulation for the future, to the effect that no one who was on the census rolls after the censors in question should make an unmarried 108 or married woman his heir. In the Voconian law there is no phrase "has made or shall make", nor in any law are past actions called to account, except those which are inherently so abominable and evil that, even if there were no law, they should have been strenuously avoided. But even in these particular cases, we see the legal sanctions in many instances framed in such a way that actions previous to their enactment are not liable to judicial scrutiny: for example, the Cornelian law dealing with the forging of wills and counterfeiting of money, and several others, which impose no new principle of law upon the people but prescribe that, in relation to a particular act that was always wrongful, the people should have the right, starting from a particular date, to take judicial 109 action. But if someone introduces some new principle into the civil law, shall he not allow all previous transactions to stand as valid? Look at the Atinian, Furian, and Fusian laws, and, as I mentioned earlier, the Voconian law itself, and all the others that deal with the civil law; you will find that, in all of them, a right to legal action is established that can only be invoked by the public for the period subsequent to the enactment of the particular law. Those who attach the greatest importance to edicts describe the praetorian edict as law that lasts for a year, but your edict encompasses a greater span of time than

lege. Si finem edicto praetoris adferunt Kalendae Ianuariae, cur non initium quoque edicti nascitur a Kalendis Ianuariis? an in eum annum progredi nemo poterit edicto quo praetor alius futurus est, in illum quo alius praetor fuit regredietur? Ac si hoc iuris, non unius hominis causa edixisses, cautius 5 composuisses. Scribis, QVI HEREDEM FECIT FECERIT. Quid, si plus legarit quam ad heredem heredesve perveniat? quod per legem Voconiam ei qui census non sit licet; cur hoc, cum in eodem genere sit, non caves? Quia non generis, sed hominis causam verbis amplecteris, ut facile 10 appareat te pretio, non iure esse commotum. Atque hoc si in posterum edixisses, etsi minus esset nefarium, tamen esset improbum; sed tum vituperari posset, in discrimen venire non posset; nemo enim committeret. Nunc est eius modi edictum ut quivis intellegat non populo esse scriptum, 15 sed P. Anni secundis heredibus. Itaque cum abs te caput illud tam multis verbis mercennarioque prooemio esset ornatum, ecquis inventus est postea praetor qui idem illud ediceret? Non modo nemo edixit, sed ne metuit quidem quisquam ne quis ediceret. Nam post te praetorem multi 20 in isdem causis fuerunt; in his nuper Annaea de multorum propinquorum sententia, pecuniosa mulier, quod censa non erat, testamento fecit heredem filiam. Iam hoc magnum iudicium hominum de istius singulari improbitate, quod C. Verres sua sponte instituisset, id neminem metuisse ne 25

5 Ac *VSDp*: At *Z al.* 6 Qui *V* (i, § 106): Si quis *SDp al.* 10 generis *SDΨp*: iuris *V* (*cf.* iii, § 58) amplecteris *V*(?) *b edd.*: complect. *SDp rell.* 11 iure *V*: om. *rell.* 12 dixisset *V* etsi *suppl. Iord.* 13 tum *VSDp*: cum *LKZ et in mg. D*: tamen *Muell., prob. May* in discrimen *V*: in dubium *SDp rell.* 16 abs te *edd.* (aps te *V*): a te *SDp rell.* caput id *V* (v, § 105) 18 inventus est *V*: est inventus *SDp rell.* 20 multi in isdem causam sis (causis?) fuerunt *V* (v, §§ 53, 111): multi testamenta eodem modo fecerunt *SDp rell.*; *Cl. Rev.* xvii. 202 21 in is *p* 23 Itaque hoc *b* 24 *Desinit in verbis* istius singu- *S plena pagina, quem sequuntur DG₂LKs et al.*: istius *Z* 25 C. π *Prisc.*: om. *Vbδ* (*Div.* § 22)

110 would a regular statute. If the first of January brings an end to a praetor's edict, why does the beginning of the edict not also date from the first of January? Or if no one can extend his edict into a year in which there will be another praetor, shall anyone be allowed apply it retrospectively to a year in which there has been another praetor? If you had issued this decree in the interests of justice and not in the interests of a single individual, you would have composed it more carefully. XLIII. You write: 'HE WHO HAS MADE OR SHALL MAKE HIS HEIR.' What if he bequeaths more in legacies than comes to the heir or heirs? This is legal under the Voconian law for anyone not on the census lists. Why do you not make provision against this, since it belongs in the same category? Because your words are not concerned with the issue of categories but with the case of an individual, and clearly show you were motivated by money, not justice. And even if you had made this proclamation as a decree to apply to the future, though it would be less scandalous, it would still be unconscionable. But in that case, though it could be faulted, its motives could not be suspect, since no one would have violated its provisions. But as the decree now stands, it is clear to anyone it was written not in the interest of the public but of the
111 reversionary heirs of P. Annius. As a result, though you embellished that section with a torrent of words and a preamble written for pay, was any subsequent praetor found willing to retain the clause in his edict? Not only did none of the praetors retain it, but no one had even a fear that any of them would. For after your praetorship there were many people in the same situation as Annius, among them a wealthy woman named Annaea, who recently, because she was not on the census rolls, made her daughter her heir in her will with the approval of many of her relatives. Now, we have here a notable judgement from the public about this man's unparalleled villainy in the fact that no one was afraid, since Verres had established the practice on his own authority, that

quis reperiretur qui istius institutum sequi vellet; solus enim tu inventus es cui satis non fuerit corrigere testamenta vivorum, nisi etiam rescinderes mortuorum. Tu ipse ex Siciliensi edicto hoc sustulisti; voluisti, ex improviso si quae res nata esset, ex urbano edicto decernere. Quam postea tu tibi defensionem relinquebas, in ea maxime offendisti, cum tuam auctoritatem tute ipse edicto provinciali repudiabas.

44 Atque ego non dubito quin, ut mihi, cui mea filia maxime cordi est, res haec acerba videtur atque indigna, sic uni cuique vestrum, qui simili sensu atque indulgentia filiarum commovemini. Quid enim natura nobis iucundius, quid carius esse voluit? quid est dignius in quo omnis nostra diligentia indulgentiaque consumatur? Homo importunissime, cur tantam iniuriam P. Annio mortuo fecisti? cur hunc dolorem cineri eius atque ossibus inussisti, ut liberis eius bona patria—voluntate patris, iure, legibus tradita—eriperes, et cui tibi esset commodum condonares? Quibuscum vivi bona nostra partimur, iis praetor adimere nobis mortuis bona fortunasque poterit? NEC PETITIONEM, inquit, NEC POSSESSIONEM DABO. Eripies igitur pupillae togam praetextam, detrahes ornamenta non solum fortunae sed etiam ingenuitatis? Miramur ad arma contra istum hominem Lampsacenos isse, miramur istum de provincia decedentem clam Syracusis profugisse? Nos si alienam vicem pro nostra iniuria doleremus, vestigium istius in foro nullum esset relictum. Pater dat filiae, prohibes; leges sinunt, tamen te interponis! De suis bonis ita dat ut ab iure non abeat; quid habes quod reprehendas? Nihil, opinor. At ego concedo; prohibe, si potes, si habes qui te audiat, si

1 istius institutum *secl. Ernesti*   2 satis non *V*: non satis π*b*
5 nata esset *V al.* : natae essent π*b*   6 tu tibi *V*, *ut videtur, al.* :
tibi tu π*b*   9 ego *om. q*   15 fecisti mortuo *b*   19 nostra
Vpb : paterna *q* : nostra paterna *r*   his *pb* : is *q*   21 Eripis *Asc.*
26 nullum *V*: non *p rell.*

112 anyone would be found willing to abide by it. You have emerged as the only person who was not content to alter the wills of the living without also rescinding those of the dead. You yourself removed this clause from your Sicilian edict; you intended, if anything unexpected arose, to decide it in accordance with your urban edict. But this line of defence that you were building for yourself for the future was fatally flawed by you when you repudiated your own precedent in your provincial edict.

XLIV. I have no doubt that, just as this affair seems cruel and shameful to me, who have a daughter especially dear to my heart, it seems the same to each of you, who are stirred by similar feelings of tenderness for your daughters. For what has nature designed to be more delightful or precious to us? What better deserves to have 113 all our attention and favour lavished upon it? You relentless villain, why have you done so great a wrong to the dead P. Annius? Why have you imprinted such anguish on his ashes and bones, snatching from children the property of their father – which was given them by their father's wishes, by the laws of justice, and by the state's statutes – and bestowing it to suit your own advantage? Shall a praetor have the power to take away our property and wealth after we are dead from those with whom we share them while alive? 'I WILL GRANT,' he says, 'NO PETITION OR RIGHT OF POSSESSION.' Will you then strip the young girl of the *toga praetexta* and remove the insignia, not only of her prosperity, but of her free birth? Do we wonder that the people of Lampsacum resorted to arms against this man? Do we wonder that, when he was departing his province, he fled from Syracuse in secret? If we grieved for the lot of others as we do for the wrongs done ourselves, no trace 114 of the man would have been left in the forum. A father makes a bequest to his daughter, you forbid it; the laws allow it, you put yourself in the way! A man divides his property without deviation from the law. What reason have you to find fault with this? None, in my opinion. But I give you leave to forbid it, if you can find or if

potest tibi dicto audiens esse quisquam. Eripias tu voluntatem mortuis, bona vivis, ius omnibus? Hoc populus Romanus non manu vindicasset, nisi te huic tempori atque huic iudicio reservasset?

Posteaquam ius praetorium constitutum est, semper hoc iure usi sumus: si tabulae testamenti non proferrentur, tum *ut*, uti quemque potissimum heredem esse oporteret, si is intestatus mortuus esset, ita secundum eum possessio daretur. Quare hoc sit aequissimum facile est dicere, sed in re tam usitata satis est ostendere omnis antea ius ita dixisse, et hoc vetus edictum translaticiumque esse. Cognoscite hominis aliud in re vetere edictum novum, et simul, dum est unde ius civile discatur, adulescentis in disciplinam ei tradite: mirum est hominis ingenium, mira prudentia. Minucius quidam mortuus est ante istum praetorem; eius testamentum erat nullum; lege hereditas ad gentem Minuciam veniebat. Si habuisset iste edictum, quod ante istum et postea omnes habuerunt, possessio Minuciae genti esset data: si quis testamento se heredem esse arbitraretur quod tum non exstaret, lege ageret in hereditatem, aut, pro praede litis vindiciarum cum satis accepisset, sponsionem faceret et ita de hereditate certaret. Hoc, opinor, iure et maiores nostri et nos semper usi sumus. Videte ut hoc iste correxerit. Componit edictum his verbis ut quivis intellegere possit unius hominis causa conscriptum esse, tantum quod hominem non nominat; causam quidem totam perscribit, ius, consuetudinem, aequitatem, edicta omnium neglegit. EX EDICTO VRBANO. SI DE HEREDITATE AMBIGITVR — — SI POSSESSOR SPONSIONEM NON FACIET. Iam qui id ad praetorem, uter possessor sit? nonne id quaeri oportet, utrum

1 quisquam *om. V*   7 ut, uti *Muell.*; *v. Stangl, Rh. Mus.* 65, *p.* 96   8 intestatus *V Asc.*: intestato *p rell.*   11 hominis aliud π: aliud hom. *bδ*   21 *glossam post* litis habent π fide iussores fructuum   et *cod.* (?) *Vrs., Asc.*: *om. p rell.*   24 his *p*: iis *b al.* 25 possit *p rell.*: posset *qr*   29 qui id ad *scripsi* (*cf.* ii, § 177): quid ad *cod. Mein , Prisc.*: quid id ad *br cum pler.*: quid ad id *pq*

you have anyone willing to listen to you, or if anyone can possibly exist who obeys your orders. Are you to deprive the dead of their last wish, the living of their property, and all men of justice? Would the Roman people not have violently punished such behaviour, if they had not reserved you for this occasion and this court?

Ever since praetorian law came into being, we have always employed this legal rule: if the documents of a will were not produced, then the right to take possession would be granted to him who would have the strongest claim to the inheritance if the person had died intestate. It is easy to explain why this is the most equitable procedure, but in a matter so familiar it is sufficient to point out that everyone previously administered the law in this manner, and that this long-standing ordinance was
115 passed down as an accepted tradition. XLV. But observe another novel proclamation of Verres in relation to an ancient practice, and at once, while there exists this fount of knowledge about the civil law, entrust our young men to his training; the man has extraordinary ability and extraordinary insights. A man named Minucius died before Verres became praetor. There was no will belonging to him to be found. Under the law the inheritance was to go to the Minucian clan. If Verres had observed the decree that everyone before and after him observed, the right to take possession would have been granted to the Minunian clan; if anyone thought he was the heir by the terms of the will which was not then available, he could take an action in law to gain the inheritance, or could pursue it by the process of offering a wager, after receiving adequate security for the disputed property and its fruits. This, in my opinion, is the form of law that our ancestors and ourselves have always employed. But observe how Verres has amended
116 the procedure. He has composed his edict in terms that allows anyone to see it was written for the benefit of one man; it merely omits the name of the individual. Indeed, he sets out the entire case in detail, ignoring law, usage, equity, and the edicts of all his predecessors. 'EXTRACT FROM THE URBAN EDICT. IF A DISPUTE ARISES CONCERNING AN INHERITANCE ... IF THE PARTY IN POSSESSION FAILS TO OFFER A WAGER.' Now, what business is it of the praetor which of the two parties is in possession? Is it not the question of which of them has

possessorem esse oporteat? Ergo, quia possessor est, non moves possessione: si possessor non esset, non dares? Nusquam enim scribis, neque tu aliud quicquam edicto amplecteris nisi eam causam pro qua pecuniam acceperas.

117 Iam hoc ridiculum est: SI DE HEREDITATE AMBIGETVR ET TABVLAE TESTAMENTI OBSIGNATAE NON MINVS MVLTIS SIGNIS QVAM E LEGE OPORTET AD ME PROFERENTVR, SECVNDVM TABVLAS TESTAMENTI POTISSIMVM POSSESSIONEM DABO. Hoc translaticium est: sequi illud oportet, SI TABVLAE TESTAMENTI NON PROFERENTVR. Quid ait? se ei daturum qui se dicat heredem esse. Quid ergo interest proferantur necne? Si protulerit, uno signo ut sit minus quam ex lege oportet, non des possessionem: si omnino tabulas non proferet, dabis? Quid nunc dicam? neminem umquam hoc postea alium edixisse? valde sit mirum neminem fuisse qui istius se similem dici vellet. Ipse in Siciliensi edicto hoc non habet; exegerat enim iam mercedem; item ut illo edicto de quo ante dixi, in Sicilia de hereditatum possessionibus dandis edixit idem quod omnes Romae praeter istum. EX EDICTO SICILIENSI. SI DE HEREDITATE AMBIGITVR —.

46
118   Ac, per deos immortalis! quid est quod de hoc dici possit? Iterum enim iam quaero abs te, sicut modo in illo capite Anniano de mulierum hereditatibus, nunc in hoc de hereditatum possessionibus, cur ea capita in edictum provinciale transferre nolueris. Vtrum digniores homines existimasti eos qui habitant in provincia quam nos qui aequo iure uteremur, an aliud Romae aequum est, aliud in Sicilia? Non enim hoc potest hoc loco dici, multa esse in provinciis aliter edicenda; non de hereditatum quidem possessionibus,

---

5 ambigetur π : ambigitur b Asc., Par. 7786   9 est om. π   10 non om. pq¹   15 sit codd. : scilicet Bake : valde hoc est mirum Prisc.   22 Ac pq : at r Par. 7786   26 esse exist. Prisc.   27 eos p (corr. nos) ... uterentur Prisc.

the right to be in possession that ought to be under investigation? So, because a man is in possession, you do not remove him from it, but if he were not in possession, would you not grant it to him? For you make no stipulation about this, nor do you cover any other matter in your edict except this case for which you had received payment. Now here is
117 an absurd clause: 'IF A DISPUTE ARISES CONCERNING AN INHERITANCE, AND THE DOCUMENTS OF THE WILL, SIGNED BY NO FEWER SIGNATORIES THAN THE LAW REQUIRES, ARE PRODUCED BEFORE ME, I WILL AS A RULE GRANT THE RIGHT OF POSSESSION IN ACCORDANCE WITH THE DOCUMENTS OF THE WILL.' This much is traditional; it should be followed by the clause: 'IF THE DOCUMENTS OF THE WILL ARE NOT PRODUCED ...' But what does Verres say? That he will grant the right of possession to him who claims to be the heir! What difference does it make then whether the documents are produced or not? If a person produced them with one signature less than the law requires, you would not grant the right of possession; if he produces no documents at all, you will grant it. Why should I bother to state that no one afterwards ever adhered to that decree? I am sure it would cause great surprise that no one wanted to be said to resemble Verres! He himself did not use the clause in his Sicilian edict, for he had already exacted his payment. Just as in the case of the clause I mentioned earlier, he issued the same edict in Sicily in relation to granting the right to take possession of inheritances as all praetors, with the exception of himself, had issued in Rome. 'EXTRACT FROM THE SICILIAN EDICT. IF A DISPUTE ARISES CONCERNING AN INHERITANCE ...'

118   XLVI. Now, in the name of the gods, what can one say about this? For, just as I asked you a short time ago in relation to the clause involving Annius and the inheritances of women, I now ask you again in relation to the clause involving the right to take possession of inheritances why you did not wish to transfer these clauses to your provincial edict. Did you consider that those living in the province were more deserving than we of a fair system of justice, or is one thing just in Rome and another in Sicily? For it cannot be said at this point that many sections of an edict are necessarily different in the provinces, not even the sections dealing with the right to take possession of inheritances or those dealing

non de mulierum hereditatibus. Nam in utroque genere video non modo ceteros, sed te ipsum totidem verbis edixisse quot verbis edici Romae solet. Quae Romae magna cum infamia pretio accepto edixeras, ea sola te, ne gratis in provincia male audires, ex edicto Siciliensi sustulisse video. 5
119 Et cum edictum totum eorum arbitratu, quam diu fuit designatus, componeret qui ab isto ius ad utilitatem suam nundinarentur, tum vero in magistratu contra illud ipsum edictum suum sine ulla religione decernebat. Itaque L. Piso multos codices implevit earum rerum in quibus ita 10 intercessit, quod iste aliter atque ut edixerat decrevisset; quod vos oblitos esse non arbitror, quae multitudo, qui ordo ad Pisonis sellam isto praetore solitus sit convenire; quem iste conlegam nisi habuisset, lapidibus coopertus esset in foro. Sed eo leviores istius iniuriae videbantur quod erat in 15 aequitate prudentiaque Pisonis paratissimum perfugium, quo sine labore, sine molestia, sine impensa, etiam sine patrono
120 homines uterentur. Nam, quaeso, redite in memoriam, iudices, quae libido istius in iure dicundo fuerit, quae varietas decretorum, quae nundinatio, quam inanes domus eorum 20 omnium qui de iure civili consuli solent, quam plena ac referta Chelidonis; a qua muliere cum erat ad eum ventum et in aurem eius insusurratum, alias revocabat eos inter quos iam decreverat, decretumque mutabat, alias inter aliquos contrarium sine ulla religione decernebat ac proxumis paulo 25
121 ante decreverat. Hinc illi homines erant qui etiam ridiculi inveniebantur ex dolore; quorum alii, id quod saepe audistis, negabant mirandum esse ius tam nequam esse verrinum; alii etiam frigidiores erant, sed quia stomachabantur ridiculi videbantur esse, cum Sacerdotem exsecrabantur qui verrem tam 30

1 in utroque *Lamb. edd.* (i, § 15) : utroque *codd.*   3 quod *p* edici *p rell.* : om. *qr*   6 quam diu fuit design. *suppl. in mg. p*² : om. *r*   13 esse solitus sit *codd.*   19 dicundo *V Prisc.* : dicendo *πb*   23 vos *p*   24 aliquos *V* : alios *p rell.*

with the inheritances of women. For I see that in both types of case not only all others, but you yourself, have issued edicts in exactly similar terms to those generally used in Rome. But the decrees you had most disgracefully issued at Rome for a bribe, these, I notice, are the only ones you removed from your Sicilian edict, seeking to avoid acquiring a bad reputation in the province for no pay.

119 And not only did he compose his entire edict as praetor-elect at the bidding of those who were purchasing justice from him for their own benefit, but in the course of his magistracy he made decisions without the slightest scruple that ran contrary to the provisions of that very edict of his. As a result, L. Piso filled several volumes with accounts of the cases in which he interposed his veto because Verres had made a decision contrary to the terms of his edict. I do not imagine you have forgotten the crowds and lines of people that regularly gathered around the tribunal of Piso when he was praetor. If Verres had not had him as a colleague, he would have been buried in the forum under showers of stones. But the wrongs he did seemed less serious because the fairness and wisdom of Piso provided a ready refuge, of which people could avail themselves without toil or trouble or expense or even the services of an advocate.

120 Now I ask you, gentlemen, to recall how arbitrarily Verres administered the law, how inconsistent were his judgements, how much trafficking took place, how empty were the houses of all those who were usually consulted about matters of civil law, how full to overflowing was the house of Chelidon. Whenever that woman came to him and whispered in his ear, he would sometimes recall parties to whom he had already given a decision and change it; at other times he would, without the slightest qualm, give others a decision directly opposite to the one he had just

121 given in the case immediately preceding. It was this which caused those people to emerge who were found to be actually witty under the spur of grief, some of whom, as you have often heard, used to say it was no wonder a boar-pig's justice was so iniquitous; others had even feebler talents, but seemed witty in their anger as they cursed Sacerdos because he had left behind such an evil

nequam reliquisset. Quae ego non commemorarem,—neque
enim perfacete dicta neque porro hac severitate digna sunt,
—nisi vos illud vellem recordari, istius nequitiam et iniquitatem tum in ore vulgi atque in communibus proverbiis esse
versatam. 5

47   In plebem vero Romanam utrum superbiam prius com-
122 memorem an crudelitatem? Sine dubio crudelitas gravior
est atque atrocior. Oblitosne igitur hos putatis esse quem
ad modum sit iste solitus virgis plebem Romanam conci-
dere? Quam rem etiam tribunus plebis in contione egit, 10
cum eum quem iste virgis ceciderat in conspectum populi
Romani produxit ; cuius rei recognoscendae faciam vobis
123 suo tempore potestatem. Superbia vero quae fuerit quis
ignorat? quem ad modum iste tenuissimum quemque contempserit, despexerit, liberum esse numquam duxerit? P. 15
Trebonius viros bonos et honestos compluris fecit heredes ;
in iis fecit suum libertum. Is A. Trebonium fratrem habuerat proscriptum. Ei cum cautum vellet, scripsit ut heredes
iurarent se curaturos ut ex sua cuiusque parte ne minus
dimidium ad A. Trebonium illum proscriptum perveniret. 20
Libertus iurat ; ceteri heredes adeunt ad Verrem, docent non
oportere se id iurare facturos esse quod contra legem Corneliam esset, quae proscriptum iuvari vetaret ; impetrant ut
ne iurent ; dat his possessionem. Id ego non reprehendo ;
etenim erat iniquum homini proscripto egenti de fraternis 25
bonis quicquam dari. Libertus, nisi ex testamento patroni
124 iurasset, scelus se facturum arbitrabatur ; itaque ei Verres

2 perfacete *V Lg.* 42 : perfacile *p rell.*   3 et iniquitatem tum
p rell. : *om. V*   4 volgi *V*   10 tr, pl. Quintius *V*   11 iste
virgis *V π* : virgis iste *bδ*   12 produxisset *V* (*Zielinski p.* 193)   14
iste *V Prisc.* : is *pδ*   16 conplures *Vbr* : plures *pq*   17 iis *V* : his
p rell.   Is Aulum *p*   20 A. *prb* : *om. Vq*   fratrem illum *nb* :
illum *V edd.*   22 id iurare *p* (*ut coni. Klotz*) : adiurare *V* : iurare
id *qr* : iurare *rell.*   acturos *V*   23 vetaret *V ut videtur* : vetat
p rell.   25 inicum *V*   26 Libertus *V edd.* : at ille libertus *r* (*ut
coni. Ern.*) : et ille lib. *p rell.*

swine. I would not be reminding you of these jokes (for they are not particularly humourous, and, moreover, they do not befit the seriousness of this occasion) were it not that I want you to recall that this man's wickedness and injustice were constantly on the lips of the general public and were bywords everywhere.

122   XLVII. As regards his treatment of the common people of Rome, should I mention first his arrogance or his cruelty? Certainly his cruelty was more serious and more atrocious. Well then, do you think those people here have forgotten how Verres used to beat the ordinary citizens with rods? A tribune of the people actually raised the matter at a public meeting when he displayed before the Roman people a man whom Verres had beaten with rods. But I will give you an opportunity to examine this issue
123 in due course. As for his arrogance, who is unaware of its extent or of the manner in which he despised and scorned all men of slender means and invariably refused to regard them as free citizens? P. Trebonius made many good and honourable men his heirs, among them a freedman of his own. He had a brother, A. Trebonius, who was on the list of the proscribed. Since he wanted to make provision for him, he stipulated that the heirs should swear to insure that not less than half their shares went to this proscribed man, A. Trebonius. The freedman took the oath. The other heirs approached Verres and pointed out that they did not have the right to bind themselves by oath to a course of action that contravened the Cornelian law, which forbade any help being given to a proscribed person. They were granted their request for exemption from the oath, and Verres gave them possession of the inheritance. I am not finding fault with this, for it was indeed unconscionable that a proscribed man in dire need should get anything from his brother's estate. The freedman thought he would be committing a crime if he did not take the oath, in
124 accordance with the terms of his patron's will. As a

possessionem hereditatis negat se daturum, ne posset patronum suum proscriptum iuvare, simul ut esset poena quod alterius patroni testamento obtemperasset. Das possessionem ei qui non iuravit; concedo; praetorium est. Adimis tu ei qui iuravit; quo exemplo? Proscriptum iuvat; 5 lex est, poena est. Quid ad eum qui ius dicit? utrum reprehendis quod patronum iuvabat eum qui tum in miseriis erat, an quod alterius patroni mortui voluntatem conservabat, a quo summum beneficium acceperat? Vtrum horum reprehendis? Et hoc tum de sella vir optimus dixit: 'Equiti 10 Romano tam locupleti libertinus homo sit heres!' O modestum ordinem, quod illinc vivus surrexerit!

125   Possum sescenta decreta proferre in quibus, ut ego non dicam, pecuniam intercessisse ipsa decretorum novitas iniquitasque declarat; verum ut ex uno de ceteris coniecturam 15
48 facere possitis, id quod priore actione didicistis, audite. C. Sulpicius Olympus fuit; is mortuus est C. Sacerdote praetore, nescio an antequam Verres praeturam petere coeperit; fecit heredem M. Octavium Ligurem. Ligus hereditatem adiit; possedit Sacerdote praetore sine ulla controversia. 20 Posteaquam Verres magistratum iniit, ex edicto istius, quod edictum Sacerdos non habuerat, Sulpici patroni filia sextam partem hereditatis ab Ligure petere coepit. Ligus non aderat. L. frater eius causam agebat; aderant amici, propinqui. Dicebat iste, nisi cum muliere decideretur, in 25 possessionem se ire iussurum. L. Gellius causam Liguris defendebat; docebat edictum eius non oportere in eas

6 lex poena est *V*   7 tum π*b* : *om. V*   9 a *r* : *om. Vpqb*
11 homo sit *V* : sit homo *p rell.*   12 surrexerit *V* (*Zielinski p.* 193) :
surrex̄ *p* : surrexit *r rell., prob.* May   13 sescenta *V* : ⅬⅩ *p* : sexaginta *rell.*   ego non dicam pecuniam *V* : ego pec. non dicam *pr rell.*
16 didicistis *V* : cognostis *p rell.* (*Am. J. Ph.* xxvi. 411)   18
coeperit π*b rell., Prisc.* : coepit *V*   19, 23 (*item* i, § 126) ligus *pq* :
ligur *rell.*   22 non *om. V* : s. l. *ut videtur p*², *dein del.*   26 ire
iussurum *Vprb* : ire missurum δ : se missurum *coni. Zumpt* (*Zielinski l. c.*)   27 ad eas heredes *pb*

result, Verres declared he would not grant him possession of the inheritance, to keep him from being in a position to help the proscribed man who was his patron, and as a punishment for obeying the terms of the will of his other patron. You granted possession to him who did not take the oath. I grant it was your right to do so as praetor. You took possession from him who took the oath. On what precedent? If he helps the proscribed man there is a law and a penalty to deal with that. What business is it of him who is interpreting a point of law? Are you disapproving the fact that he was helping the patron who was then in pitiable circumstances, or that he was respecting the last wish of the other patron who was dead and from whom he had received the greatest possible benefit? Which of these is it that you disapprove? And what is more, this most estimable of men voiced the following sentiment from his judgement-seat: "A freedman should not be the heir of so wealthy a Roman knight." What a restrained class of men, to allow him to rise from that seat alive!

125   I can lay before you countless decrees which, by their very novelty and inequity, make plain, without any words of mine, that money played its part in them; but, that you may infer the character of the others from one instance, listen to an incident that you were informed about at the first hearing. XLVIII. There was a man named C. Sulpicius Olympus. He died when C. Sacerdos was praetor, probably, I think, before Verres became a candidate for the praetorship. He made M. Octavius Ligus his heir. Ligus took up the inheritance and held possession of it without any controversy while Sacerdos was praetor. After Verres assumed office, the daughter of Sulpicius' patron, on the basis of a clause in Verres' edict that Sacerdos had not employed, claimed one-sixth of the inheritance from Ligus. The latter was absent, and his brother Lucius pleaded his case. Friends and relatives appeared in support. Verres declared that, if a settlement was not reached with the woman, he would decree that she should take possession. L. Gellius defended Ligus' case. He pointed out that the edict of Verres should not

hereditates valere quae ante eum praetorem venissent; si hoc tum fuisset edictum, fortasse Ligurem hereditatem aditurum non fuisse. Aequa postulatio, summa hominum 126 auctoritas pretio superabatur. Venit Romam Ligus; non dubitabat quin, si ipse Verrem convenisset, aequitate causae, auctoritate sua commovere hominem posset. Domum ad eum venit, rem demonstrat, quam pridem sibi hereditas venisset docet; quod facile homini ingenioso in causa aequissima fuit, multa quae quemvis commovere possent dixit; ad extremum petere coepit ne usque eo suam auctoritatem despiceret gratiamque contemneret ut se tanta iniuria adficeret. Homo Ligurem accusare coepit, qui in re adventicia atque hereditaria tam diligens, tam attentus esset; debere eum aiebat suam quoque rationem ducere; multa sibi opus esse, multa canibus suis, quos circa se haberet. Non possum illa planius commemorare quam 127 ipsum Ligurem pro testimonio dicere audistis. Quid est, Verres? utrum ne his quidem testibus credetur, an haec ad rem non pertinent? non credemus M. Octavio, non L. Liguri? quis nobis credet, cui nos? quid est quod planum fieri testibus possit, si hoc non fit? An id quod dicunt leve est? Nihil levius quam praetorem urbanum hoc iuris in suo magistratu constituere, omnibus quibus hereditas venerit coheredem praetorem esse oportere. An vero dubitamus quo ore iste ceteros homines inferiores loco, auctoritate, ordine, quo ore homines rusticanos ex municipiis, quo denique ore, quos numquam liberos putavit, libertinos homines solitus sit appellare, qui ob ius dicendum M. Octavium Ligurem,

1 venissent] fuissent *V contra codd. et Prisc.*   5 causae *V Non.* : causae et *pr rell.* (i, § 137 : *Am: J. Ph.* xxvi. 414)   8 fuit in causa aequissima *pr*   11 gratiamque *prb* : gratiam *V* (i, § 145)   17 Quid est *V* : quid ẽ *p* : quid enim *bδ*   18 crederetur *pδ*   19 credemus *V* : credimus *π* : *om. bδ*   21 est *V* : est Verres *pr*   23 urbanum *V* : ūrb. *p* : urbis *bδ* (i, § 143)   29 dicendum *Vπb* : dicundum *δ*

126 apply to inheritances that had been received before his praetorship and that, if the decree had been in force at the time, Ligus would, perhaps, not have taken up the inheritance. It was a reasonable appeal, but the weightiest influence that men could bring to bear was overcome by money. Ligus returned to Rome, confident that, if he met Verres face to face, he could influence him by the justice of his case and by his own personal authority. He went to his house, explained the matter, pointed out how long ago the inheritance had come his way, and, as was easy for an intelligent man arguing a totally just case, said many things capable of influencing just about anyone. Finally, he began to plead with him not to scorn his prestigious position or show contempt for his influence to the extent of doing him so great an injury. The man began to berate Ligus for being so anxious and concerned about an adventitious legacy and told him he should also consider his, Verres', side of things: he had many needs, as did the jackals that he had around him. I cannot recount the matter more clearly than did Ligus himself in the evidence you heard him give.

127 What do you say to this, Verres? Shall we not believe even these witnesses, or are these matters not relevant to the case? Shall we not believe M. Octavius or L. Ligus? Who will believe us, whom shall we believe? What can the evidence of witnesses make plain, if not this? Or is it a trivial matter that they speak about? It is no less a charge than that the urban praetor imposes the rule during his tenure in office that he has the right to be the co-heir of everyone who receives an inheritance. Or do we really have any doubt about the tone in which he addresses the other people of more lowly status, influence, and rank, or the peasants from the communities of Italy, or indeed those whom he never considered free citizens, the freedmen, when he had no hesitation in demanding money for administering the law from M. Octavius Ligus,

hominem ornatissimum loco, ordine, nomine, virtute, ingenio, copiis, poscere pecuniam non dubitavit?
49 In sartis tectis vero quem ad modum se gesserit quid ego dicam? Dixerunt qui senserunt; sunt alii qui dicant;
128 notae res ac manifestae prolatae sunt et proferentur. Dixit Cn. Fannius, eques Romanus, frater germanus Q. Titini, iudicis tui, tibi pecuniam se dedisse. RECITA. CN. FANNI TESTIMONIVM. Nolite Cn. Fannio dicenti credere, noli, inquam, tu, Q. Titini, Cn. Fannio, fratri tuo, credere; dicit enim rem incredibilem; C. Verrem insimulat avaritiae et audaciae, quae vitia videntur in quemvis potius quam in istum convenire. Dixit Q. Tadius, homo familiarissimus patris istius, non alienus a matris eius genere et nomine; tabulas protulit, quibus pecuniam se dedisse ostendit. RECITA. NOMINA Q. TADI. RECITA. TESTIMONIVM Q. TADI. Ne Tadi quidem tabulis nec testimonio credemus? Quid igitur in iudiciis sequemur? Quid est aliud omnibus omnia peccata et maleficia concedere nisi hoc, hominum honestorum testimoniis et virorum bonorum tabulis non credere?
129 Nam quid ego de cotidiano sermone querimoniaque populi Romani loquar, de istius impudentissimo furto seu potius novo ac singulari latrocinio? ausum esse in aede Castoris, celeberrimo clarissimoque monumento—quod templum in oculis cotidianoque aspectu populi Romani positum est, quo saepe numero senatus convocatur, quo maximarum rerum frequentissimae cotidie advocationes

1 ordine *om. pq*   2 dubitavit Vpq^1: dubitarit *rb*   3 se Vqr: sese $p\delta$ 5 ac *p*: atque *qr*: *om. V*   6 C. Fannius π*b*: Cn. Phaenius *V*   7 iudiciis (*corr.* iudicis) tuis *Vb*: iudici is tuis *p* pec. se dedisse *ed. Venet.* 1483, *Zielinski* (*p.* 193): se pec. dedisse *codd.* R. Cn. Faeni test. *V*: Recita test. Cn. Faen. *pb*   8 dicenti *pr rell.*: *om. V*   10 Verrem p^2 *s. l.*   12 histum *p*   16 Ne Tadi quidem tab. *V edd.*: Ne tabulis quidem Quinti (Q.) Tadii *pr rell.* credemus *V*: credetur π*b*δ (i, § 127)   19 honestorum *V*: honestissimorum *pr rell.*; *cf. Cluent.* § 202, *Har. Resp.* § 19

a man most distinguished for his position, rank, reputation, virtue, abilities, and resources?

128 XLIX. What should I say about his behaviour in relation to the repair of public buildings? Men who have had experience of it have already spoken; there are others still to speak. Well-known and clearly-proven incidents have been related and will be related. Cn. Fannius, a Roman knight and the brother of Q. Titinius, one of your judges, has said he gave you money. Read the section beginning: 'THE EVIDENCE OF CN. FANNIUS.' Refuse to believe the evidence of Cn. Fannius, refuse – I mean you, Q. Titinius – to believe Cn. Fannius, your own brother. For he speaks the incredible; he accuses C. Verres of greed and of brazenness, vices which seem more appropriate to anyone than to him. Q. Tadius, a close friend of Verres' father and no stranger to his mother's family and name, has given evidence and has produced accounts which show that he handed over money. Read the section beginning: 'THE ACCOUNTS OF Q. TADIUS.' Read the section beginning: 'THE EVIDENCE OF Q. TADIUS.' Shall we not believe even the accounts and evidence of Q. Tadius? What then will we be guided by in court? What else is a refusal to believe the evidence of honourable men and the accounts of honest individuals but the granting of a licence to all to commit all forms of wrongdoing and criminality?

129 Now, what should I say about a matter that is a subject of constant talk and complaint among the Roman people, the matter involving a most shameful theft by Verres, or rather a novel and unparalleled act of brigandage? To think that in the temple of Castor, a most celebrated and renowned monument, located where the Roman people see it daily in full view, where the senate often meets, where every day throngs of people receive legal counselling about affairs of the highest importance,

50

130 fiunt—in eo loco in sermone hominum audaciae suae monumentum aeternum relinquere. Aedem Castoris, iudices, P. Iunius habuit tuendam de L. Sulla Q. Metello consulibus. Is mortuus est; reliquit pupillum parvum filium. Cum L. Octavius C. Aurelius consules aedis sacras locavissent neque potuissent omnia sarta tecta exigere, neque ii praetores quibus erat negotium datum, C. Sacerdos et M. Caesius, factum est senatus consultum, quibus de sartis tectis cognitum et iudicatum non esset, uti C. Verres P. Caelius praetores cognoscerent et iudicarent. Qua potestate iste permissa sic abusus est ut ex Cn. Fannio et ex Q. Tadio cognovistis, verum tamen cum esset omnibus in rebus apertissime impudentissimeque praedatus, hoc voluit clarissimum relinquere indicium latrociniorum suorum, de quo non audire aliquando sed videre cotidie 131 possemus. Quaesivit quis aedem Castoris sartam tectam deberet tradere. Iunium ipsum mortuum esse sciebat; scire volebat ad quem illa res pertineret. Audit pupillum esse filium. Homo qui semper ita palam dictitasset, pupillos et pupillas certissimam praedam esse praetoribus, optatum negotium sibi in sinum delatum esse dicebat. Monumentum illa amplitudine, illo opere, quamvis sartum tectum integrumque esset, tamen aliquid se inventurum in 132 quo moliri praedarique posset arbitrabatur. L. Habonio aedem Castoris tradi oportebat: is casu pupilli Iuni tutor erat testamento patris: cum eo sine ullo intertrimento convenerat iam quem ad modum traderetur. Iste ad se Habonium vocat; quaerit ecquid sit quod a pupillo traditum non sit, quod exigi debeat. Cum ille, id quod erat, diceret facilem pupillo traditionem esse, signa et dona com-

3 de *Vpq* : *om. rb*δ   5 aedis *V* : aedes *p*   7 hi *p*   10 Celius *p* : Coelius *q*   11 sic abusus est π ('*est nova lectio*') : *om. b*δ *edd.* (*Cl. Rev.* xvii. 202)   14 iudicium *Zumpt al.*   24 Habonio π *Prisc.* : Rabonio δ (*ut V*, i, § 150)   29 id *om. pq*   30 comparare *fb*

to think that in this place he dared to leave for men to talk about an everlasting memorial of his effrontery.
130 L. The task of maintaining the temple of Castor, gentlemen, was held by P. Junius, a task given him by the consuls L. Sulla and Q. Metellus. He died, leaving a young son under the care of guardians. When the consuls L. Octavius and C. Aurelius, who had let the contracts for the maintenance of temples, proved unable to insure the completion of all repairs, as did the praetors C. Sacerdos and M. Caesius, to whom the task had been assigned, the senate decreed that, in cases where inspections and evaluations of repairs had not been made, the praetors C. Verres and P. Caelius should make them. How Verres abused this authority entrusted to him you have learned from Cn. Fannius and Q. Tadius, but, though in all his dealings he had most openly and shamelessly acted the brigand, he still wanted to leave this gleaming memorial of his pillagings, which we would be able not simply to hear about occasionally but to see
131 before us every day. He inquired who had responsibility for handing over the temple of Castor in a state of good repair. He knew that Junius himself had died and wanted to know who was now concerned in the matter. He heard it was the son who was in the care of guardians. So this fellow, who had always quite openly stated that young boys and girls in the care of guardians were the surest prey for praetors, told himself that a most welcome piece of business had been tossed into his lap. He considered that in a public building of such size and workmanship, however well-repaired and flawless it might be, he would
132 find some basis for scheming and pillaging. The temple of Castor was due to be handed over to L. Habonius, who happened to have been made a guardian of the young Junius by the father's will. An agreement had already been made with him for the transfer of the building without any loss to either side. Verres summoned Habonius and asked him if there was anything the boy had failed to deliver that ought to be extracted from him. When Habonius told him what was, in fact, the truth, that it was a straightforward transfer for the boy, with

parere omnia, ipsum templum omni opere esse integrum, indignum isti videri coepit ex tanta aede tantoque opere se non opimum praeda, praesertim a pupillo, discedere. Venit ipse in aedem Castoris, considerat templum; videt undique tectum pulcherrime laqueatum, praeterea cetera 5 nova atque integra. Versat se; quaerit quid agat. Dicit quidam ex illis canibus quos iste Liguri dixerat esse circa se multos, 'Tu, Verres, hic quod moliare nihil habes, nisi forte vis ad perpendiculum columnas exigere.' Homo omnium rerum imperitus quaerit, quid sit 'ad perpendicu- 10 lum': dicunt ei fere nullam esse columnam quae ad perpendiculum esse possit. 'Nam mehercule,' inquit, 'sic agamus; columnae ad perpendiculum exigantur.' Habonius, qui legem nosset—qua in lege numerus tantum columnarum traditur, perpendiculi mentio fit nulla—et qui non putaret 15 sibi expedire ita accipere, ne eodem modo tradendum esset, negat id sibi deberi, negat oportere exigi. Iste Habonium quiescere iubet et simul ei non nullam spem societatis ostendit; hominem modestum et minime pertinacem facile coercet; columnas ita se exacturum esse confirmat. Nova 20 res atque improvisa pupilli calamitas nuntiatur statim C. Mustio, vitrico pupilli, qui nuper est mortuus, M. Iunio patruo, P. Titio tutori, homini frugalissimo; hi rem ad virum primarium summo officio ac virtute praeditum, M. Marcellum, qui erat pupilli tutor, deferunt. Venit ad 25 Verrem M. Marcellus; petit ab eo pro sua fide ac diligentia pluribus verbis ne per summam iniuriam pupillum Iunium fortunis patriis conetur evertere. Iste, qui iam spe atque opinione praedam illam devorasset, neque ulla aequitate orationis neque auctoritate M. Marcelli commotus est; 30

2 ĕ, corr. isti, *p*   4 vidit *p*   6 dicit *pq* : dicit ei *q²r rell. edd.*
7 ipsis π   8 nihil *pbδ* : non *q edd.*   17 deberi *b* : debere *p* (*corr.*
i, *ut videtur*) *qr*   23 P. Titio *ut V infra,* § 137; *cf.* § 139 : P.
Tettio *pq* : P. tertio *r* : Potitio δ

133 all the statues and offerings accounted for and the temple itself immaculate in all its features, it began to seem shameful to him that he should walk away from so great a building, involving so much work, without collecting ample spoils, especially from a boy in the care of guardians. LI. He paid a visit himself to the temple of Castor and surveyed the sacred structure. He saw the ceiling splendidly panelled throughout and also the fresh and flawless condition of the rest of the building. He paced around and asked what action he might take. One of those jackals that he had told Ligus he kept about him in large numbers spoke up: "There is no move you can engineer in this matter, Verres, unless, perhaps, you want to demand that the columns should be plumb." The stupid fellow, who has no knowledge of anything, asked what being plumb meant. They told him practically no column existed capable of meeting this criterion. "Then, by Hercules," he says, "Let this be our move; let us demand that the columns

134 should be plumb." Habonius, who was aware of the terms of the contract, in which only the number of columns was recorded without any mention of their being plumb, and who did not consider it in his interest to accept charge of the temple on these terms in case he should have to hand it over on similar terms, said that he was not entitled to this stipulation and that it was not right to demand it. Verres ordered Habonius to be quiet, while at the same time suggesting there was some hope of a partnership between them. He easily imposed his control on a man who was unassuming and lacking in any strength of will. Habonius gave assurances he would demand the columns

135 should be plumb. This fresh development and unexpected disaster for the boy was immediately reported to his stepfather C. Mustius, who died recently, and to his uncle M. Junius, and to his guardian P. Titius, a man of the highest character. They carried the news to M. Marcellus, who was also a guardian of the boy, and an eminent and highly conscientious and virtuous man. M. Marcellus went to see Verres and, with characteristic integrity and diligence, pleaded with him at great length not to attempt by an act of gross injustice to deprive the young Junius of his father's property. Verres, who had already swallowed up in his hopes and thoughts this potential loot, was unmoved either by any aspect of the justice of the plea or by the personal authority of M.

itaque quem ad modum ostendisset se id exacturum esse
136 respondit. Cum sibi omnis ad istum adlegationes difficilis,
omnis aditus arduos ac potius interclusos viderent—apud
quem non ius, non aequitas, non misericordia, non propinqui oratio, non amici voluntas, non cuiusquam auctoritas
[pro pretio], non gratia valeret—statuunt id sibi esse 5
optimum factu, quod cuivis venisset in mentem, petere
auxilium a Chelidone, quae isto praetore non modo in iure
civili privatorumque omnium controversiis populo Romano
praefuit, verum etiam in his sartis tectisque dominata est.
52
137 Venit ad Chelidonem C. Mustius, eques Romanus, publi- 10
canus, homo cum primis honestus; venit M. Iunius,
patruus pueri, frugalissimus homo et castissimus; venit
homo summo pudore, summo officio, spectatissimus ordinis
sui, P. Titius tutor. O multis acerbam, o miseram atque
indignam praeturam tuam! Vt omittam cetera, quo tandem 15
pudore talis viros, quo dolore meretricis domum venisse
arbitramini? qui numquam ulla condicione istam turpitudinem subissent nisi offici necessitudinisque ratio coegisset.
Veniunt, ut dico, ad Chelidonem. Domus erat plena;
nova iura, nova decreta, nova iudicia petebantur. 'Mihi 20
det possessionem, mihi ne adimat, in me iudicium ne det,
mihi bona addicat.' Alii nummos numerabant, ab aliis
tabellae obsignabantur; domus erat non meretricio con-
138 ventu sed praetoria turba referta. Simul ac potestas primum
data est, adeunt hi quos dixi. Loquitur C. Mustius, rem 25
demonstrat, petit auxilium, pecuniam pollicetur. Respondit
illa ut meretrix non inhumaniter; libenter ait se factu-

3 vident *p*   6 pro pretio *auct. Garat. secl. edd.*   esse optimum *pbr*: opt. esse *edd.*   13 venit *Vb* : *om.* π   14 pudore *V* (i, § 126): pudore et π   16 mittam π*b*   17 talis viros quo dolore *p*² *s. l.*   18 numquam ulla π : numq. nulla *V* : nulla *b*   22 mihi adimat *pq*¹   23 ab aliis tab. obsign. *V* : alii tabulas obsignabant *p rell.*   28 inhumaniter *V Prisc.* : inhumane π *rell.*   se facturam *V et Donat.* : se esse facturam *pr rell.*, *prob. May* (i, § 142)

136 Marcellus. Accordingly, he replied that he intended to demand what he had indicated. Since it seemed to them that any form of representation to Verres was difficult, and that all approaches to him were precipitous, or, to be more exact, closed off (for he was a man on whom neither law, nor equity, nor pity, nor the pleading of relatives, nor the wishes of friends, nor the personal authority or influence of anyone had any effect), the men decided that the best course of action was the one that might have suggested itself to anyone, namely to seek help from Chelidon, who, while Verres was praetor, not only presided over the Roman people in matters of civil law and in all disputes between private citizens, but ruled supreme even in matters relating to the maintenance of public buildings.

137 LII. C. Mustius, who was a Roman knight and public contractor and among the most honourable of men, approached Chelidon. So did M. Junius, the boy's uncle, a most moderate and blameless individual. So did P. Titius, the boy's guardian, a man who had the deepest sense of propriety and duty and was a most distinguished member of his order. What a wretched, shameful praetorship was yours, and what a source of grief to many! Not to mention anything else, with what feelings of shame and grief do you think such men approached the house of a prostitute? They would never have submitted to such a disgrace, if consideration of duty and necessity had not compelled them. But, as I say, they made their way to Chelidon. The house was full; new laws, new decrees, new decisions were being sought. "Ask him to give me the right of possession; ask him not to take the right of possession from me; ask him not to decide against me; ask him to assign the property to me." Some were paying over money, others were signing agreements; the house was packed, not with the gathering that associates with prostitutes, but with the throng that 138 attends a praetor. As soon as the opportunity arose, those I mentioned approached her. C. Mustius spoke, explained the matter, asked her help and promised money. She replied in a manner that, for a prostitute, was not ungracious; she said she would gladly do what was asked, and would discuss the matter thoroughly with

ram, et se cum isto diligenter sermocinaturam; reverti
iubet. Tum discedunt: postridie revertuntur. Negat illa
posse hominem exorari; permagnam eum dicere ex illa re
pecuniam confici posse.

53 Vereor ne quis forte de populo, qui priore actione non
adfuit, haec, quia propter insignem turpitudinem sunt
incredibilia, fingi a me arbitretur. Ea vos antea, iudices,
cognovistis. Dixit iuratus P. Titius, tutor pupilli Iuni,
dixit M. Iunius tutor et patruus; Mustius dixisset, si
viveret, sed recenti re de Mustio auditum est; dixit L.
Domitius, qui cum sciret me ex Mustio vivo audisse, quod
eo sum usus plurimum (etenim iudicium, quod prope
omnium fortunarum suarum C. Mustius habuit, me uno
defendente vicit), cum hoc, ut dico, sciret L. Domitius, me
scire ad eum res omnis Mustium solitum esse deferre,
tamen de Chelidone reticuit quoad potuit, alio responsionem
suam derivavit. Tantus in adulescente clarissimo ac principe
iuventutis pudor fuit ut aliquam diu, cum a me premeretur,
omnia potius responderet quam Chelidonem nominaret;
primo necessarios istius ad eum adlegatos esse dicebat,
deinde aliquando coactus Chelidonem nominavit. Non te
pudet, Verres, eius mulieris arbitratu gessisse praeturam
quam L. Domitius ab se nominari vix sibi honestum esse
arbitrabatur?

54 Reiecti a Chelidone capiunt consilium necessarium, ut
suscipiant ipsi negotium. Cum Habonio tutore, quod erat
vix HS quadraginta milium, transigunt HS ducentis milibus.
Defert ad istum rem Habonius: ut sibi videatur, satis
grandem pecuniam et satis impudentem esse. Iste, qui
aliquanto plus cogitasset, male accipit verbis Habonium,

---

1 se cum isto Vpb : cum isto se qr 8 Iuni V : Iunii p 10 sed
recenti re de M. auditum est V : · sed pro Mustio · rec. re de Mustio
aud. pb (*Act. Pr.* § 33)   titus dom. pbr 21 actus π *al.*   28 defert π :
refert $b\delta$ videatur *coni. Ernesti*: videbatur p *codd.*   30 accepit pb

Verres. She told them to come back. They then left and returned the following day. She said the man could not be persuaded; his comment was that he stood to make a great deal of money from this transaction.

LIII. I am afraid that perhaps some members of the public, who were not present at the first hearing, will think that these events, because their extraordinary vileness makes them incredible, are being invented by me. But you, gentlemen, have learned about them previously. P. Titius, a guardian of the young Junius, has recounted them under oath; M. Junius, a guardian and an uncle, has recounted them. C. Mustius would have recounted them if he were alive, but the story was heard from him while the matter was still fresh. L. Domitius has recounted them, who, though he knew that I had heard from Mustius when he was alive, because I was very friendly with him (for C. Mustius had won a case involving practically all his possessions with me as his one defending advocate), though L. Domitius, as I was saying, knew I was aware of the fact that Mustius was in the habit of reporting everything to him, he still kept silent about Chelidon as long as he could and channelled his response in another direction. Such was the sense of shame felt by this most illustrious young man, a leading light of the younger generation, that for a considerable time, as I kept pressing him, he would answer anything rather than speak the name of Chelidon. At first he kept saying that friends of Junius had made representations to Verres, then at last he mentioned, under pressure, the name of Chelidon. Are you not ashamed, Verres, to have conducted your praetorship at the bidding of this woman, whom L. Domitius considered he could scarcely mention by name without dishonour?

LIV. Rebuffed by Chelidon, they made the unavoidable decision to conduct the matter themselves. They reached agreement with Habonius to pay two hundred thousand sesterces for a matter that entailed scarcely forty thousand. Habonius reported the transaction to Verres, indicating that, in his opinion, it was a pretty large and a pretty shameless amount of money. Verres, who had been thinking of a somewhat larger sum, greeted

negat eum sibi illa decisione satis facere posse; ne multa,
141 locaturum se esse confirmat. Tutores haec nesciunt; quod
actum erat cum Habonio, putant id esse certissimum;
nullam maiorem pupillo metuunt calamitatem. Iste vero
non procrastinat; locare incipit non proscripta neque edicta 5
die, alienissimo tempore, ludis ipsis Romanis, foro ornato.
Itaque renuntiat Habonius illam decisionem tutoribus.
Accurrunt tamen ad tempus tutores; digitum tollit Iunius
patruus; isti color immutatus est, vultus, oratio, mens denique
excidit. Quid ageret coepit cogitare; si opus pupillo 10
redimeretur, si res abiret ab eo mancipe quem ipse adposuisset,
sibi nullam praedam esse. Itaque excogitat —
quid? Nihil ingeniose, nihil ut quisquam posset dicere,
'Improbe, verum callide'; nihil ab isto vafrum, nihil veteratorium
exspectaveritis; omnia aperta, omnia perspicua 15
142 reperientur, impudentia, amentia, audacia. 'Si pupillo
opus redimitur, mihi praeda de manibus eripitur. Quod
est igitur remedium? quod? Ne liceat pupillo redimere.'
Vbi illa consuetudo in bonis praedibus praediisque vendundis
omnium consulum, censorum, praetorum, quaestorum 20
denique, ut optima condicione sit is cuia res sit, cuium
periculum? Excludit eum solum cui prope dicam soli
potestatem factam oportebat. Quid enim? quisquam ad
meam pecuniam me invito adspirat, quisquam accedit?
Locatur opus id quod ex mea pecunia reficiatur; ego me 25
refecturum dico; probatio futura est tua, qui locas; praedibus
et praediis populo cautum est; et, si non putas
cautum, scilicet tu, praetor, in mea bona quos voles

2 hec *p* (haec δ): hoc *qb*   10 nesciit quid ageret *H. G. Koch*
13 ut quisquam posset π : quod qu. possit *al.*   14 vafrum *Madvigius*
(ii, § 132 ; iii, § 35) : fabrum *Asc.* : verum π : tectum *al.*   19
vendundis *V Asc.*,: vendendis *p rell.*   21 res sit *pbδ* : res *V*: res est
Prisc.   23 factam *V* : factam esse *p rell.*   24 quisquam acc. *V* :
quid acc. *p rell.*   26 refecturum *V* (i, § 138) : ref. esse *p rell.*   27
pupillo *V*   28 [et] ... ilico tu praetor *Kays.* : cautum esse, tu
Stuerenb. : et si non putas (sc. cautum esse) caveas licet. Tu praetor
... immittes? *Halm*   cauta *p*

141 Habonius with a tongue-lashing and said he could not be satisfied with this agreement; to cut the story short, he declared he would invite tenders for the job. The guardians knew nothing about this; they thought the agreement made with Habonius was absolutely firm, and they had no fear of any greater calamity befalling the young boy. But Verres did not delay. He commenced the taking of bids, on a day that had not been posted or announced, and was a most inappropriate time, in the very midst of the Roman festival, with the forum all decked out for the celebrations. Habonius accordingly cancelled his agreement with the guardians. But they rushed to the spot in time for the bidding. The uncle Junius raised his finger. Verres changed colour, he lost control of his face, speech, and indeed his mental faculties. He began to consider what he should do. If the contract was acquired by the young Junius and it left the hands of his appointed agent, there was no profit in it for him. He therefore contrived a solution - and what was it? Nothing ingenious, nothing that would allow anyone to say: "dishonest but clever"; expect no cunning or wiliness from this fellow; you will find everything about him is open and clear: just plain shamelessness, frenzy, 142 and effrontery. "If the contract is acquired by the boy, the loot is snatched from my hands. What then is the remedy? The boy must not be allowed to acquire the contract." What has happened to the practice employed by every consul, censor, praetor, and indeed quaestor in selling property and land furnished as appropriate security, whereby first preference is given to him to whom the property and the liability belong? Verres excluded the one person who, I might almost say, was the only one who should have been given the opportunity to bid. But why? Is there someone who has designs on my money against my wishes, and is taking steps to get it? A contract is being awarded that involves repairs at my expense. I say that I will make the repairs. You, who are awarding the contract, will have the right to approve the work. The public interest has been safeguarded by guarantors and their property; even if you do not think it has been safeguarded, can it be that you, as praetor, will send anyone you wish to seize my property and that

55
143 immittes, me ad meas fortunas defendendas accedere non sines. Operae pretium est legem ipsam cognoscere; dicetis eundem conscripsisse qui illud edictum de hereditate. Recita. LEX OPERI FACIVNDO. QVAE PVPILLI IVNI —. Dic, dic, quaeso, clarius. C. VERRES PRAETOR VRBANVS 5 ADDIDIT. Corriguntur leges censoriae! Quid enim? video in multis veteribus legibus, CN. DOMITIVS L. METELLVS CENSORES ADDIDERVNT, L. CASSIVS CN. SERVILIVS CENSORES ADDIDERVNT: vult aliquid eius modi C. Verres. Dic: quid addidit? Recita. QVI DE L. MARCIO M. 10 PERPERNA CENSORIBVS — — SOCIVM NE ADMITTITO NEVE PARTEM DATO NEVE REDIMITO. Quid ita? ne vitiosum opus fieret? At erat probatio tua. Ne parum locuples esset? At erat et esset amplius, si velles, populo cautum
144 praedibus et praediis. Hic te si res ipsa, si indignitas 15 iniuriae tuae non commovebat, si pupilli calamitas, si propinquorum lacrimae, si D. Bruti, cuius praedia suberant, periculum, si M. Marcelli tutoris auctoritas apud te ponderis nihil habebat, ne illud quidem animadvertebas, eius modi fore hoc peccatum tuum quod tu neque negare posses, 20 —in tabulas enim legem rettulisti,—neque cum defensione aliqua confiteri? Addicitur opus HS DLX milibus, cum tutores HS CCIƆƆ CCIƆƆ CCIƆƆ CCIƆƆ id opus ad illius iniquissimi hominis arbitrium se effecturos esse clamarent.
145 Etenim quid erat operis? Id quod vos vidistis; omnes 25 illae columnae, quas dealbatas videtis, machina adposita

  2 sinas $b\delta$ ipsam legem $b\delta$ 4 R (= Recita) V: *om. p rell.*
(i, § 106)   Lex operi V: ex opere *pr rell.*   5 urbanus V: urb.
pr: urbis $b\delta$ (i, § 127; § iii, 123)   6 Quid enī uedeo (*corr.* uideo) in multis *p rell.* (i, § 157): Quid eni multis V: quid est in multis *Halm, May*: Quod esse video in multis ... *vult Muell.*   7 Cn. Met. L. Cass. Cn. Serv. censores addid. *mediis omissis p*   10 R (= Recita) V: *om. p rell. ut supra*   11 Perpenna *pqb*   admitto *p*   14 pupillo V 16 si (*ante* propinq.) *et in sqq.* V: *om. p rell.*   17 suberant *Vqr Asc.*: subierant *p*   20 tu *om. pq^1*   21 legem *om. $b\delta$*   neque cum V: nec cum *prb*   22 opus V: id opus *p rell.* cum totores H. S. $\overline{\text{LXXX}}$ milibus id opus *p rell., edd.* (*contra* V)   24 iniq. hominis V: hom. iniq. *p rell.*

143 you will refuse to allow me to take steps to defend my possessions? LV. It is worth while examining the contract itself; you will affirm that the same man wrote it as wrote that edict about inheritance. Read the section beginning: 'THE CONTRACT RELATING TO THE PERFORMANCE OF THE WORK. IN AS MUCH AS THE WARD JUNIUS ...' Speak, please speak more clearly. 'C. VERRES, THE URBAN PRAETOR, HAS ADDED THE PROVISION.' The censors' regulations are being amended! But what of it? I notice in many contracts from the past the clauses: 'THE CENSORS CN. DOMITIUS AND L. METELLUS HAVE ADDED THE PROVISION; THE CENSORS L. CASSIUS AND CN. SERVILIUS HAVE ADDED THE PROVISION.' Verres' wish is something of this sort. Tell me what it is he has added. Read it out. 'ANYONE WHO HAS RECEIVED A CONTRACT FROM THE CENSORS L. MARCIUS AND M. PEPERNA ... LET HIM NOT BE ADMITTED AS A PARTNER, LET HIM NOT BE GIVEN A SHARE IN THE CONTRACT, LET HIM NOT BE ALLOWED TO ACQUIRE THE CONTRACT.' Why this provision? So that the work would not be faulty? But the right to approve it belonged to you. So that the contractor would not lack adequate security? But the public interest had been safeguarded by guarantors and their property, and would have been 144 more amply safeguarded had you wished. If at this point the nature of the matter itself, if the outrageousness of the wrong you were doing had no impact upon you, if the misfortune befalling a young boy, if the tears of his relatives, if the risk to D. Brutus, whose land stood as security, if the personal authority of the guardian M. Marcellus carried no weight with you, did you not even take note of the fact that this wrongdoing you were contemplating would be such that you could neither deny it (because the contract was entered in your records) nor admit it with any semblance of a defence? The contract was awarded for five hundred and sixty thousand sesterces, though the guardians loudly declared they would carry out the work to the satisfaction of this most 145 prejudiced arbiter for forty thousand. For what work was involved? That which you see before you. All those columns, which you see freshly whitened, were taken

nulla impensa deiectae eisdemque lapidibus repositae sunt. Hoc tu HS DLX milibus locavisti. Atque in illis columnis dico esse quae a tuo redemptore commotae non sint; dico esse ex qua tantum tectorium vetus deiectum sit et novum inductum. Quodsi tanta pecunia columnas dealbari putassem, certe numquam aedilitatem petivissem.

56
At ut videatur tamen res agi et non eripi pupillo: SI QVID OPERIS CAVSA RESCIDERIS, REFICITO. Quid erat quod rescinderet, cum suo quemque loco lapidem reponeret? QVI REDEMERIT SATIS DET DAMNI INFECTI EI QVI A VETERE REDEMPTORE ACCEPIT. Deridet, cum sibi ipsum iubet satis dare Habonium. PECVNIA PRAESENS SOLVETVR. Quibus de bonis? Eius qui, quod tu HS DLX milibus locasti, se HS CCIↃↃ CCIↃↃ CCIↃↃ CCIↃↃ effecturum esse clamavit. Quibus de bonis? Pupilli, cuius aetatem et solitudinem, etiamsi tutores non essent, defendere praetor debuit. Tutoribus defendentibus non modo patrias eius fortunas, sed etiam bona tutorum ademisti. HOC OPVS BONVM SVO CVIQVE FACITO. Quid est 'suo cuique'? Lapis aliqui caedendus et adportandus fuit machina sua; nam illo non saxum, non materies ulla advecta est; tantum operis in ista locatione fuit quantum paucae operae fabrorum mercedis tulerunt, et manuspretium machinae. Vtrum existimatis minus operis esse unam columnam efficere ab integro novam nullo lapide redivivo an quattuor illas

1 eisdemque *p* : eisdem (*ut vid.*) *V* (i, § 126) 4 deiectum *pq Prisc.* (*in V littera tertia incerta est*) : delectum *b*, deletum δ 6 petivissem *Vpr* : petissem *q Prisc.* May 11 accepit *V Asc.* : acciperet π (*cf.* susceperis *Div.* § 37) : *num* acceperit? 13 solvetur *V* : solvitur *pr rell.* 14 milibus *pr rell.* : om. *V* se *V* : om. *p rell.* 18 tutorū ademisti *pr* : tutorum una adem. *q* 19 facito... cuique *V sol.* : om. (*ex homoeoteleuto*) *p rell.* 20 aliqui *Vπ* : aliquis *bδ* apportandus fuit? machina una; nam *Orelli, Kays.* 21 ulla *V sol.* : secl. *Muell.* 22 et in ista π*b* fabrorum *secl. Bake, Kays.* 23 *Post* tulerunt *habet* manispraetium machinae *V* : .et manus. pretium machinae *prb* (*Act. Pr.* § 33; i, § 139): manu pretii (praedii *Asc.*) machina *Asc., Madv., Kays., Muell.* (*i. e. quantum manupretii machina tulit*)

down without any expense by moving in a machine, and were rebuilt using the same stones. This is the job you contracted to have done for five hundred and sixty thousand! And among those columns I maintain there are some that were never touched by your contractor, and I maintain there is one that merely had the old plaster removed from it and a fresh coat applied. But if I had thought that it cost so much money to have columns whitened, I would certainly never have become a candidate for the aedileship.

LVI. But that it might nonetheless seem a piece of public business was being transacted and not the robbery of a young boy, there was the clause: 'IF ANYTHING IS CUT AWAY IN THE COURSE OF THE WORK, IT SHALL BE REPAIRED.' What was there to cut away when each stone was being put back in its own place? 'HE WHO TAKES THE CONTRACT SHALL GIVE SECURITY FOR APPREHENDED DAMAGE TO HIM WHO TOOK OVER FROM THE ORIGINAL CONTRACTOR.' What a mockery! An order to Habonius to give security to himself! 'THE MONEY SHALL BE PAID IN CASH.' From whose property? From the property of him who loudly declared he would carry out for forty thousand sesterces the work that you contracted to have done for five hundred and sixty thousand. From the property of a young boy whose tender age and orphaned state the praetor should have protected even if there were no guardians. But you, though his guardians were protecting him, stole away not only the possessions he inherited from his father but even the property of his guardians. 'THE WORK MUST BE SOUND, CARRIED OUT WITH THE MATERIAL APPROPRIATE TO EACH PART OF IT.' What is this 'material appropriate to each part'? Some stones had to be cut and put in place with appropriate machinery; but no stone and no material were transported there. The only effort involved in that contract was paying whatever the workmen earned for a few days work along with the cost of the machinery. Do you think it takes less work to build one new column from the beginning using no second-hand stone, or to put back in place four such as

reponere? Nemo dubitat quin multo maius sit novam facere. Ostendam in aedibus privatis longa difficilique vectura columnas singulas ad impluvium HS CCIƆƆ CCIƆƆ 148 non minus magnas locatas. Sed ineptum est de tam perspicua eius impudentia pluribus verbis disputare, praesertim 5 cum iste aperte tota lege omnium sermonem atque existimationem contempserit, qui etiam ad extremum adscripserit: REDIVIVA SIBI HABETO; quasi quicquam redivivi ex opere illo tolleretur ac non totum opus ex redivivis constitueretur. At enim si pupillo redimi non licebat non necesse erat rem 10 ad ipsum pervenire; poterat aliquis ad id negotium de populo accedere. Omnes exclusi sunt non minus aperte quam pupillus. Diem praestituit operi faciundo Kalendas Decembris, locat circiter Idus Septembris; angustiis temporis excluduntur omnes. Quid ergo? Habonius istam 15
57
149
diem quo modo adsequitur? Nemo Habonio molestus est neque Kalendis Decembribus neque Nonis neque Idibus; denique aliquanto ante in provinciam iste proficiscitur quam opus effectum est. Posteaquam reus factus est, primo negabat se opus in acceptum referre posse; cum instaret 20 Habonius, in me causam conferebat, quod eum codicem obsignassem. Petit a me Habonius et amicos adlegat: facile impetrat. Iste, quid ageret, nesciebat; si in acceptum non rettulisset, putabat se aliquid defensionis habiturum; Habonium porro intellegebat rem totam esse patefacturum,— 25 tametsi quid poterat esse apertius quam nunc est?—ut uno minus teste *ag*eret, Habonio opus in acceptum rettulit 150 quadriennio post quam diem operi dixerat. Hac condicione, si quis de populo redemptor accessisset, non esset usus; cum die ceteros redemptores exclusisset, tum in eius arbi- 30 trium ac potestatem venire nolebant qui sibi ereptam

3 HS quadragenis milibus *pb*   5 eius *V* : istius *pr rell.*   20 se π : om. δ   21 eum π *Prisc.* : tum *bδ*   27 ageret *scripsi* : haberet *codd.* (*Act. Pr.* § 36) *Arus. Mess.* : haberem *Lamb.* (*Cl. Rev.* xix. 160)

these? No one has any doubt that it is a far greater task to make a new one. I will show that individual columns no less in size, in instances involving long and difficult transport, have been set in place by the *impluvium* in private houses for twenty thousand sesterces. But it is silly to argue any further about such conspicuous shamelessness, especially since he himself has openly shown his contempt by this entire contract for what anyone says or thinks. Even at the end he dared add the clause: 'HE MAY KEEP THE SECOND-HAND MATERIALS'; as if there were any second-hand materials to be taken from that operation, and the work in its entirety were not constructed from second-hand products. But, it may be suggested, even if the boy was not permitted to acquire the contract, that did not necessarily mean the matter passed into the hands of Verres; any member of the public could have become involved in the transaction. But all were excluded no less openly than the boy. He set the Kalends of December as the date for completion of the work; he awarded the contract around the Ides of September; everyone was excluded by the shortness of the time. LVII. Well then, how did Habonius meet the deadline? No one troubled Habonius on the Kalends of December or on the Nones or Ides; in the end Verres set out for his province some time before the work was finished. After he was indicted, he denied at first that he could record the work as completed; when Habonius kept pressing him, he referred the case to me on grounds that I had sealed the record-book. Habonius asked me for it and sent his friends to intercede. He gained his request without difficulty. Verres was uncertain what to do. If he did not record the work as completed, he reckoned he would have some measure of defence. But he also realized Habonius would expose the whole affair (though how could it be more exposed than it is now?) so, in order to have one less witness against him he gave Habonius credit for completion of the work four years after the deadline he had stated for the contract. If any ordinary contractor had come forward he would not have experienced such treatment; he had indeed excluded the other contractors by his deadline, but they were also unwilling to place themselves under his control and authority since he would consider they had snatched his

praedam arbitraretur. Nunc ne argumentemur, quo ista pecunia pervenerit facit ipse indicium. Primum cum vehementius cum eo D. Brutus contenderet, qui de sua pecunia HS DLX milia numeravit, quod iam iste ferre non poterat, opere addicto, praedibus acceptis de HS DLX milibus 5 remisit D. Bruto HS CX milia. Hoc, si aliena res esset, certe facere non potuisset. Deinde nummi numerati sunt Cornificio, quem scribam suum fuisse negare non potest. Postremo ipsius Haboni tabulae praedam illam istius fuisse clamant. Recita. NOMINA HABONI. 10

58
151
Hic etiam priore actione Q. Hortensius pupillum Iunium praetextatum venisse in vestrum conspectum et stetisse cum patruo testimonium dicente questus est, et me populariter agere atque invidiam commovere, quod puerum producerem, clamitavit. Quid erat, Hortensi, tandem in illo puero 15 populare, quid invidiosum? Gracchi, credo, aut Saturnini aut alicuius hominis eius modi produxeram filium, ut nomine ipso et memoria patris animos imperitae multitudinis commoverem. P. Iuni erat, hominis de plebe Romana, filius, quem pater moriens cum tutoribus et propinquis, tum legibus 20 tum aequitati magistratuum, tum iudiciis vestris commenda- **152** tum putavit. Hic istius scelerato nefarioque latrocinio bonis patriis fortunisque omnibus spoliatus venit in iudicium, si nihil aliud, saltem ut eum cuius opera ipse multos annos esset in sordibus paulo tamen obsoletius vestitum videret. 25 Itaque tibi, Hortensi, non illius aetas, sed causa, non vestitus, sed fortuna popularis videbatur, neque te tam com-

1 Nunc ne π (*p post levem rasuram*) : nonne (argumentamur) *bδ* : nos ne *Muell.*   4 HS IƆLX *ed. Venet.* 1483 : HS CCLƆƆƆ *p*   9 istius *p rell.* : huius *V*   9. 10 Haboni *V* : -ii *p*   12 praetext. ven. *V* (*ut videtur*) : ven. praet. *pr rell.*   stetisse cum *V* : stet esse cum *p* (*ut Par. Lall.*) : tet esse cum *p*² : ter esse cum *qr* : testes secum *bδ*   17 eius modi *p rell.* : huius modi *V* (i, § 17 ; iv, § 6)   18 commoverem *Vπ* : concitarem *bδ*   19 Iuni *V* : Iunii *p*   21 commendatum fuisse *V*   24 eum *om. pq*¹   25 esset *V* : est *pr*   27 te tamen monebat *V*

booty from him. Now in case there should be any argument as to where that money went, he himself provides the evidence. First of all, when D. Brutus, who had paid the five hundred and sixty thousand sesterces out of his own pocket, was vigorously contesting the matter with him, and he could no longer endure the pressure, he repaid, after the contract had been awarded and guarantors had been accepted, one hundred and ten of the five hundred and sixty thousand to D. Brutus. This he certainly could not have done, if he was no longer involved in the matter. Secondly, the money for the contract was paid to Cornificius, who he cannot deny was his clerk. Finally, the accounts of Habonius himself loudly proclaim that the loot from that affair fell to Verres. Read the section beginning: 'THE ACCOUNTS OF HABONIUS.'

151 LVIII. I might add that at this point in the course of the first hearing Hortensius complained about the fact that the young Junius came before you dressed as a minor and stood with his uncle while the latter was giving evidence, and he loudly protested that, by bringing the boy into court, I was conducting the case in a demagogic fashion and arousing hostility against his client. Now what was it about that boy, Hortensius, that was likely to excite public sympathy or stir resentment? I suppose it was the son of a Gracchus or a Saturninus or some such person that I had brought into court in an attempt to arouse the undiscerning multitude by the very name and memory of his father. He was in fact the son of P. Junius, one of the ordinary people of Rome, whom his father at his death thought he had entrusted to the protection not only of guardians and relatives but also of the laws, of
152 fair-minded magistrates, and of your courts. This boy, who had been robbed of all his father's property and wealth by Verres' vile and abominable pillagings, came into court, if for no other reason, that he might at least see the man whose actions had kept him for many years in the shabby garb of mourning dressed in clothes that were a bit shabbier still. It was therefore not the boy's age, Hortensius, but his cause, not his clothing but his circumstances that seemed to you likely to win public sympathy, nor was it the fact that he came in the dress

movebat quod ille cum toga praetexta, quam quod sine bulla venerat. Vestitus enim neminem commovebat is quem illi mos et ius ingenuitatis dabat ; quod ornamentum pueritiae pater dederat, indicium atque insigne fortunae, hoc ab isto praedone ereptum esse graviter tum et acerbe homines 5 153 ferebant. Neque erant illae lacrimae populares magis quam nostrae, quam tuae, Q. Hortensi, quam horum qui sententiam laturi sunt, ideo quod communis est causa, commune periculum ; communi praesidio talis improbitas tamquam aliquod incendium restinguendum est. Habemus enim 10 liberos parvos ; incertum est quam longa cuiusque nostrum vita futura sit ; consulere vivi ac prospicere debemus ut illorum solitudo et pueritia quam firmissimo praesidio munita sit. Quis est enim qui tueri possit liberum nostrorum pueritiam contra improbitatem magistratuum? Mater, 15 credo. Scilicet magno praesidio fuit Anniae pupillae mater, femina primaria : minus illa deos hominesque implorante iste infanti pupillae fortunas patrias ademit. Tutoresne defendent ? Perfacile vero apud istius modi praetorem, a quo M. Marcelli tutoris in causa pupilli Iuni et oratio et 20 voluntas et auctoritas repudiata est !

59
154 Quaerimus etiam quid iste in ultima Phrygia, quid in extremis Pamphyliae partibus fecerit, qualis in bello praedonum praedo ipse fuerit qui in foro populi Romani pirata nefarius reperiatur ? Dubitamus quid iste in hostium praeda 25 molitus sit, qui manubias sibi tantas ex L. Metelli manubiis fecerit, qui maiore pecunia quattuor columnas dealbandas quam ille omnis aedificandas locaverit ? Exspectemus quid dicant ex Sicilia testes ? Quis umquam templum illud aspexit quin avaritiae tuae, quin iniuriae, quin audaciae 30

2 commovet *V*   5 tum *V*π : *om.* *bδ*   6 illae *V* : eae *p* : hae *bδ*
10 restinguendum sit *V* : -enda est *prb rell.*   11 cuiusque nostrum *Vpq* : nostrum cuiusque *bδ*   12 proficere *rb*   14 est enim *pbδ* : enim est *qr*   19 defendent *p* (*ut coni. Madv.*) : defenderent *rell.*
22 quaerimus *Prisc.* : quaeremus *p rell.*

153 of a minor that disturbed you so much as the fact that he came without his locket. For the clothing that convention and the priviliges of free birth entitled him to wear bothered no one, but people were seriously and indeed bitterly upset that the childhood ornament his father had given him, as a sign and symbol of good fortune, had been snatched from him by this pirate. Nor were the tears of the people any more in evidence than ours, or than yours, Hortensius, or than the tears of those who will soon give their verdicts, and for the reason that this is a case and a danger that affects us all, and it is by the help of us all that such wickedness must be stamped out like a destroying fire. For we have small children and no certainty as to how long the life of any of us will be. While we are alive we have a duty to plan and make provision to insure that those children, if orphaned at a tender age, are protected by the strongest possible safeguards. But who can protect our children in their early years against the wickedness of magistrates? The mother, no doubt. A fine protection, indeed, the mother of the young Annia proved, though she was a prominent lady! Verres was, of course, deterred by her calls for help to gods and men from robbing the infant girl of the wealth her father left her! Will the guardians protect them? With the greatest of ease, no doubt, when they are dealing with a praetor of Verres' ilk, who spurned the pleadings, and wishes, and personal authority of the guardian M. Marcellus in the case of the young Junius!

154 LIX. Do we still continue to investigate what he did in remotest Phrygia and in the farthest reaches of Pamphylia, or the manner in which he himself played the pirate in a war against pirates, when he is seen to behave like a villainous brigand in the forum of the Roman people? Are we in any doubt about his machinations to secure booty taken from the enemy, when he created such rich spoils for himself from the spoils taken by L. Metellus and contracted to have four columns whitened for a greater sum than Metellus paid for the construction of all of them? Should we wait to see what the witnesses from Sicily have to say? Who has ever looked at that temple without becoming a witness to your greed, to your wrongdoing, to your effrontery? Who has

testis esset? quis a signo Vortumni in circum maximum venit quin is uno quoque gradu de avaritia tua commoneretur? quam tu viam tensarum atque pompae eius modi exegisti ut tu ipse illa ire non audeas. Te putet quisquam, cum ab Italia freto diiunctus esses, sociis temperasse, qui aedem Castoris testem tuorum furtorum esse volueris? quam populus Romanus cotidie, iudices etiam tum cum de te sententiam ferent, videbunt.

60
155 Atque etiam iudicium in praetura publicum exercuit; non enim praetereundum est ne id quidem. Petita multa est apud istum praetorem a Q. Opimio; qui adductus est in iudicium, verbo quod, cum esset tribunus plebis, intercessisset contra legem Corneliam, *re vera* quod in tribunatu dixisset contra alicuius hominis nobilis voluntatem. De quo iudicio si velim dicere omnia, multi appellandi laedendique sint, id quod mihi non est necesse; tantum dicam, paucos homines, ut levissime appellem, adrogantes hoc adiutore Q. Opimium per ludum et iocum fortunis omnibus evertisse.

156 Is mihi etiam queritur quod a nobis IX solis diebus prima actio sui iudici transacta sit, cum apud ipsum tribus horis Q. Opimius, senator populi Romani, bona, fortunas, ornamenta omnia amiserit? cuius propter indignitatem iudici saepissime est actum in senatu ut genus hoc totum multarum atque eius modi iudiciorum tolleretur. Iam vero in bonis Q. Opimi vendendis quas iste praedas, quam aperte, quam improbe fecerit, longum est dicere: hoc dico, nisi vobis id hominum honestissimorum tabulis planum fecero, fingi

1 Vortumni *Asc.* : Vertumni *Prisc.* : vertuñi *p* : vertuni *qr*   2 quin in uno *coni. Halm*   4 tu *om. Prisc., secl. Iord.*   5 diiunctus π : disiunctus *bδ* (iv, §§ 103, 117)   6 furtorum tuorum *Prisc.*   8 terrent viderunt *p*   13 re vera *add. Prisc.*   16 sint *Ern., Kays.* : sunt *p rell.*   id quod π : quod *b rell.*   17 appellem π : dicam *Asc.*   20 ab nobis *pq et (corr. ex* ab omnibus*) r*   21 ipsum *p rell.* : istum ipsum *Prisc.*   25 eius modi iud. *pq Prisc.* : iud. eius modi *bδ*

walked from the statue of Vortumnus to the Circus Maximus without being reminded of your greed at every step? You oversaw the repair of that road, which carries our sacred chariots and possessions, in such a manner that you do not dare to travel on it yourself. Is anyone to imagine that, when a sea separated you from Italy, you treated the allies with moderation, when you were willing to have the temple of Castor as a witness to your thefts? It is a temple the Roman people gaze on every day, as will the jurors also when they pronounce their verdict on you.

155 LX. And he also conducted a criminal trial during this praetorship, for not even this incident should be left without mention. Q. Opimius was brought before Verres as praetor in a suit involving a fine. Opimius was brought to trial ostensibly because, when tribune of the plebs, he had used his veto contrary to the provisions of the Cornelian law, but in reality because, in the course of his tribunate, he had opposed the wishes of a certain nobleman. If I wanted to tell the whole story of this trial, I would have to name and cause hurt to many people. I have no need to do that and will merely say that a few arrogant individuals (to describe them in the mildest possible terms), with the cooperation of Verres and for their amusement and diversion, evicted Q. Opimius from all his possessions.

156 Does he still complain to me because I brought the first stage of his trial to completion within nine days when, before his court, Q. Opimius, a senator of the Roman people, lost all his goods, property, and furnishings in three hours. Because of the outrageous character of this trial, it was repeatedly urged in the senate that all fines and all trials of this type should be abolished. How he further made profit from the sale of Q. Opimius' property and how openly and shamelessly he did so is a long tale to tell, but I say this, if I do not give you proof of the matter from the records of highly honourable men, you may consider that this whole affair

157 a me hoc totum temporis causa putatote. Iam qui ex calamitate senatoris populi Romani, cum praetor iudicio eius praefuisset, spolia domum suam referre et manubias detrahere conatus sit, is ullam ab sese calamitatem poterit deprecari? 5

61 Nam de subsortitione illa Iuniana iudicum nihil dico. Quid enim? contra tabulas quas tu protulisti audeam dicere? Difficile est; non enim me tua solum et iudicum auctoritas, sed etiam anulus aureus scribae tui deterret. Non dicam id quod probare difficile est; hoc dicam quod ostendam 10 multos ex te viros primarios audisse, cum diceres ignosci tibi oportere quod falsum codicem protuleris; nam qua invidia C. Iunius conflagravit, ea, nisi providisses, tibi ipsi 158 tum pereundum fuisset. Hoc modo iste sibi et saluti suae prospicere didicit referendo in tabulas et privatas et publicas 15 quod gestum non esset, tollendo quod esset, et semper aliquid demendo, mutando, interpolando; eo enim usque progreditur ut ne defensionem quidem maleficiorum suorum sine aliis maleficiis reperire possit. Eius modi subsortitionem homo amentissimus suorum quoque iudicum fore 20 putavit per sodalem suum Q. Curtium, iudicem quaestionis suae; cui ego nisi vi populi atque hominum clamore atque convicio restitissem, ex hac decuria vestra, cuius mihi copiam quam largissime factam oportebat, quos iste adnuerat in suum consilium sine causa subsortiebatur. 25

4 sit *pr Asc., Prisc.*: est *codd. pler.*   13 conflagravit *pq*: -arit *rδ*   17 mutando interpolando *pq*: *post* mutando *habent brδ* curando ne litura appareat, *quae verba reperiuntur in margine cod. p (manu prima scripta)*   19 possit *π*: posset *bδ*   subsortitionem *Asc.*: sortitionem *p rell.* (i, § 51)   22 suae *V*: om. *p rell.*: *v. Am. J. Ph.* xxvi. 416   ego nisi *V*: nisi ego *p rell.* (ii, § 64)   atque hominum *Vπ*: et hom. *b rell.* (*v. Iordanum ad loc.*)   23 vestra *Vπb*: nostra *Asc.* (*Div.* § 73)   copiam *codd.*: potestatem *Asc.*   24 largissime *codd.*: -am *Asc.*   factam *codd.*: fieri *Asc.*   oportebat quos *V*: oportebat erepta esset facultas eorum quos *p rell.*: *v. Am. J. Ph. l. c.*

157 was invented by me to suit the occasion. Now, will a man who attempted to bring home spoils and make profit from the ruin of a senator of the Roman people, at whose trial he was presiding as praetor, succeed in diverting from himself by his pleas any form of ruin you might care to mention?

LXI. Again, I am saying nothing about that supplementary selection of jurors conducted by Junius. How could I? Should I dare gainsay the records you produced? It is a difficult task, for not only your personal authority and that of the jurors but also the gold ring of your clerk deter me. I will not mention anything that is difficult to prove, but I will mention something that I will show many leading men heard from your lips, when you were asserting you ought to be pardoned for producing false records, since, if you had not taken precautions, you would yourself inevitably have been destroyed by the hatred that was engulfing Junius.
158 Verres has learned to look out for his interests and his safety by this device of recording in private and public records what has not been done, and erasing what has, and always removing, changing, or inserting something; indeed he is being carried so far in this direction that he cannot find any defence for his misdeeds without further misdeeds. The mindless fool thought there would be a similar supplementary selection of jurors in his own case through the cooperation of his fraternal associate, Q. Curtius, who presides over a criminal court of his own. If I had not resisted the latter, supported by a vigorous public response and by people's shouts and taunts, he would have arbitrarily taken from this panel of yours, to which I should have been given the freest possible acccess, the supplementary jurors for his tribunal that Verres had agreed he should select.

COMMENTARY

1-23: *A prefatory review of the importance of the case and the villainy of the accused joined to reassertions of Cicero's aims and resolve, and of the consequences for the senatorial order of an unjust acquittal.*

1. common talk: *sermo* frequently has the meaning of "gossip" in Cicero, and is commonly linked to *fama*. Cf. *Q.F.* 1.1.17. *Par. St.* 43. *Cael.* 38. *Mur.* 38. The phrase "belief of the Roman people" repeats the idea expressed in *sermonem vulgi* and represents one of the many forms of redundancy prominent in Cicero's style of oratory. Quintilian comments on this passage (9.4.119) and defends the repetition as a form of doubling of words or phrases (*geminatio*) to satisfy the needs of rhythm and please the ear. Cicero relates in *Brut.* 316 how Molo of Rhodes checked his tendencies towards redundancy as a young orator. He did not eliminate them.
second stage: there was a mandatory adjournment (*comperendinatio*) and second stage in extortion trials. Verres, of course, did not appear for the second stage, and Cicero never got the opportunity to deliver this or the other four speeches he had so painstakingly prepared. Cf. Intro. p. 10.
definite and deliberate decision: this translates Cicero's verbs *statuerat* and *deliberaverat*, virtual synonyms in this context. This type of grouping of words of similar meaning is another example of Cicero's copious style. Quintilian defended the practice on grounds that it made the sense stronger and clearer. He maintained that it should not be called pleonastic, since it was not purely superfluous, but a form of the figure of speech he called *adiectio*, the addition of seemingly superfluous words for reasons of elegance or cogency. Cf. 9.3.18, 28, 46ff. Examples abound throughout this speech.
brazen: *audax* and *audacia* were favourite terms in Cicero's vocabulary of personal and political abuse.

Audacia in its most general sense was a reckless and irresponsible daring receptive to any form of criminality. It was a product of *avaritia*, a greed for money that broke down restraint (*continentia*). Cf. *Rosc.* 75, 87-88. *Verr.* 2.1.87, 128. *Cael.* 13. In a narrower political sense it was a perversion of true ambition and fortitude (*magnitudo animi* and *fortitudo*), a reckless pursuit of power without regard for the common good. Cf. *Off.* 1.62-65. *Sest.* 139. Wirszubski, 12-22. Badian (1), 72-74.

prepared to hear: the striving for aural effect in this sentence is noteworthy. The word-play in *audendum* ... *audiendum* is combined with alliteration and chiasmus. Cf. *ora* ... *os* in 1.9, and *impudentiae* ... *pudentem* in 2.5. Cicero, as Quintilian noted (9.3.74), delighted in word-play (paronomasia), but, contrary to Quintilian's opinion, he did not always use it with restraint. Cf. below 53.9; 62.6.

he offers a defence: *defendere* sometimes occurs in the passive form with a middle sense, "to make one's defence", "defend oneself". Cf. *Quinct.* 66.

reap the reward: Cicero frankly acknowledges the benefits to a rising politician like himself from success in an *illustris accusatio* such as this. Cf. Intro. p.7.

Roman people: Cicero constantly harps on the theme throughout the Verrines that the Roman people are awaiting definite proof of the integrity of senatorial juries, and he presents the case of Verres as a golden opportunity for the jury of senators to vindicate their order and stave off the impending threat to the senate's monopoly of the courts. This was, of course, a line of argument of obvious benefit to Cicero's case, and need not be taken to represent the facts. Cf. *Verr.* 1.46-49; 2.1.21-23 and Intro. p.11.

No, rather: *immo vero*, a common phrase in Cicero to modify a preceding statement or idea or introduce a preferable suggestion. Cf. *Mil.* 64. *Planc.* 33.

very powerful men: it was conventional to attack the actions and motives of the opposing side in Roman trials. Cf. Cicero's line of defence in the *Pro Caelio*, and the attacks on himself by the prosecutor Torquatus, who was supposedly his friend, in the trial of P. Sulla. Cicero makes full use of the convention in the Verrines. He repeatedly tries to arouse ill-feeling (*invidia*) against

Verres' *patroni* by presenting them as exclusive, cliquish oligarchs of great *potentia*, a word that connoted dangerous unofficial power derived from such sources as high birth, wealth, and factional intrigue. In *Verr.* 1.35 he accuses Hortensius of wielding *intolerabilis potentia*, and uses even stronger language in *Verr.* 2.5.175, where he speaks of his despotic domination of the courts and of the state in general. He argues that it is the arrogance and power-hungry exclusiveness of such men which is the cause of the disrepute afflicting the senate and the courts. In contrast, he presents himself as a new man, who relies only on his talents and industry and is determinedly pitting them against the *potentia* of the partisan elite backing Verres in an effort to restore the popularity and authority of the senate (cf. esp. *Verr.* 1.35ff.; 2.5.180ff.). It was potent rhetoric, exploiting fertile political themes and designed to reach a broad audience in published versions of the speeches and to establish Cicero as an exemplar of old-fashioned *virtus*, standing forth, in the best traditions of the Republic, as the enemy of corruption and abuse of power.

diligence ... integrity ... steadfastness: a good example of the tricolon, the structural device that grouped words, phrases, or clauses in threes. It was considered a highly pleasing literary figure (cf. *Ad Her.* 4.26), and is common throughout Latin literature. Ideally each member of the triad should be longer than the preceding (*De Or.* 3.186), or the third one, as in the present instance, should be longer than the rest, embracing, as it were, the others (Demetrius, *Eloc.* 18). The thought should also rise in force, building to a climax (Quint. 9.4.23). These principles also applied to larger groupings of cola. Cf. Wilkinson, 178.

test of a legal battle: translates *contentionem certamenque*, another instance of *adiectio*, this time an alliterative one which recurs in *Verr.* 2.2.177.

4. without appearing: the argument is that Verres would have gained nothing by failing to appear, but would have deprived the senators of the opportunity to give firm proof of their integrity. Once a prosecution passed the stage of the *nominis delatio* (cf. Intro. p.2.), the absence of the accused could not prevent the proceedings going ahead, and, in fact, must have meant summary

conviction. Cf. Greenidge (1), 473.

<u>challenging of jurors</u>: cf. Intro p.4. Greenidge (1), 440. Jones (1), 68. The challenging was especially important in the case of senatorial juries because of their relatively small size.

5. <u>good conscience</u>: *religio* commonly signifies a scrupulous regard for obligations and for right, a strict adherence to conscience. It is often linked to *fides* in Cicero. Cf. *Verr.* 2.1.22. *Deiot.* 16. *Fam.* 11.29.1.

<u>part of the state:</u> Cicero presents himself as a healer, seeking to restore health to an important arm of the state, the judiciary, that had lost the confidence of the people. Cf. Intro. p.8.

<u>however the case was finally decided:</u> the reading of the manuscripts, *postremo ut*, does not give the required sense, nor does the emendation of Peterson, *perperam si*, meaning "if the case is decided wrongly". It is, besides, palaeographically difficult. Cicero states that he undertook the case hoping to remove, with credit to himself, the ill-will against the courts by achieving a conviction. He goes on to say he had a second motive, to end the dispute over juries. The sentences following show, however, that he was not maintaining, as Peterson's emendation would suggest, that this result would follow only from a wrongful verdict, but that it was inevitable whatever the judgement of the jury. The best sense therefore for the corrupt passage is "however the case was decided", a meaning obtained by the simple change, first suggested by Manutius, of *ut* to *utut*. Cf. Peterson, *CR* 17 (1903), 201.

6. <u>brought to a resolution:</u> the phrase *in discrimen adducere* recurs in Cicero with the sense "taking to the point of decision". Cf. *Phil.* 3.29. *Fam.* 5.21.3.

<u>money rules supreme:</u> *pecuniam plurimum posse*. Alliteration and the other common and closely related form of euphony, assonance, were features of Latin writing from earliest times. Although by Cicero's day the rhetoricians were warning against excessive use of either (cf. *Ad Her*. 4.18), the orator had a weakness for both. Cf. *Tusc*. 1.119. Quint. 9.4.41. Wilkinson, 25-31.

<u>we will stop</u>: note the broad parallelism in the structure of the conditional sentences, which is also evident in the sentence following. This form of balance is common in

Cicero, especially when he is presenting contrasting or opposing ideas, though he rarely strives for the exact symmetry associated with the Gorgianic figure of isocolon. Cf. *Orator* 38, 164-66. Laughton (1), 44-45. Gotoff, 49-54.

7. punishments of Roman citizens: the power of a governor over Roman citizens in his province was a somewhat vexed question in Cicero's day because, in a common pattern in Roman public life, the law had become overlain by convention. Our evidence indicates that the right of appeal (*provocatio*) had never been extended to the provinces and that governors therefore had, from a strict legal point of view, unlimited powers over Roman citizens living within their jurisdiction. But a convention had arisen that a governor should refer capital cases to Rome and should not inflict punishments to which citizens in the capital would not be liable. Cf. *Verr.* 5.140-44, 163-70. *Fam.* 10.32.3. Roman sentiment against inflicting degrading punishments, such as crucifixion, on citizens was especially strong. Cf. *Rab.* 16. Greenidge (1), 410-12.

8. ordinary penalty: the penalty in cases of extortion was the payment of damages, the assessment made by the jury that tried the case. Under the *Lex Acilia* of 123-22, double the amount of the assessment had to be paid, and it seems likely that this stipulation was retained by Sulla in his revision of the law in the *Lex Cornelia* of 81. Cicero claimed that Verres illegally extorted 400,000 sesterces from Sicily (*Verr.* 1.56) and called for an assessment of one million (*In Caec.* 19), probably a loose round figure. It is possible there was an additional criminal penalty for extortion, but the overall evidence, and especially the evidence of the Verrines, seems against it. Cf. Sherwin-White (1) and (2). Henderson, 41ff. Alexander (1), 527-29. The damages assessed, however, might cause bankruptcy, which brought *infamia*, involving a reduction in civil rights.

9. we have brought before your court: in the preceding sentences Cicero, using the grand manner, which sought by the solemnity and impassioned vigour of its language and sentiments and the smooth-flowing sweep of its sentence structure to sway the mind and stir the emotions (cf. *Orator* 97), attempts to convey the unique vileness

and the variety of Verres' crimes. This sentence is the climax of the indictment and is fittingly the most elaborate. It presents a series of contrasting pairs, in ascending phrases, with words of similar ending, building to a climax in the description of Verres as not a mere killer but a butcher of citizens. The sentence resembles a passage from the *Pro Milone* quoted by Cicero in *Orator* 165 as an example of his use of the Gorgianic figures of isocolon, antithesis, and homoeoteleuton to achieve an harmonious rhythmical sentence structure. Quintilian (8.3.2) cites the passage as an example of a particular form of amplification through use of strikingly descriptive terms that are made even more striking by following a strong word with a still stronger one.

<u>benefit</u>: Verres would suffer lighter penalties in the extortion court than in others before which he might be arraigned. It was, therefore, to his benefit to be convicted there rather than elsewhere. Cf. Ps. Asconius 226, Stangl.

<u>who does not know</u>: the rhetorical question (*interrogatio* or *percontatio*), liberally employed in the next several sentences, was a recognised figure in antiquity. It had many purposes: to increase the vigour of an argument, press home a fact with greater emphasis, arouse pity, embarrass an opponent, express astonishment or indignation. Cf. Quint. 9.2.6-10. *Ad Her.* 4.22. Other noteworthy examples occur in 47-48, 77-78, 87-88, 113.

10. <u>this is not the defendant</u>: the sentence contains an anacolouthon, a structural inconsistency that leaves the construction with which a sentence begins grammatically incomplete. In this sentence Cicero switches attention entirely to the last named subject, the prosecutor, with a relative clause that grammatically refers only to him, and in sense cannot be joined with *reus* or *tempus*. The meaning is clear and the emphasis on the prosecutor rhetorically effective. This kind of structural anomaly is relatively common in Greek and Latin, and is more acceptable in inflected than in non-inflected languages. Cf. 23, 139.

<u>here I fear</u>: there are many examples in the speech of this type of parenthesis which totally interrupts the thought but heightens anticipation, or scores a point arising from, but not directly relevant to, the subject in

hand. It was a recognised rhetorical figure known as *digressio*. Cf. *De Or*. 3.203. *Orator* 137. Quint.9.2.56.
have the gall: *sustinere* in the unfavourable sense of having the audacity to do something. Cf. Ovid, *Met*. 11.322. Val.Max. 9.4.3. Juvenal 15.88.

11. before another court: the embezzlement court (*quaestio de peculatu*). It was likely established in 103 B.C. in conjunction with the treason court (*quaestio de maiestate*) in a major drive by the radical faction led by Saturninus to limit the power of the oligarchy by judicial curbs. Cf. Gruen (1), 177, 263. Extortion trials often brought to light actions that rendered the accused liable to later prosecution in other courts on charges such as embezzlement, treason, or murder. Cf. *Cluent*. 114, 116. Sherwin-White (2), 43-55.
in his quaestorship: for Verres' quaestorship cf. Intro. p.5. and sections 34-40.
Cn. Carbo: served as Cinna's colleague in the consulship in 85 and 84. He became consul again in 82 but, after suffering several defeats at the hands of Sulla's forces, he fled first to Africa and then to Sicily, where he was captured and executed by Pompey.
grain tithe: under the system of taxation operating in Sicily one-tenth (*decuma*) of harvested crops was owed to the Roman state (*Verr*. 3.12-14, 18). A further one-tenth of the grain harvest was subject to compulsory purchase at a price of 3 sesterces per *modius*. An additional requisition of grain, up to 800,000 *modii*, could be made, for which a rate of $3\frac{1}{2}$ sesterces was paid (*Verr*. 2.3.163). A fixed amount of grain for the governor's needs also had to be supplied, though it was customary for governors to accept money instead (*Verr*. 2.3.188ff.,225). The collection of the *decuma* was farmed out to local agents, who were able to make reasonably accurate estimates of what the tithe would yield in a given year from careful records kept by local officials of the acreage of each crop planted by each farmer in their districts. Using this information and making allowance for profit, the contractors made their bids, undertaking to deliver a set amount of produce to the Roman authorities. The highest bidder got the contract. He then fixed the amount of the tithe with each farmer. In cases of dispute the determination of the amount could be deferred until

the harvest was gathered. In theory the system was fair and efficient, but could easily be abused by a dishonest governor. The possibilities for abuse were revealed by Verres, and are spelled out in great detail in *Verr.* 2.3. A governor could cheat the state, as the present passage accuses Verres of doing, by recording a figure for the tithe below that for which it had been sold (*Verr.* 2.3.49, 77,81-2), or by selling the tithe cheaply to increase the collector's profit (*Verr.* 2.3.148). He could also enable the tax-farmers to take more than they were owed by failing to provide any effective legal protection against unfair exactions (*Verr.* 2.3.25-35). The system of compulsory purchase could also be abused by simple refusal to pay the full amount for grain received under the scheme or indeed to pay anything at all (*Verr.* 2.3.165). The practice of paying cash instead of grain for the support of the governor's household (the *pecunia cellae nomine*, as it was known) left scope for unjust extortions of money. Provincials were at the mercy of rapacious governors, with no mode of redress other than the slow, uncertain process of seeking reparation in the extortion court after a governor's term expired.

M. Marcellus and P. Africanus: M. Claudius Marcellus captured Syracuse in 211 B.C. in one of the most important developments of the Second Punic War. He treated the wealthy and richly endowed city generously, leaving untouched many of its art treasures. P. Cornelius Scipio Africanus Aemilianus, after his capture of Carthage in 146, recovered many of the treasures taken from Sicily by the Carthaginians and restored them to the Sicilian communities. Cf. *Verr.* 2.4.73ff., 116-23, 130-31; 2.5.124ff.

12. Let him think: here begins a long series of jussive clauses piled up without connectives, an effective use of asyndeton to add intensity and make the series seem even longer. Cf. Quint. 9.3.50.

counteracting: *mederi* with the meaning "to remedy" or "to amend", governs both *crimini* and *confessioni*, but is strictly appropriate only to *confessioni*, a form of condensed expression or brachyology known as *zeugma*.

for as long as I allowed him: Cicero secured an order from the presiding praetor M'. Acilius Glabrio, removing the pirates from Verres' custody and committing them to prison (*Verr.* 2.5.76).

treason court: to harbour or release a *hostis* was an obvious act of treason. Cf. *Verr*. 2.5.76-79. Ps. Asconius 227, Stangl.
I will then embark: Cicero declares that, if he fails to get a conviction in any of the three *quaestiones* within whose jurisdiction fell the varied crimes of Verres, he will use his powers as aedile to prosecute Verres in a *iudicium populi*. Cf. *Verr*. 2.5.151. The charge would apparently be that Verres had summarily executed Roman citizens in violation of the *Lex Porcia* and the *Lex Sempronia*, which forbade the scourging or execution of citizens without allowing appeal to the people or trial by a *iudicium* established by the people. Cf. *Verr*. 2.5.163. In the *actio prima* (36) he made similar threats to prosecute before the people anyone attempting by any means to corrupt a jury. Cicero seems to be claiming for the aedileship the broad powers of criminal jurisdiction in relation to offences against the rights of citizens that tribunes had acquired, but which, to our knowledge, had never been exercised by aediles. Only one instance of an aedilician prosecution before the people is known to us in the entire history of the Republic, i.e. the prosecution of Milo *de vi* by Clodius in 56, and there is some doubt that this was a prosecution before the people. Cf. Gruen (2), 298, n.139. One may fairly assume Cicero was stretching the aediles' prerogatives and engaging in rhetorical bluster in his pledges to act as public prosecutor and use the people to punish abuses of the people's rights. Cf. Greenidge (1), 340ff. Lintott (1), 95ff. Jones (1), 15ff.

13. guarantors: *cognitor* in the technical sense of one who guarantees a person's identity. Cf. *Verr*. 2.5.168 and the use of *cognoscerent* below (14.6).
14. quarries: described in *Verr*. 2.5.68ff.
loftier platform: the Rostra, from which he would conduct the prosecution before the people. Cf. *Verr*. 2.5.151.
public show: cf. *Verr*. 1.36. One of the major tasks of aediles was the organisation, largely at their own expense, of the entertainment at the *Ludi*, the Games associated with major religious féstivals. There were six such Games in Cicero's day. In *Verr*. 2.5.36 Cicero says he would have responsibility for the *Ludi Cereales*, the *Ludi Florales*, and the *Ludi* in honour of the Capitoline Triad. Since the first two, and possibly all three, were

traditionally the responsibility of the plebeian aediles, it seems certain that it was the plebeian and not, as many scholars used to believe, the curule aedileship that Cicero held. Cf. Taylor (1), 194-202. Cicero's tenure of the office was uneventful. He later boasted (*Off.* 2.58) that he had refrained from extravagance in the entertainments he provided.

15. let anyone try anything: *conari* can have the meaning of venturing, attempting something daring or wrongful (cf. Livy 26.43.1. Quint. •5.13.30), and that seems clearly the force of it here. Cicero is restating the point that wrongdoing in this case will not achieve much and will not pass unpunished. The other translation sometimes proferred, "let everyone do his utmost", strains the Latin and does not fit the context well.

ancient practice: cf. *Cael.* 73, where Cicero speaks of the *vetus institutum* according to which young men sought to demonstrate their industry to the Roman people by an *illustris accusatio*. Cicero seems to be asserting the practice had fallen into disuse, though our evidence, which records more than twenty criminal trials in the seventies, would not especially suggest this. Cf. Gruen (2), 32ff.

friends and allies: Cicero's favourite way of describing provincial communities. Cf. sections 45, 54, 56, 59, 76, 78. By the first century B.C. the words had become a euphemistic formula with which to describe Rome's subjects. It implied no special relationship or formal commitments. For recent discussions of the history and significance of the terms in Roman diplomacy cf. Gruen (4), I. 54-95. Sherwin-White (3), 58-70.

quaestor: Quintus Caecilius Niger, who had served as Verres' quaestor in 72 and had sought leave to bring the prosecution or, as this passage indicates, at least to act as a subordinate prosecutor (*subscriptor*). Cicero, using the licence accorded the orator's craft to draw opposite conclusions, as the occasion demanded, from the same facts (cf. Asconius 70, Clark: *oratoriae calliditatis ius*), here presents Caecilius as having a just grievance, something he had denied in *In Caec.* 58ff. There is no question of *inimicitias iustas* being ironic.

16. restraint: *pudor* was the quality underlying *modestia*. It gave rise to a sense of decency and propriety that

shrank from any form of unbecoming behaviour. Cf. *Inv.* 2. 164. *Fin.* 2.113. *Sulla* 15. *Fam.* 11.27.4.
as much authority: Cicero is saying he could have uncovered a wider range of crimes than those he was specifically authorised to investigate in connection with the charge of extortion.

17. When I returned: here begins a highly complex sentence, containing thirteen clauses smoothly interwoven into an integral whole by a system of hypotaxis or subordination that leads the reader towards the main statement at the end through a series of ancillary statements that qualify or elucidate it. The sentence has many features of the classic period. Cf. *Orator* 221ff. Quint. 9.4.121ff. Gotoff, 66ff. Wilkinson, 167ff.
respectability and refinement: heavily ironic, their conduct conflicting with their pretensions to urbane gentility.
right up to the time: translates *usque eo ... donec*. Note the wide separation of these closely related words, an example of the figure of *hyperbaton*. The device is a feature of Cicero's style, sometimes used to give a smoother, more elegant word order (cf. *Quint.* 8.6.62), sometimes to give emphasis to the words placed between the related elements. A further use is illustrated in the present instance, where the *hyperbaton* serves to signal the temporal clause that concludes the sentence and, characteristic of the period, keeps the sense incomplete until the very end. Cf. 56.9; 149.3.

18. present constitution: refers to the constitutional settlement of Sulla, passed into law in 81-80. One of its reforms was the restoration of control of the courts to the senate.
M. Lucretius: otherwise unkown. P. Sulpicius Galba went on to hold the praetorship in the mid-sixties, and became one of Cicero's competitors for the consulship of 63. He was regarded as an honest man, but he lacked popularity and eventually withdrew from the race. Cf. Asconius 82, Clark. *Att.* 1.1.1. *Mur.* 17.
Sex. Peducaeus: served as governor of Sicily in 76-75. Cicero served under him as quaestor in 75, and thought highly of him. Cf. *Verr.* 2.2.138; 2.3.216; 2.4.142. *Att.* 10.1.1. Nothing is known of the other two senators mentioned, Q. Considius and Q. Junius.

19. **too independent and opinionated:** translates *nimium sui iuris sententiaeque*. The force of the genitive is possessive. They were men who belonged to, were attached or subject to their own authority and opinions.
In any event: *itaque* carries this meaning when used to resume the main narrative after some insertion or digression. Cf. *Am.* 3. Livy 2.12.3.
at my election: Cicero tells us in *Pis.* 2 that he was the first of the candidates for the College of Aediles for which he was standing to win a majority of the tribes and be declared elected. For Verres' efforts to prevent his election cf. *Verr.* 1.23-24.
which had had no influence: an effective antithesis accentuated by the parallel structure of the clauses. Cf. 31.7; 55.9; 72.5.

20. **diligence:** refers to his care in challenging the jurors and securing a tribunal of such high *dignitas*.
wealthy and wanton: the triple alliteration and asyndeton gives a sense of the vigour and intensity of Cicero's onslaught on Verres in the first hour of his first speech against him.
festival: the Games in celebration of Pompey's victory over Sertorius, which began on August 15. Cf. Intro. p.9.

21. **good opinion:** *existimatio populi Romani* is often translated "good name of the Roman people" (cf. Taylor (2), 115; Greenwood, 141; Yavetz, 253). *Existimatio*, a very common term in writings from the late Republic, did generally mean "reputation" or "public image" or "good name", and was often linked to *fama*, which carried similar meanings. (For a recent, detailed discussion cf. Yavetz, 214-27). But *existimatio* could also mean "good opinion", the way one regarded someone else rather than the way in which one was oneself regarded (cf. below 87.11; 93.7; also *Verr.* 1.20; 2.3.146. *Planc.* 6). This seems clearly the meaning of *existimatio* in this passage. Cicero's point is that he has done everything that could possibly be expected of him in the case, and has, as a result, achieved what was most important to him, the acclaim of the public. He goes on to say the jurors should take thought for their standing with the public, and should now do what is expected of them, namely convict Verres.

The word *spolia* in this passage is sometimes

170

taken to refer to specific rewards Cicero stood to gain if Verres was convicted. The evidence for such rewards in Roman criminal law comes mainly from Cicero (cf. *Balb.* 57. *Sulla* 50. *Rosc.Am.* 8,83. *Verr.* 2.5.173), and was first assembled by Mommsen (*Strafrecht*, 504-11), who put forward the view that there existed a single system of rewards that offered successful prosecutors a higher civic status and specifically entitled them, in cases where loss of civil rights was involved, to the status of the accused. L.R. Taylor (*Party Politics*, 112-16), accepting and developing this view, argued that Cicero, as a result of Verres' conviction, acquired the latter's place among the praetorians in the senate. Mommsen's theory has been recently challenged by M. Alexander [*CP* 80 (1985), 20-32], who rejects the idea of a uniform system of rewards and argues that different incentives were offered to prosecutors by different criminal statutes, depending on the gravity of the crime and the perceived need to encourage prosecutions. Alexander makes a strong case and, since there survives no explicit statement of the rewards offered Roman prosecutors in extortion cases, and since, moreover, it is far from certain that any loss of civil rights was necessarily involved in such cases (cf. note on 8.3), there are no adequate grounds for asserting that Cicero joined the ranks of the praetorians in the senate in 70. The absence of any reference to such a change in status or to any use of it in senatorial debates in the early sixties, and a generally contemptuous attitude by Cicero towards advancement by such means (cf. *Rosc.Am.* 83. *Balb.* 57) further lessen the likelihood that he acquired such 'spoils'. *Spolia* is best taken in this passage as a mere continuation of the metaphor introduced by *vici*.

<u>My duty demanded</u>: Cicero once more makes elaborate use of the rhetorical question, this time to provide an emphatic concluding statement of a central theme of the first section of the speech, his concerns and actions as prosecutor. Characteristically, the questions form a triad, and increase in length and rhetorical intensity.

22. <u>provident consideration</u>: translates *prospicite atque consulite*, a common combination. Cf. *Verr.* 2.1.153. *Cat.* 2.26; 4.3. *Fam.* 3.2.1.

<u>burden</u>: while the conservative *nobilitas* considered that

control of the criminal courts was an important bulwark of senatorial supremacy, there were obviously many senators who found jury service a burden, and who very likely welcomed the compromise offered by the *Lex Aurelia*. Cf. Intro. p.4.

how much danger: this was the most serious issue at stake in the jury question for the ruling class, the likelihood that, if the *equites*, comprised largely of *publicani*, gained control of the criminal courts, they would use them to intimidate political leaders and to further personal interests. The conviction of Rutilius Rufus in 92 had shown how real and serious this danger was. Cf. Intro. p.3.

will have declared they wish: translates *voluerit*, a verb that often represents an authoritative statement of a wish that is almost equivalent to a command.

23. **certain people:** refers, no doubt, to the succession of anti-senatorial tribunes and their supporters who led the continuing agitation in the latter half of the seventies for the restoration of tribunician powers and reform of the courts. There is no reason to believe that Cicero has Pompey in mind. Cf. Mitchell (1), 113ff.

rather many words: Cicero has, in fact, taken twenty-three sections, roughly one-seventh of the speech, to restate, in an extended *exordium*, themes he had concentrated on in the *actio prima*. His purpose, as in all *exordia*, was to win the sympathetic attention and goodwill of the jurors (cf. *De Or.* 2.318-25. *Ad Her.* 1.7. Quint. 4.1.1-71), and, in line with the precepts of the rhetoricians, he drew his main themes from the persons involved in the case and from the case itself. Cf. Quint. 4.1.6. His own honourable purposes and conscientious efforts in face of dishonourable attempts to obstruct him by powerful men are emphasized, as are Verres' unparalleled wickedness and brazen contempt for the laws and institutions of Rome. He makes several direct appeals to the jurors themselves to stand with him, combining two approaches emphasized by Quintilian (4.1.16, 20; 6.1.13), praise or flattery and the inducement of fear by clear warnings of the dire consequences of a wrong decision. With regard to the case itself, the most notorious forms of wrongdoing involved in it are highlighted, as are relevant external considerations such as public sentiment and,

above all, the standing of the senate and its control over juries. Cf. Quint. 4.1.23, 30-31. This last topic, which Cicero obviously considered his most effective means of pre-disposing the jury to convict, keeps recurring, as Cicero makes good use of the techniques of *repetitio* and *commoratio*, which were designed firmly to implant one overriding consideration in the listener's mind by lingering over it and repeatedly returning to it. Cf. *Ad Her.* 4.58. *De Or.* 3.202. Quint. 9.2.4.
which ... led: the sentence provides another example of anacolouthon, arising in this instance, as often, from a change in subject. The relative *quae* is left dangling, as the subject is changed to *nonnulli*. There is no obscurity and the change of subject creates a greater directness and forcefulness.

24-31: *Digression to defend the omission of a detailed indictment at the first hearing.*

24. Now, so that: Cicero now prepares to begin the detailed, continuous exposition of Verres' crimes (*oratio* or *accusatio perpetua*) that he had deliberately omitted in the *actio prima* (cf. Intro. p.10), but first he digresses to defend that earlier omission and rebut Hortensius' charge that it was a violation of due process. He presents Hortensius' complaint as an unheard of and perverse line of reasoning that assumes a defendant is helped by having his crimes paraded, and hurt by having them left unmentioned. He goes on to argue that his avoidance of an *oratio perpetua* was his right, and, in any event, no more advantageous to the prosecution than to the defence. It is a protracted and somewhat laboured argument, and shows a tendency of Cicero to stretch a good point too far and overindulge in subtleties of argumentation. The first sentence with its repetitious uses of oxymoron, seeking to highlight from several angles the ridiculous quality of Hortensius' criticism, sets the tone of this rather tedious section.
did not speak: cf. Plutarch, *Cic.* 7.4, where he says Cicero secured the conviction of Verres not by speaking, but, in a way, by not speaking.

25. **not because**: *non quo*, followed by the subjunctive, commonly introduces clauses that state a rejected reason.
legally allotted hours: by 59 B.C. the legal limit for the speech of the prosecutor in an extortion trial was six hours (*Flacc.* 82). This almost certainly did not include the time taken to read documents and written evidence. The time allowed at the second hearing may have been different, though there is no reason to suppose it was. The limit that applied in 70 is unknown, but may well have been the same as in 59. Even the extraordinary long and detailed indictment contained in the speeches of the *actio secunda* would not have taken more than eight hours to deliver. Cicero saved more than six hours, however, by dispensing with the *accusatio perpetua* at the first hearing, since his action also precluded a detailed rebuttal by Hortensius.
have the right: *posse* occurs commonly with the meaning "to be able legally", "to have the legal right". Cf. *Prov.Cons.* 45. *Sest.* 73. *Att.* 9.9.3.
should be heard: *cognoscere* is used here in the special sense of examining judicially, giving a case a hearing. Cf. below (27) *se ipsum cogniturum*, also *Verr.* 2.2.20. *Flacc.* 47.
to make the conviction ... impossible: Greenwood translates "to make his conviction more difficult", but *quo minus ... posset* conveys the meaning of preventing or removing the possibility of something being done.
while many: Cicero's fondness for antithesis sometimes leads him to stretch logic in pursuit of neat verbal contrasts. The first element of the antithesis, that hearing a case allows the possibility of acquittals, has no great relevance to his main point that no one can be condemned without a hearing.

26. **adjournment**: Hortensius argued that, by failing to give the charges a full airing in the *actio prima*, Cicero was defeating the purpose underlying the practice of *comperendinatio* or *comperendinatus*, which was to have the arguments and evidence heard twice. Cicero responds that a double hearing benefits the prosecution as much, and probably more, than the defence, since it allows the prosecutor, who has to speak first, the opportunity to rebut at the second hearing the arguments of the defence. Ps. Asconius 230, Stangl totally misrepresents

the sense of this passage, as do some modern commentators. Cf. Carcopino, 205-34.

Glaucia: C. Servilius Glaucia, the turbulent demagogic ally of Saturninus in the final years of the second century B.C., passed a bill, the *Lex Servilia repetundarum*, restoring control of the extortion court to the *equites* and, as Cicero indicates here, making *comperendinatio* compulsory. (Cf. Asconius 21, Clark. *Brut.* 224). The date of the bill remains a matter of lively controversy. No precise answer is possible, but the evidence points to a date between 105 and 100. Cf. Gruen (1), 166-67. Balsdon (1), 107.

further hearing: *amplius* was a legal formula indicating judgement was being deferred pending a further hearing. It was used when a jury returned the verdict *non liquet*, "the case is not proven". The process is sometimes represented by the verb *ampliare* or the noun *ampliatio*. It would appear the *Lex Acilia repetundarum* of 123-22 restricted the number of such postponements to two. Cf. Greenidge (1), 499. The precise meaning of this section and its implications for the history of the extortion court have been widely discussed. Cf. Balsdon (1), 108-13. Carcopino, 205-35. Greenidge (1), 498-502. Mattingly (1), 481-86. The sense seems to be as follows: Glaucia introduced a compulsory adjournment. Previously, i.e. under the *Lex Acilia*, a verdict could be given at the first hearing or judgement could be deferred. That was a less harsh procedure, since it meant an innocent defendant could get a fast acquittal, and a guilty one could prolong the process of conviction. But Cicero would be happy to accuse Verres under the milder law, since many far less guilty than he had been convicted under it on the first hearing, and Verres certainly would be, because the jury, once they heard Cicero's presentation of the case, would be ashamed to resort to *ampliatio* and would convict immediately.

Restituo does not, as Balsdon thinks, mean Cicero is claiming by his conduct of the case to be restoring, in effect, the milder procedure of the *Lex Acilia*. That would be a patently ridiculous claim, since Cicero's handling of the prosecution extended none of the supposed benefits of the *Lex Acilia* to Verres. *Restituo* goes closely with *puta*, part of an imaginary scenario indicating what Cicero would be willing to concede, and making the point that, even under a less rigid procedure that allowed *ampliatio*, Cicero would be able to persuade the jury to convict at the earliest possible opportunity.

The main historical significance of the passage is that it appears to show beyond reasonable doubt that Glaucia's law abolished *ampliatio* as it had functioned under the *Lex Acilia*. Cicero indicates that *comperendinatio* introduced a tougher procedure, tougher in that it insisted on a most thorough airing of the facts through two full hearings of the evidence and of the pleas of the advocates, and tougher especially in that it precluded long delays in conviction. Since such delays were brought about by *ampliatio*, which could force two postponements of indefinite duration, their elimination must have involved the elimination of their source. Further, the whole point of Cicero's imagined prosecution of Verres under the *Lex Acilia* was that he was willing to revert to a milder procedure that allowed *ampliatio*, something obviously precluded by the law actually governing the case. The conclusion indicated, therefore, is that *comperendinatio* was introduced as a substitute for *ampliatio*, providing for one postponement of fixed duration in place of two of indefinite duration, and making the adjournment compulsory to insure that jurors had ample opportunity to assess the evidence and make a decision.

27. keep quiet: Cicero is himself engaging in *dissimulatio*. For a very different view of the advocate's importance in moving a jury cf. *De Or*. 2.178-216.

    Sacerdos: C. Licinius Sacerdos was urban praetor in 75 and governed Sicily in 74. He was therefore Verres' immediate predecessor in the island. He gave evidence against Verres at the trial. Cf. *Verr*. 2.2.119.

    despatched letters: a characteristic use of asyndeton in the triad of main clauses to achieve the vigour and rapidity especially suited to narration. Cf. 91.6ff.; 138.

28. when Dio: the sentence provides a notable example of anaphora, the form of *repetitio* that used the same word to begin a succession of clauses. It was thought to add grace, majesty, and vigour, and was recommended as a means of ornamentation and amplification. Cf. *Ad Her*. 4.19. Quint. 9.3.45.

30. you put forward: cf. Intro. p.9 for the obstructive tactics of Verres and his supporters and for the timetable of the trial.
M'.Glabrio: son of the author of the *Lex Acilia*, he went on to hold the consulship in 67. From the allusions to him in the Verrines, he was not particularly well-disposed towards Verres.
31. If I had not seen: an elaborate sentence with its extensive use of anaphora, its jingling *i* sounds (most striking in the homoeoteleuton of the triad of passive infinitives) and its balanced antithesis at the end. Its point, ironically expressed, as often, by ironic use of *credo* to indicate incredulity, is that it was hardly any fear of insufficient ability or material that caused Cicero to forego his speech for the prosecution but the realisation, obvious to all, that every effort was being made by the opposition to delay the proceedings.
proviso: *cautio* meant the taking of precautions, and in its legal sense represented an exception or special condition limiting the terms of a law or contract. Cicero is referring here to the bribery-agents (*divisores*), whom he alleges Verres hired to bribe the jury. Cf. *Verr.* 1.5-8,23.

32-34: *The four divisions (*partitiones*) of the* accusatio.

32. I will therefore: Cicero comes at last to the *accusatio perpetua*, the detailed, continuous exposition of Verres' crimes from the beginning of his public life through his governorship of Sicily. The present speech traces the catalogue of misdeeds to the end of Verres' praetorship in 74. It is a noteworthy aspect of Roman criminal procedure that a prosecutor was entitled to lay before the court all violations of the law in question that the defendant could be alleged to have committed at any period in his life (excepting any on which he had been tried previously), and that the jury could convict if they believed any one of the allegations. Crimes unrelated to the law under which the case was being tried could also be introduced, but these served only to impugn the character and credibility of the accused, and could not form a basis for conviction. Cf. Alexander (3), 164-66. Quint. 7.1.12.

177

pass over: this and the following sentences provide examples of the somewhat artificial rhetorical device of *paralipsis* or *antiphrasis* or *occultatio*, which stated a resolve to avoid mentioning something while doing precisely that. It was considered useful as a mode of innuendo when lengthier discussion might prove embarrassing, or the matters alluded to were unfounded or unclear. Cf. *Ad Her.* 4.37. Quint. 9.2.47; 9.3.98-99. Cicero uses the figure frequently, despite its transparently contrived character. Cf. 49, 86, 95.
brought forth: it is uncertain whether *produxit* means "brought into court" or "brought into the world". Children were commonly brought into Roman courts in an attempt to arouse sympathy (cf. *Verr.* 2.1.151. Quint. 6.1.30; 11.3.174), but since Cicero was accused by Hortensius of using this ploy against Verres and made no counter-accusation (cf. 151 below) and since in a later derogatory comment about the boy (*Verr.* 2.3.159-63) he gives no indication he was actually present, it seems unlikely that Verres brought his son to court, or that Cicero wanted to pretend he had.

33. nocturnal revels: such charges were commonplace in Roman invective in allusions to an opponent's early life. Cf. *Cael.* 6,25,29,35.
will permit: the MSS read *patiatur*, but the future indicative *patietur*, conjectured by Schuetz, gives a far stronger and more positive ending to the sentence.

34. robbery ... wickedness: this piling up of words of related or similar meaning Quintilian (8.4.26) called *congeries*, and saw as one of the main modes of enhancing or augmenting the force of language.

34-40: *Verres' quaestorship.*

34. as quaestor: quaestors on election drew lots to determine their sphere of duty. Two were allotted to oversee the treasury at Rome, the others assigned to consuls and praetors who held military commands, or to promagistrates. Their duties were primarily financial. The quaestor took charge of the funds allocated to his superior; he made the necessary disbursements and had the responsibility of filing accounts at the end of his term

in his own name and that of his commander. In the provinces he might be assigned military or judicial duties by the governor, and generally became acting-governor with the title *quaestor pro praetore* in cases where a governor left his province before his successor arrived. If he died while serving in a province his duties were normally transferred to one of the *legati*, who then held the title *legatus pro quaestore*. Cf. Stevenson, 86. Greenidge (2), 212ff.

civil dispute: the conflict between Sulla and Cinna, which was threatening to erupt into civil war in 84 with Sulla's impending return from the East.

self-indulgence: *luxuria* is a common term in Cicero, representing the vice that he and many of his contemporaries saw as a primary cause of the moral degeneration underlying the evils of the late Republic. It signified an immoderate attachment to physical pleasure and material splendour, the antithesis of the austere dedication to duty and achievement characteristic of the old morality. Cf. Mitchell (2), 27ff.

not to detain: this sentence, with its directness, plainness, and economy of language, and staccato style of sentence structure is typical of Ciceronian writing in narrative and explanatory passages, and a strong contrast to the fulsome, liberally embellished, and intricately structured style he employs in more emotional contexts. He discusses this plainer mode of oratory in detail in *Orator* 78-90. Cf. *Ad Her.* 4.14. Other good examples of this plain narrative style occur in 46, 66, 125, 138.

35. hard to fathom: a good illustration of Cicero's use of irony, which he termed *dissimulatio* and described as a most effective means of penetrating people's minds. Cf. *De Or.* 3.203. Quint. 8.6.54; 9.2.44. Verres was a *novus homo* or new man in the sense that his family had only recently become involved in politics and had achieved no great distinction. For a recent discussion of *nobilitas* and *novitas* cf. Brunt (1), 1-17.

36. Ariminum: modern Rimini, taken over by Cinna in 87, betrayed to Sulla in 82 by P. Albinovanus, an officer serving under the proconsul C. Norbanus. Cf. Appian, *BC* 1.67,91. Ps. Asconius 234, Stangl.

37. **rank and prestige:** Cicero consistently portrays Sulla's side as the side of the *nobilitas*, aiming to restore the standing and authority of those of greatest *dignitas*, the word he used to denote the esteem and standing derived from one's own and one's family's merits and achievements. Cinna he considered had destroyed a sacred principle of republicanism by oppressing the most distinguished citizens, and establishing a rule of the *indigni* in which *humilitas* (low status) prevailed over *dignitas*. Cf. Mitchell (1), 82-83,199.

But if: Cicero's crowning denunciation of Verres' behaviour as quaestor is replete with rhetorical artifice. He begins by using the figure of *anteoccupatio* or *praesumptio*, the anticipation of an opponent's argument, in this case forestalling an obvious rejoinder from Hortensius that Carbo was unworthy of Verres' loyalty. Cf. *De Or*. 3.205. Quint. 9.2.16-17. He follows this with the figure of *comparatio*, using the analogous situation of Piso and his response to it to show what Verres should have done. Cf. Quint. 8.4.13-14. He then employs one of his favourite modes of ornamentation, which he called *thesis*, and which consisted in divorcing an issue from a particular person and particular circumstances and discussing its universal implications. Cf. *Orator* 46, 125-26. *De Or*. 3.120ff. Betrayal, whatever the reason, is revealed as invariably evil and the act of an evil man, threatening all civilised life and the basis of human relationships. He returns from these general implications of treachery to the specific vileness of the instance of it exemplified by Verres, adding force to the indictment by means of the rhetorical question and another favourite device, *apostrophe*, as he turns away from the jury to address Verres directly. Cf. Quint. 9.2.38ff. He concludes with another common figure, the *exclamatio* (cf. *Orator* 135. Quint. 9.2.26; 9.3.97), followed by a triad of clauses repeating the same point from different angles, an example of *expolitio*, the refining of a general sentiment by presenting it in different guises. It was a favourite preliminary exercise or *progymnasma* in the rhetorical schools. Cf. *Ad Her*. 4.54. The style is perhaps more forced and artificial than that of his later speeches, but its skill and power are undeniable.

disloyal: *malus, improbus, seditiosus, audax, perditus, perniciosus* were the most common terms in a rich vocabulary of derogatory catchwords used by the defenders of traditional republicanism, the self-styled *boni* or *optimates*, to describe the varied class of politicians of the late Republic who promoted popular social or political change against the wishes of the senate. For Cicero's opinion of these so-called *populares* cf. Mitchell (1) 196ff. Seager, 328-38.
Piso: M. Pupius Piso, quaestor in 83, a close friend of Cicero in the eighties (*Brut.* 236,310), who, though married to the widow of Cinna, deserted to Sulla. He served as a *legatus* of Pompey in the sixties and became consul in 61.
Scipio: L. Cornelius Scipio Asiaticus, consul in 83 with the *novus homo* C. Norbanus. His army defected to Sulla. The latter released him unharmed, but he was later proscribed and went into exile at Massilia.

38. the lot: Cicero here and elsewhere in the Verrines (cf. *In Caec.* 46. *Verr.* 1.11) attributes a sacred character to the lot, implying the result of the drawing of lots represented the will of the gods. Cf. *In Caec.* 65. In *Phil.* 3.24-26 he makes references to *religiosa sortitio* and *sors divina* which imply a Roman belief that the gods had a hand in the workings of chance.
general welfare: *summa res* or *summa res publica* are common phrases meaning "the general good" or "the welfare of the state", *summa* carrying the sense of "general", "collective".
honour: the chiasmus, which arranges the contrasting pairs in reverse order, heightens the antithesis by varying the emphasis in the two clauses, and iuxtaposing the words denoting the primary contrast.

39. title that implies: e.g. the title of quaestor.
one can: *possis* is an example of the use of the subjunctive in generalising statements where the subject is the indefinite second person. Cf. Woodcock, 90.

40. as a son: Cicero frequently alludes to a quasi-filial relationship, generally referred to as *necessitudo*, that Roman tradition prescribed should exist between a quastor and his commander. It was, of course, in his interest to make the most of any such tradition in his efforts to magnify Verres' treachery towards Carbo and Dolabella,

but the frequency of his allusions to the idea throughout his writings leaves little doubt that it was firmly established in the *mos maiorum*. Cf. *In Caec.* 61, 65. *Planc.* 28. *Red.in sen.* 25. *De Or.* 2.200. *Fam.* 13.10.1. Pliny, *Ep.* 4.15.9; 10.26. Thompson, 339-55.

<u>41-61</u>: *Verres' thefts of paintings and statues as a legate of Dolabella.*

41. <u>Dolabella</u>: Cn. Cornelius Dolabella was praetor in 81 and proconsul in Cilicia in 80-79. He was prosecuted for extortion on his return to Rome in 78 by M. Aemilius Scaurus. He was convicted and went into exile. For a detailed discussion of the man and his trial cf. Gruen (3), 389-99.
<u>Malleolus</u>: nothing is known of him beyond what Cicero tells us in this speech.
<u>while it is true:</u> *cum* ... *tum* indicating that while something is indeed the case, something else of equal or greater significance is also the case. Cf. below 150. *Dom.* 32. *Cluent.* 197.
<u>vile betrayal:</u> to injure an *amicus*, especially a benefactor, was a serious breach of *fides*, perhaps justified if the interests of the state were at stake (cf. *Phil.* 5.6. *Am.* 37), but otherwise deplorable. In *Phil.* 2.3 Cicero calls the violation of *amicitia* a *gravissimum crimen*. Cf. Brunt (2), 12ff.

43. <u>legate:</u> in addition to the quaestor, a governor had on his staff a number of *legati*. Propraetors normally had one, proconsuls three. These officials were originally senatorial commissioners, representatives of the government at Rome, but the practice developed of allowing governors to nominate them, though their appointment was always ratified by the senate. They had no specific duties, but the governor could delegate any of his own responsibilities to them. Cf. Stevenson, 86-87. Greenidge (2), 323-24.

44. <u>After ... Cilicia was assigned:</u> the clause has been taken to mean "after the province of Cilicia was created for Dolabella", and has been used as evidence that Cilicia was first constituted as a territorial province in 80, with Dolabella as its first governor (Sherwin-White, *JRS* 1976,

10). Why Cicero should say the province was created for Dolabella is, however, unclear, and it is far easier to take *constituere* in its common meaning of "assign" or "allot". Besides, the extant evidence, recently expanded by discovery of a new inscription, now seems strongly to favour the view that Cilicia had been established as a territorial province by the end of the second century. Cf. Hassall, Crawford, and Reynolds, *JRS* 1974, 195-220. Harris, 153. The new province did not, however, initially comprise Cilicia proper, but areas farther west, principally Pamphylia and southern Pisidia. Cf. Magie, II.1165.

with what: the sudden switch from direct statement to exclamation is a familiar narrative technique in Cicero. The delivery in such instances was carefully modulated to enhance the emotional impact of *exclamatio* and accentuate the astonishment it conveyed at the facts being narrated. Cf. *Ad Her.* 3.24.

demanded money: besides the extortions of resident governors, the provinces suffered greatly from burdens imposed by Roman officials travelling through them. Free lodgings and entertainment had to be provided under the law, but these were often only a minor part of the cost of official visitors. The *Lex Julia* of 59 attempted to curtail abuses, but by no means freed the provincials from this menace. In addition to the evidence of this speech, cf. *Leg.Agr.* 1.8; 3.45. *Att.* 5.10.2; 5.16.3; 5.21.5, 7. Arnold, 74-75. Shatzman (1), 53ff. Broughton (2), 574.

47. I have no doubt: the style changes markedly from the elegant plainness and directness of the preceding narrative, as Cicero reverts to the more vigorous, opulent mode to drive home the shocking implications of the facts so crisply recounted. He resorts again to apostrophe and liberal use of the rhetorical question. Tricola and the periodic sentence structure reappear. Mythology and history are enlisted to accentuate the enormity of Verres' wrongdoing. There is a tone of indignation (*iracundia*) and reprimand (*obiurgatio*), a common aspect of the rhetorical decoration of such passages. Cf. *De Or.* 3.205. *Orator* 138. Quint 9.2.3, 26.

before your mind: the phrase *in mentem venire* used impersonally with the genitive of the thing remembered, is

common in Cicero. Cf. *Verr.* 2.4.110. *Fin.* 5.2. *Fam.* 7.3.1.
arts and studies: the *artes liberales* or *artes ingenuae* that Cicero continually emphasised as an indispensable training for the orator and statesman. Cf. *Inv.* 1.35. *De Or.* 1.20, 72-74, 158; 2.72; 3.54, 127, 140. *Arch.* 2, 12-16. *Brut.* 322.

48. Latona: the Roman name for Leto, daughter of the Titans Phoebe and Coeus. She conceived by Zeus and incurred the wrath of Hera. The sufferings brought on her by Hera and the birth on Delos are told, in somewhat differing versions, in the Homeric hymn to Delian Apollo and the fourth hymn of Callimachus.

49. Asia: the province of Asia came into being as a consequence of the bequeathal to Rome of the kingdom of Pergamum by its king Attalus III, who died suddenly in 134 at the age of 36. Rome's plans for the area were complicated by a revolt, which was organized soon after publication of the will by a pretender named Aristonicus, and which won support from many of the major cities. The revolt was finally crushed in 129 by the consul M'. Aquillius, who then, with the help of senatorial commissioners, organized the new province. The more remote and less valuable areas to the east and southeast, i.e. the east of Phrygia and all of Lycaonia, were given to Pontus and Cappadocia. The western, more accessible districts, stretching from the Hellespont to the Gulf of Cos, and including Mysia and the Troad, Lydia, the southwest of Phrygia, and Caria, were incorporated in the province, though within this area many cities were left free, enjoying full self-government and independence of the Roman governor, and possibly exemption from paying tribute to Rome. Cf. Magie, I.154ff. Jones (2), 58ff. Sherwin-White (3), 80ff.
I see no reason: this type of paralipsis, cast in the form of a question, is a standard Ciceronian device. Cf. Quint. 9.2.47.
Comitium: the open area in front of the senate-house, northeast of the forum proper. It measured about three hundred feet across and was the principal meeting place of the tribal legislative assemblies and of informal public gatherings (*contiones*) until the middle of the second century B.C., when increasing numbers necessitated use

of the forum. The Rostra stood between the *comitium* and the forum, until the new Rostra was built by Julius Caesar in the forties at the west end of the forum. Cf. Taylor (3), 21ff. It was customary for aediles to decorate the *comitium* and the forum for major festive occasions, and they often had to resort to borrowing works of art from friends and from provincial and allied communities to secure the necessary adornments. Cf. below 58-59. *Verr.* 2.3.9; 2.4.6, 126. *Dom.* 111.

50. Samian Juno: called by Herodotus (3.60) the largest of all the Greek temples he had seen.
 seal evidence: cf. below 60-61, 98, 149. *Verr.* 2.2.182, 186ff.; 2.4.140, 149. The prosecutor also had authority from the court's president to compel the presence of witnesses. Cf. *Verr.* 2.2.64-65.

51. have allotted: the reading of the MSS, *subsortitus es*, has been rejected by many editors, but can stand as a vivid statement of Cicero's recurrent allegation that Verres had a set of jurors of his own ready to take over if the case extended into the following year.
 use our witnesses: a reference to Cicero's decision to forego the usual *accusatio perpetua* and proceed, after a relatively brief introductory statement, to the questioning of witnesses.

52. quaestor and public bidder: the urban quaestors had the responsibility of collecting the payments imposed on those convicted in the extortion and embezzlement courts. Cf. Livy 38.58.1; 38.60.8. Greenidge (2), 214. *Sectores* were speculators who bought at public auction property seized by the state. Cicero is saying that Verres' action in hiding the statues was proof he had accepted defeat and was now concentrating on keeping his loot from being seized.

53. I am not going to say: an effective form of *comparatio*, rising from a lesser variety of wrongdoing to a greater. Cf. below 54.4, and Quint. 8.4.9.
 music inside: the phrase *intus canere* came to mean singing for oneself, or acting in one's own interest. Cf. *Leg.Agr.* 2.69. According to Ps. Asconius 237, Stangl, it was used to describe the plucking of the strings of the lyre with the fingers of the left hand as distinct from striking the strings with a *plectrum* held in the right hand, which was described by the phrase *foris canere*.

<u>deep inside:</u> a strained play on words (*paronomasia*), as <u>Cicero says</u> Verres showed himself more skilful than the lyre-player in keeping things inside to benefit himself alone.

54. <u>scoundrel:</u> Cicero has now concluded his skilfully varied narrative of the thefts from Asia, and proceeds, in a familiar pattern, to the orator's greatest task, manipulation of the facts and the identification and the amplification of arguments to produce the desired effect on the hearers. Cf. *Orator* 136. *De Or.* 2.178,291; 3.104. Quint. 8.3.89. He begins with an indignant *exclamatio*, which he follows with a variety of *comparatio* already noted in 53.2, the citing of a lesser form of a crime to heighten the gravity of the form in question. He then adduces a rapid succession of historical parallels (*exempla* or *similitudines*) in the form of rhetorical questions with parallel structure. The historical *exemplum* was another variety of *comparatio* much favoured by Cicero, its purpose to drive home a point by the similarity or, as here, the contrast offered by the example. Cf. Quint. 5.11.5-7; 8.4.13. *Ad Her.* 4.57, 59-62. He rounds off by anticipating two lines of defense (*anteoccupatio*) that he is able to turn against Verres to discredit him further.

<u>you should ... not have conveyed:</u> *deportasses* is an example of the pluperfect subjunctive used in a jussive sense to indicate what should or should not have been done. Cf. *Verr.* 2.3.195. *Fin.* 4.57. Woodcock, 86-87.

<u>property of the nation:</u> Cicero is demanding more than law or convention required. Other evidence shows commanders had virtually unlimited control over war booty and commonly used it to enrich themselves and their soldiers and officers as well as the treasury. Some commanders might, for reasons of patriotism or self-advertisement, surrender all the booty or their share of it to the treasury or might use it for public purposes such as the building or decoration of temples and monuments, but such actions were wholly discretionary and were by no means the accepted norm. For a well-documented example of a commander's use of war booty cf. Pompey's actions after the Mithridatic war. Appian, *Mith.* 116. Plutarch, *Pomp.* 45. Pliny, *NH* 37.16. The entire question of the disposition of booty has been discussed in detail by Shatzman, *Historia* 21 (1972), 177-205.

55. **M. Marcellus:** cf. 11n.
L. Scipio: L. Cornelius Scipio Asiaticus, brother of Scipio Africanus. As consul in 190 and proconsul in 189 he led the war against Antiochus, defeating him at Magnesia.
Flamininus: T. Quinctius Flamininus became consul in 198 and was placed in command of the Second Macedonian War. He defeated Philip V decisively at Cynocephalae in 197 and liberated Greece from Macedonian control.
L. Paulus: L. Aemilius Paulus Macedonicus, father of Scipio Aemilianus, became consul for the second time in 168 and was given command of the Third Macedonian War. He defeated Perseus, the Macedonian king, at Pydna in June 168, which ended the war.
Mummius: L. Mummius Achaicus became consul in 146 and took command of the war against the Achaean Confederacy. He captured and destroyed Corinth and dissolved the Confederacy. Later in his life, Cicero expressed disapproval of Mummius' action. Cf. *Off.* 1.35; 3.46.

56. **their times:** closely similar sentiments recur in *Off.* 2.75-76. Cf. *Cael.* 39-40. Cicero was a confirmed *laudator temporis acti*, who saw in the disciplined dedication instilled by the *mos antiquus* the chief reason for Rome's greatness, and attributed the evils of his time primarily to the erosion of the old ideals and the growth of self-indulgence and greed. Cf. 34n.
P. Servilius: P. Servilius Vatia Isauricus, consul of 79, served as proconsul in Cilicia in 78 and 77 and waged successful campaigns against the pirates and the tribes of Lycia and Pamphylia. Olympus was situated on the Lycian coast.
to give his verdict: *laturus* is the only example in Cicero of the use of the future participle to convey the idea of purpose. Cf. Laughton (2), 120 for a discussion of this passage. The construction is common from the time of Livy onwards.
in the period since: note the hyperbaton. *Postea ... quam* brackets the main clause and signals the upcoming temporal clause. Cf. 17n.

57. **The treasures:** the comparison is developed with careful precision, as each of three aspects of Verres' behaviour is compared in turn with corresponding aspects of the Servilian *exemplum*. Cf. Quintilian's analysis in 8.4.13 of

a similarly precise use of *comparatio* by Cicero in *Cat.* 1.3.
58. **adorned:** Cf. 49n.
59. **and they kept paying worship:** the relative *qui*, as often from Cicero's time onwards, serves here as a coordinating conjunction = *et ei*. Cf. Woodcock, 188.
the very place: the indicatives *fecerant* and *solebant* show this is Cicero's own comment, not part of what the allies said. He is getting in another reminder that the court in recent times had been failing in its duty to protect the allies.
60. **all the accounts:** the evidence of the Verrines, and of Latin writers generally, shows that Romans kept, and were expected to keep, detailed accounts of all their business transactions. Cf. *Rosc.Com.* 2. *Caec.* 17. *Font.* 3, 12. Catullus 28.6.
Antonius: the orator M. Antonius, a patron of Cicero in the nineties. Cf. *De Or.* 2.97.
M. Terentius and C. Cassius: consuls in 73. Verres was therefore claiming he had kept accounts to the end of his praetorship, but had none for the years in Sicily. Cf. *Verr.* 2.4.36.
61. **pool:** the *impluvium* was a rectangular tank, often with elaborately decorated sides, cut into the floor of the *atrium* to catch the rainwater from the opening in the roof overhead. In some designs there was a column at each of the four corners. Cf. below 147.9 and Vitruvius, *De Arch.* 6.3.1.
you cannot show: sc. *ostendere* with *habes*. Such ellipsis of a verb, when it can be supplied from a preceding or following clause or from the context, is common.

62-85: *The episode at Lampsacum.*

62. **But I suppose:** a deft transition to a new form of wrongdoing by Verres in Asia. Irony, the rhetorical question, and paralipsis are used to create an image of numberless transgressions, only one of which Cicero has time to recount.
63. The story which follows provides one of the finest examples of Cicero's skill in *narratio*. It is in two parts, the first (63-69) dealing with Verres' attempt to

seize the daughter of Philodamus, the second (72-76) with the subsequent trial and execution of Philodamus and his son. The first part, where the facts were easily assembled into a damning tale of Verres' lechery, is told in a reasonably direct, though carefully manipulated, manner. The scene and tone are set with the description of a distinguished, peace-loving community whose tranquillity is about to be shattered by the arrival of Verres on an unwarranted self-serving mission. The tense then changes to the historic present to enhance the vividness of the events that follow. The pace of the narrative quickens, the style clear and direct, with little obvious ornament or amplification. There is, however, enough detail and comment to direct the hearers' sympathies and add life and plausibility to the particular version of events being created. The characters are sharply drawn and starkly contrasting, as the well-bred, gracious, and wholly honourable Philodamus strives to maintain his dignity and protect his family against the tyrannous authority of a sordid and depraved *legatus* and his equally unprincipled minions. Time is also taken to develop carefully the reactions of the townspeople and Roman citizens, presenting two external judgements of the atrociousness of Verres' behaviour. All the characteristics traditionally associated with good narrative are here: lucidity, brevity, plausibility, vividness, the unobtrusive combining of persuasion with narration. Cf. *Topica* 97. *De Or.* 2.326-30. Quint. 4.2.31-132.

The narrative is interrupted at a natural stopping point following Verres' escape from retribution, as Cicero pauses to illustrate Verres' deserts by an historical example, and to emphasise the supporting evidence for the story and Verres' inability to deny it. Such pauses to argue particular points or indicate the strength of one's case were common in lengthy narrations (cf. Cicero's treatment of the Samian statues in the tale of the Asian thefts and Quint. 4.2.54). But Cicero is also building the transition that he wants to the second part of the story. Verres was basing his defence on the argument that the conviction of Philodamus represented a declaration by the courts that he had suffered rather than perpetrated an injustice at Lampsacum. Cicero wanted to confront this seemingly reasonable argument at the beginning, and the second part of the story is carefully directed towards disproving it and showing that the trial was a sham and a further indictment rather than a vindication of Verres. This special purpose brought some changes in the narrative technique. The tone is more argumentative; the directness and economy of the narrative style is interrupted by freer use of rhetorical figures, by a more elaborate, forceful style of sentence structure, and by more obvious efforts to stir the emotions. Cf. Quint. 4.2.79-80, 111-115, where he discusses the use of such techniques in *narratio*.

Lampsacum: the form Lampsacus also occurs. The city was situated at the eastern entrance to the Hellespont, a position that gave it commercial and historical importance and high prosperity. Magie (cf. I. 234, 247) believes it had the status of a free city at the time of this incident, but there is no clear evidence to support this, and Cicero's failure to stress such a status makes it virtually certain the city did not possess it.

relaxed way of life: Cicero often speaks disparagingly of the Greeks, presenting them as lazy, self-indulgent, untrustworthy, irresponsible. Cf. *Verr.* 2.2.7. *Flacc.* 9-12, 16-20, 23-24, 57, 61-66, 71. *De Or.* 1.47. *Fam.* 16.4.2. Balsdon (2), 30-54. Petrochilis, *passim*. Guite, 142-59. But here, appropriate to the occasion, he presents a more positive view of their easygoing character; they are peaceable, compliant subjects. Cf. below 81.6-8.

Nicomedes: Nicomedes IV Philopator, king of Bithynia 94-75/74 B.C., who became embroiled in 88 in the First Mithridatic War with the king of Pontus, Mithridates VI Eupator. He was restored to his throne by Sulla in 85 and, at his death in late 75 or early 74, he bequeathed his kingdom to Rome. Sadala was a Thracian king about whom very little is known. Embassies to allied or client states could be highly profitable. Cf. the manoeuvring of Clodius to secure a *legatio* in 59. *Att.* 2.4.2; 2.7.2-3.

64. precious favourite: the mocking irony in Cicero's allusions to Rubrius shows one of the many faces of the famed Ciceronian wit. Cf. above *miro artificio*. *De Or.* 2.235-89.

65. as might be expected: *ut* here has a causal force, indicating what was natural or what was to be expected in the circumstances. For other examples cf. *OLD*, 2114.
66. Greek style: what this meant is not certain, but the likeliest explanation is that suggested by *Tusc.* 1.96, which indicates it was a custom of the Greeks at banquets to name the person whose health one wished to drink and then pass him the glass to empty after taking a sip from it.
 the host: this alliterative tricolon without connectives shows Cicero's eye for graphic detail and his capacity to depict atmosphere as well as action with elegant conciseness.
 they called: *poscunt maioribus poculis* is an elliptical, probably colloquial, phrase, with *bibere* or *propinare* understood. Cf. *Verr.* 2.3.105, *cum ... maximis poculis ministraretur*.
 a practice of the Greeks: cf. Isaeus 3.13-14. There was far greater separation of the sexes and far more social restrictions on women in Greece than in Rome. Cf. Lacey, 158ff. Pomeroy, 79ff.
67. host: Cicero omits no opportunity to highlight the full measure of Verres' misconduct. Here he weaves in a reminder that this incident, in addition to its other vicious aspects, involved a violation of the sacred bond that existed between host and guest. For other allusions to the bond cf. *Verr.* 2.5.108-09. *Fam.* 13.19.1; 13.78.1. Recurring allusions to Philodamus' high position are similarly used to add to the general atrociousness of the affair.
69. the Roman citizens: by the 70's B.C. there were large numbers of Italians resident in all the major cities of the province of Asia. They were organised in associations known as *conventus civium Romanorum* and worked closely together to promote their interests. Cf. Magie I. 162ff.; II.1615. Broughton (2), 543ff.
70. Hadrianus: C. Fabius Hadrianus as praetor or propraetor in Africa in 84 B.C. prevented Metellus Pius taking control of the province for Sulla. He continued to govern Africa until burnt to death in his praetorium in 82 (Livy, *Per.* 84, 86). Cicero naturally omits any reference to his political affiliations, almost certainly the reason his murder went unpunished.

perilous blaze: translates *flamma periculoque*, an example of *hendiadys*, which uses two nouns joined by a conjunction to express a single idea whose sense is more naturally represented by making one of the nouns dependent or converting it to an adjective. Cf. 91.5.

71. But now: Cicero makes frequent use of the fluid, vigorous periodic style to enclose in a single complex but carefully integrated sentence a summarizing statement of a particular point. The dependent clauses lead in the classic manner towards the main statement at the end. Verres' lack of a defence, stated in the first clause, is followed by two closely parallel statements of Cicero's proofs, all building to the conclusion that Verres' conviction is beyond question, the will of fortune herself. The ending or *clausula* of the sentence has a rhythmical pattern especially favoured by Cicero, cretic and trochee -u -u. Cf. Wilkinson, 153-64. This gathering of the various elements of an argument into a compelling resumé was known as *frequentatio* (*Ad Her.* 4.52). Cf. 74.7n.

72. that you: once again the contrast is rendered in exactly parallel phrases, combining the figures of antithesis and isocolon. Cf. above 6n.; 19n.
    all of Asia: Cicero commonly cites the *sermo vulgi* or the reactions of certain people and communities to reinforce the particular impression he is seeking to create. Cf. 68-69; 73.2; 76.8.

73. creditors: money-lending to individuals and communities in the provinces was a common activity of both senators and members of the equestrian order in the late Republic. Twelve per cent was considered the legitimate rate of interest, but much higher rates were commonly charged and creditors often needed the help of the Roman authorities in the province to enforce their usurious demands. Moneylenders were especially active in Asia because of the needs of the Asian cities for funds to pay the huge indemnities imposed by Sulla in 85 after the First Mithridatic War. Cf. Plutarch, *Luc.* 20. Appian, *Mith.* 63. *Att.* 5.21.10-13; 6.1.3, 16. Magie, I. 237. Broughton (2), 518. Shatzman (1), 75ff.

74. despite the fact: another example of the summarizing period, bringing together the various factors that insured Verres' control over the decision of the court and contrasting with them the helplessness of Philodamus. Cf.

71. Anaphora is a common feature of such sentences. Cf. 28. 82. 139.
75. what need: the allusive brevity achieved by the paralipsis is a highly successful means of conveying the desired impression of feverish effort by Dolabella and Verres to compel conviction at the second hearing.
were condemned: the story has now reached its climactic point, and the emotional level rises sharply. Cicero describes the scene at Laodicea in the vived fashion he called *sub oculos subiectio,* a technique otherwise described as *evidentia, repraesentatio,* or *demonstratio.* It sought not merely to recount events, but to show them happening before the eyes of the mind. Cf. *De Or.* 3.202. Quint. 4.2.63-64; 8.3.61-71; 9.2.40. *Ad Her.* 4.68. The switch to the historic present, the accumulation of words signifying pain and grief, the description of the honourable actions of father and son so sharply at variance with their fate, the image, expressed as a chiasmus, of each weeping for the other, the grief-stricken reaction of others to their punishment, the concluding indignant *exclamatio* summarizing the abominable character of the entire episode all combine to produce a graphic and poignant description designed to have a powerful, emotional impact. Quintilian (4.2.114) picked out the passage as an example of a successful appeal to the emotions in the course of a *narratio.* Cf. Quint. 6.1.54; 11.3.162. This method of moving an audience, commonly referred to as *pathos,* represented one of three main modes of persuasion identified in ancient rhetorical theory. The others were rational proof (*probatio*) and *ethos,* the effective presentation of the moral character of oneself and one's clients so as to win credibility and goodwill. Cicero acknowledged the importance of all three modes, but considered the capacity to stir emotion the greatest test and the greatest gift of eloquence. Cf. *Brut.* 89, 279. *Orator* 128. *De Or.* 2.115, 182, 185-215. Quint. 6.2. Kennedy, 222ff., 505.
76. Laodicea: one of the assize cities in the province of Asia, situated on the river Lycus in Caria. It was the judicial centre closest to Dolabella's province of Cilicia, and was far removed from Lampsacum.
77. No longer: the narrative is followed in the usual manner by a passage (77-85) designed to enhance the emotional

impact and persuasiveness of the facts related. Cf. 47n.; 54n.; 87.8; 93.6. Characteristically, it combines rhetorical expressions of outrage and reprimand with more reasoned argument. The familiar devices of exclamation, apostrophe, and the chain of indignant rhetorical questions accentuate the baseness of Dolabella's conduct and the unworthiness of the man on whose behalf he had acted so improperly. Cf. Quint. 9.1.1. The same techniques are used to underline the wanton arrogance and the monstrous implications of Verres' misdeeds. This is followed by an *argumentatio* (cf. *Inv.* 1.74), the development of arguments to show that the riot at Lampsacum could only be explained as an understandable response to the intolerable wrong done by Verres and could not be presented as an unjustified attack on grounds of Philodamus' conviction, since, by Verres' own admission, it was not Philodamus who inspired it.
his accounts: cf. 98.6-14.

78. to become: the future indicative is not uncommon in indignant rhetorical questions of this sort where the deliberative subjunctive might be expected. Cf. *Cat.* 1.27. Virgil, *Aen.* 4.546. Livy 21.10.11.
If everything: anaphora, homoeoteleuton, and asyndeton increase the vigour and impact of this hyperbolic representation of Verres' intemperance and its consequence. For the ancient view of hyperbole and its uses cf. Quint. 8.6. 67ff. *Ad Her.* 4.44.

79. was the state: Cicero now advances two standard forms of conjectural proof (*coniectura*) based on motive or intention (*causa* or *animus*) and character or way of life (*persona* or *vita*), as he argues that the people of Lampsacum were provoked beyond endurance by Verres, since their action otherwise lacked any logical motive and was, besides, incompatible with their placid and compliant nature. Cf. *Inv.* 1.16ff. *Ad Her.* 2.3ff. Quint. 7.2.7ff.
has been insulted: for the sanctity of legates, particularly in their capacity as official envoys of the state, cf. below 84.10. *Man.* 11. *Phil.* 9.4. Livy 4.17. Caesar, *BG* 3.9. Dion.Hal. 11.25.3. Tacitus, *Hist.* 3.80.

80. would have come: the use of the imperfect subjunctive, as in *venirent*, was common in past unreal conditions up to the time of Livy. It carried the suggestion that an action was likely to have happened. Cf. below 85.11. Woodcock, 155.

1. legally appointed hour: the normal and only lawful process would have involved taking the case to Rome and initiating a prosecution under the *lex de repetundis*. Theoretically, the provincials, as the injured party, could conduct the prosecution themselves, but such a course would be highly unusual and unlikely to succeed, and in practice, as in the case of the Sicilians, aggrieved provincials had to try to find an able or influential Roman to conduct the case for them. Cf. above 50. 7-8. *In Caec.* 11.14.

   By whom: an example of the figure Cicero called *sibi ipsi responsio*, answering one's own question, or reasoning by question and answer. Cf. *De Or.* 3.207. Quint. 9.3.90. *Ad Her.* 4.23. For other examples cf. 83.11ff. 146. 8ff.

   more powerfully influenced: the antithesis between hate and fear is elegantly expressed by a chiasmus in an alliterative clause ending with the common cadence cretic + trochee.

2. Do not ... force: Cicero repeatedly urges protection of the right of the provincials in the Verrines and decries what he sees as growing abuses in provincial government and declining control of provincial administrators. Such sentiments suited his case, but they are consistent with his views elsewhere and with his liberal and benevolent administration as a provincial governor in Cilicia in 51-50. He believed both honour and expediency required that the government of the provinces should be conducted with equity and good faith (*aequitas* and *fides*), and he maintained this was the view of empire that had prevailed in earlier generations, producing what was in reality a protectorate rather than an empire. The abandonment of this concept for a more exploitative and oppressive regime in his own day he considered ruinous, and a further symptom of the moral degeneration and surrender to self-indulgence and greed that were undermining the strength and stability of the empire. Cf. *Verr.* 2.3.217-19. *Man.* 6,12-14, 37-38. *Off.* 1.35; 2.23-28, 75-77. *Att.* 5.10.2; 5.11.5; 5.13.1; 5.14.2; 5.15.2; 5.16.3; 5.17.2; 5.20.6; 5.21.7; 6.1.2, 16; 6.2.4; 6.3.3. The idea of Rome as a benevolent protectorate growing tyrannous amidst a general decline in moral standards was not peculiar to Cicero. Cf. Sallust, *Cat.* 9.5.

And do you: once more the summarizing period, its various components accented by anaphora. Cf. 74n.
83. what I mean is: translates *inquam*, often used in the 1st person to emphasize or explain a word or phrase, or resume after a digression with the sense "I mean" or "I repeat". For examples cf. *OLD*, 918.
84. Let us have: *cedo* and the plural *cette* are rare imperative forms meaning "give" or "produce".
Why have you: Cicero magnifies the gravity of Verres' inaction by descanting upon the one point in a skilful use of the figure of refinement (cf. 37n.). One triad of questions, each accented in familiar fashion by anaphora, sets forth from slightly differing angles the positive consequences of Verres' omission, while a second triad, similarly punctuated by anaphora, focuses on the omission itself and the action, variously described, that should have been taken to avert those consequences. The cumulative effect is one of manifold and inexcusable misbehaviour.
85. M. Aurelius Scaurus: Broughton (*MRR* 1.529) places his quaestorship in 117 B.C. He went on to become *consul suffectus* in 108.
refuge: all sacred places were considered in the Greek world to afford a certain measure of protection to those who took refuge in them, but true sanctuary was provided only by those on whom the privilege of inviolability (*asylia*) and official status as *asyla* were conferred by law. The shrine of Artemis at Ephesus was one of the earliest and most famous of these *asyla*. It later lost the status under Augustus, when the city began to fall under the control of criminals. Cf. Strabo 14.1.23. Tacitus, *Ann*. 3.61. Livy 35.51.2. Smith, I.234. Scaurus' disregard of the inviolability of the temple showed contempt for the beliefs and traditions of the Greeks, as did the senate's reaction to the affair, another indication of the oppressive and insensitive character of Roman rule.
law-abiding states: the meaning of *sociorum iura* is debatable, but the contrast with *hostium tela* indicates *iura* here means "laws" not "rights", and has a pregnant sense, representing situations where laws rather than weapons hold sway.

86–90: *The theft of the Milesian galley.*

86. **the Milesians:** Miletus was one of the great Ionian cities with a famous history as a sea-power and centre of trade and industry. It was especially renowned for its woollens. Cf. Horace, *Ep.* 1.17.30. Virgil, *Georg.* 3.306. Columella 7.2,3. Broughton (2), 817. It lost its status as a free city in the eighties because of support for Mithridates. Cf. Magie, I.237.
    Myndus: located south of Miletus in Caria, a journey of about forty miles along the coast.
    one could speak: cf. 32n.
87. **L. Magius:** According to Ps. Asconius 244, Stangl, L. Magius and L. Fannius were refugees from the army of L. Valerius Flaccus, the *consul suffectus* of 86, who had been sent by Cinna to the East to counteract his arch-enemy Sulla, the commander of the war against Mithridates. Valerius was killed in a mutiny and his army surrendered to Sulla in 85. Magius and Fannius retained their Cinnan sympathies, and in the mid-seventies persuaded Mithridates to seek an alliance with the Cinnan commander, Q. Sertorius, who was still holding out in Spain. Mithridates sent ambassadors to Sertorius and an alliance was made, but it had little actual effect. Cf. Appian, *Mith.* 68. Plutarch, *Sert.* 23-24. Florus 2.10.4.
    in Spain: the bracketed sections are considered by most editors to be scribal glosses. They were not in the text used by Ps. Asconius.
    Good heavens: cf. 77n.
88. **did you think:** a finely balanced period that progresses through two broadly parallel causal clauses, each interrupted at the same point by relative clauses, to the main statement, with the main verb reserved to the very end. Once again the cadence of the *clausula* is the cretic + trochee.
    that it would be a sufficient provision: translates *satis cautum fore*. The past participle + *fore* corresponds in indirect speech to the future perfect passive form of direct speech.
89. **Murena:** L. Licinius Murena, who served as a *legatus* of Sulla in the First Mithridatic War, was left in command of Asia by Sulla in 74 and also commissioned to take action against the pirates, who were now a formidable military

power in the eastern Mediterranean, securely based in western Cilicia. Piracy had been on the increase in the Mediterranean since the middle of the second century, the rugged, indented coastline of western Cilicia providing safe defensible havens for the marauding fleets. Towards the end of the century the Romans had made a significant effort to confront the problem, dispatching a special expedition under the praetor M. Antonius in 102, and establishing Cilicia as a separate territorial province about the same time. Cf. 44n. The pirates had continued to flourish, however, and in the First Mithridatic War had cooperated with Mithridates who, in turn, had lent them aid in equipping their ships (cf. Plutarch, *Luc*. 2.5. Appian, *Mith*. 63). Murena, as Cicero's evidence indicates, raised a fleet to combat the pirates by requiring maritime cities like Miletus to build ships with the money they owed in tribute to Rome. He seems to have made little use of the fleet, however, and certainly did not succeed in breaking the power of the pirates. Cf. Appian, *Mith*. 93. Magie, I.241; II.1121.

89. tempest: Cicero uses metaphor (*translatio*) sparingly. He considered it a most appealing figure that added colour and brilliance, and he especially favoured single-word metaphors, but he gives many warnings about extravagant or inappropriate uses of the figure, and recommends that, in general, metaphor should enter demurely and should even, on occasion, be given an apologetic introduction (*De Or*. 3.155-66). Cf. *Ad Her*. 4.34. Quint. 8.6.4-18.

90. February: the month in which the senate traditionally received foreign embassies. Cf. *Att*. 1.14.5; 1.18.7. *Fam*. 1.4.1.

    consuls-elect: Q. Hortensius and Q. Caecilius Metellus, due to enter office on January 1st 69. Both were supporters of Verres, and the Milesians were therefore nervous about giving evidence against Verres, in case it would lose them the favour of the new consuls and adversely affect whatever representation they were planning to make to the senate in February.

99-102: Verres' misdeeds as a guardian and proquaestor.

90.   guardianship: Roman law required that males under the

age of puberty (fixed at 14 in the late Republic) who were not under the power of the father (*patriapotestas*) should have at least one guardian (*tutor*). Guardians were generally appointed by the *paterfamilias* in his will, but if no such testamentary guardians existed, the nearest agnates assumed the position. If there were no testamentary guardians and no agnates, the praetor was entitled to appoint a guardian. The primary duty of guardians was to administer the property of the ward in the interests of the ward. Wards could perform no legal act before age seven, and after seven required the approval of the guardians for any act that involved a risk of loss. Guardians could be called to account for their management of the ward's property and required to show they had administered it in accordance with the principles of good faith. Females who were not in *patriapotestas* were required to have a guardian throughout their lives, but by the late Republic ways had been found to insure that adult women had virtually complete independence and that the role of their guardians was little more than a formality. Cf. Schulz, 162-202. Watson (1), 40-42.

91. loaned money: cf. 73n. For the phrase *pecuniam occupare* cf. *Flacc.* 51.
    comrade: *sodalis* had the general meaning of a close companion, but also meant a member of a *sodalitas*, a social or religious fraternity or club. *Sodalitates* (as distinct from *collegia*, which were trade or religious clubs of the lower classes) catered for the wealthier and more influential Romans, and had become important in the public life of Rome in the first century B.C., acting as pressure-groups at elections and at trials involving their members or friends. The bonds of *amicitia* between *sodales* were considered especially close, demanding loyal mutual support, especially in times of crisis. Cf. *Cael.* 26. *Sulla* 7. *Mur.* 56. *Brut.* 166. *De Or.* 2.200. Verres and Malleolus were *sodales*, as the following sections show, which prompts Cicero to remark they were also *sodales* in their pathological greed for money and possessions.

92. no record: Cicero once again makes use of anaphora to accent each element of a tricolon and reinforce the overall impact. Cf. 84n.; 93. 11ff.
    received on behalf of his ward: Greenwood translates

"received from his ward", but surely *pupillo* is a dative of advantage, and the money involved is that received by Verres for the sale of property in Asia in the name of the young Malleolus. Chrysogonus was presumably a slave of Malleolus, who received the money on his master's behalf. Cicero's insinuation about an erasure would seem to be implying that Verres had originally entered one million as the sum due to Malleolus and had later substituted 600,000.

You can imagine: an example of *permissio*, a form of argument that pretends to leave certain things to the judgement of the hearers. Like paralipsis, it was a mode of persuasion by implication and suggestion, when detailed argument might prove tedious or inconclusive. Cf. Quint. 9.2.25. *De Or.* 3.207.

93. personal funds: *peculium* meant money or property managed by a person who in law did not possess the right of ownership. Slaves commonly had *peculia* in Rome, consisting of earnings allowed them by their masters. But in the late Republic a slave's *peculium* might include much more than that. Masters increasingly used slaves as agents, setting them up in a business or a craft with a *peculium* adequate to the needs of the enterprise. The profits went, of course, to the master. The law expedited this development by recognising the right of slaves to manage the *peculium*, and to form valid agreements in the process. The master, who technically remained the owner of the *peculium*, could sue the other party to such agreements, and could himself be sued for sums up to the value of the *peculium*, if the slave had acted independently, and for the full amount, if the slave had acted on his orders. Cf. Crook, 188-89. Finley, 82, 102.

under-slaves: translates *vicarii*. A *vicarius* was a slave of a slave, a not uncommon phenomenon in Rome after the emergence of slaves as agents and managers.

Behold a man: cf. 77n.

to despoil and pillage: *spoliandam* and *vexandam* are examples of the gerundive used predicatively in agreement with the object to express purpose. The construction is common after verbs of giving, sending, undertaking, demanding. Cf. Woodcock, 164.

94. to come forth from the dead: summoning witnesses from the dead to speak directly was a bold form of the device

of impersonation (*prosopopoeia*) associated with the grand style and highly regarded by Cicero as a tool of persuasion. Cf. *Orator* 85. *Brut.* 322. *Cael.* 33–38. *Fin.* 4.61. Quint. 9.2.29–37; 11.1.39; 12.10.61. *Ad Her.* 4.66. In this case, however, Cicero wanted only to imagine Malleolus present, so that he could more vehemently and dramatically upbraid Verres on his behalf. He proceeds to descant in the grand manner upon the betrayal of a *sodalis*, using the familiar triad of rhetorical questions punctuated by anaphora. Cf. 84n. This entire amplification of the crimes of Verres' guardianship in 93–94 is another elaborate appeal to the emotions, as Cicero exploits the piteous consequences of Verres' betrayal of trust as seen in the helplessness of a minor deprived of his father and his father's possessions, and in the vulnerability of his distraught mother and grandmother, forced to put aside their innate modesty and defend their rights in the unfamiliar world of men.

95. commune: comprised a group of villages in the area of Milyas just north of Lycia that had organized themselves into a federation for common action. Cf. Jones (2), 145ff.
requisitioning grain: Cicero is referring to the grain requisitioned for the governor's needs, the *frumentum aestimatum* or *frumentum cellae nomine*, which was, apparently, regularly demanded in all provinces. Provincials were supposed to be paid for this grain, as for all requisitions that were not part of the taxation system, but many farmers preferred themselves to pay money rather than take responsibility for securing and delivering the levy. Cicero describes in *Verr.* 3.188ff. how Verres extorted large sums of money from farmers in Sicily in place of this grain. Cf. 11n. Here he is claiming Verres began this practice in Cilicia, and further extended it to other requisitions such as hides, blankets, sacks.
three million: an astonishing figure in light of the fact that Cicero asked for a total assessment of only one million against Verres (*In Caec.* 19). It is not surprising that Dolabella's name remained for centuries a synonym for an extortionate governor.

97. Scaurus: son of M. Aemilius Scaurus, the consul of 115 who went on to become *princeps senatus* and one of the most influential ex-consuls of the final decade of the

second century and of the nineties. The young Scaurus was about twenty years of age at the time of Dolabella's trial, launching himself into public life in typical fashion with an *illustris accusatio*. But he also had more personal motives, as was so often the case in criminal trials of the late Republic. Dolabella had participated in a prosecution of his father, and was, in the words of Cicero, a *paternus inimicus* (Asconius 26, Clark).

98. role of defender: a lifelong attitude of Cicero. He had avoided prosecutions in his twenties, the age when most aspiring politicians sought them as a means of proving their worth, and, besides the case of Verres, undertook only one other prosecution in his entire career, the case of T. Munatius Plancus Bursa in early 51. He was driven to this second prosecution by a hatred for Plancus that he claimed exceeded even his hatred for Clodius (*Fam.* 7.2.3). Plancus, whom he had earlier defended, had violated the laws of *amicitia* by attacking Cicero in the course of a rowdy tribunate in 52. Cicero charged him with political violence and won the case. His attitude towards prosecutions is most clearly stated in the *De Officiis* (1.50) where he says it is acceptable to prosecute on the rare occasion, but not often, since it is a sign of heartlessness to endanger people's vital interests and the name of prosecutor carries not only danger but disrepute.

99. portended: there is compression of thought here bordering on obscurity, a rare phenomenon in Cicero. The meaning is that the precedent of Dolabella, who was allowed to defer submission of his accounts and was then convicted, presaged a similar fate for Verres, which moved senators to allow him a similar deferral.

cesspool: *faex*, which signifies the dregs, offscourings, refuse, was Cicero's strongest metaphor for the world of the sordid and the seamy. Cf. *Att.* 2.1.8. *Q.F.* 2.4.5. *Pis.* 9. He did not approve of metaphors that entailed indecency or vulgarity (*De Or.* 3.163-64).

100. unrecorded: *extraordinarius* had a technical meaning in relation to money, indicating sums that were outside the record, unaccounted for. Cf. *Verr.* 2.2.170. *Rosc.Com.* 4.

purchase of the praetorship: Cicero repeatedly accuses Verres of having bribed his way into the praetorship. Cf. *Verr.* 1.22; 2.4.45. The allegation likely had some foundation. Verres' father had been a *divisor*, one of the tribal officials whose original function had been to distribute gifts from leading tribesmen to less fortunate members, but who had become the main agents of electoral bribery in the late Republic. It would hardly be surprising if Verres had used his riches from the East and his father's expertise to advance his political career. Cf. Intro. p.6.

101. He was a man: this convoluted period contains another example of anacolouthon. The relative *qui* gets lost in the catalogue of clauses refuting any possible reason other than bribery for Verres' election, and Cicero switches at the end of the long series of concessive clauses to a new construction and a new subject. The sentence works well from a rhetorical point of view, but is structurally awkward and unsatisfactory.

industry: Cicero frequently sounded the theme that the traditional and proper criteria for political preferment in the Roman Republic were *virtus* and *industria*, by which he meant worth or all-round ability coupled with a spirit of initiative that looked for challenging, worthwhile undertakings and pursued them vigorously. Cf. *Verr.* 2.5.180ff. *Mur.* 16. *Sest.* 137. *Planc.* 62. *Off.* 2.36.

sobriety: *frugalitas* and the adjective of closely similar meaning, *frugi*, were an important element of the *prisci mores* or old morality so frequently extolled by Cicero. They had some positive nuances of goodness and moral integrity, but their central meaning was a sobriety and self-discipline that rejected all forms of excess. They incorporated the virtue of *temperantia*, which stood for a style of life marked by restraint and a spirit of asceticism, the antithesis of the immoderate self-indulgence and materialism represented by *luxuria* and *avaritia*. Cf. *Tusc.* 3.16-18; 4.36. *Off.* 1.15, 93, 102, 106. *Man.* 40-41. *Verr.* 2.4.98.

diligence in canvassing: *adsiduitas* is commonly used as an attribute of politicians who were constantly present in Rome and constantly promoting their claims to office. Cf. *Planc.* 67. *Mur.* 21. *Com.Pet.* 43.

additional money: Cicero elsewhere alleges Verres used various forms of bribery in efforts to impede the prosecution or influence its outcome. He had hired bribery agents to prevent Cicero's election to the aedileship, to insure the election of Hortensius and Q. Metellus to the consulship and of M. Marcellus to the praetorship, and to insure a compliant jury, especially if the trial extended into the following year. Cf. *Verr.* 1.17-27; 2.1.19, 31, 51, 158.

<u>103-127:</u> *Verres' praetorship: abuses of his judicial powers.*

103. <u>praetorship:</u> after Sulla's reform of the constitution in 81-80, eight praetors were elected each year. Since they held *imperium*, they were, strictly speaking, colleagues of the consuls, though subordinate to them, and were theoretically empowered to fulfil any of the functions of consuls. They were given particular spheres of duty, however, on entering office, and, in the post-Sullan era, those *provinciae* were almost always judicial. Two praetors were assigned by lot to administer the civil law (*ius civile*), the other six to act as presidents of standing criminal courts (*quaestiones perpetuae*). The praetors administering the civil law were known as the *praetor urbanus* and *praetor peregrinus*, the former dealing with cases between citizens, the latter with cases involving foreigners (*peregrini*). They outranked their colleagues, the *praetor urbanus* holding the highest position of all. Cf. Appian, *BC* 2.112. Livy 24.9.5.
<u>many will say</u>: an example of *sermocinatio*, or simulated dialogue, a livelier means than indirect statement of raising and refuting a possible criticism or objection. Quintilian considered it a form of *prosopopoeia*, though he acknowledges the latter term was generally reserved for situations where the speakers and speeches were wholly imaginary. Cf. Quint. 9.2.31. *Ad Her.* 4.65. This entire section represents an unusual but effective form of paralipsis, building an impression of countless crimes and masses of evidence that required the prosecution to select only the most egregious offences for investigation and presentation to the court.
<u>maintenance of public buildings</u>: the repair of public buildings was normally the responsibility of the censors, who controlled the letting of most state contracts, but no censors were elected between 86 and 70, and their duties in relation to contracts must have devolved on the consuls

and urban praetors and aediles. Cf. *Verr*. 2.3.16-18. Astin, 183.
104. with favourable omens: a common meaning of the adverb *auspicato*. Magistrates were required to take the auspices before entering office. Cicero is suggesting Verres looked for and found his good omens in the embraces of a prostitute, and went on to secure the urban praetorship, a most inauspicious development as far as the Roman people were concerned. The relative *qui* is concessive, linked with *nactus est*, not *factus est*, as sometimes suggested.

edict: Roman magistrates above the level of quaestor possessed the *ius edicendi*, the right to issue proclamations setting forth the rules and principles by which they proposed to discharge the duties of their office. The edict of a magistrate was theoretically not binding on his successor, but in practice the main features were maintained and became established tradition, producing an *edictum translaticium*. The edict of the urban praetor had particular importance, since it dealt with administration of the civil law, and gradually, by granting new remedies and developing new forms of action, it became a means of changing and developing the *ius civile*, producing a body of law separate from the statutes and known as the *ius honorarium* or *praetorium*. Cf. Watson (2), 31-87.

census rolls: failure to register at a census was a most serious offence in the early Republic, punishable by enslavement and confiscation of property (Livy 1.44.1. Dion. Hal. 4.15.6). Although Cicero elsewhere indicates (*Caec*. 99) that these penalties still applied in his day, the manner of his reference to Annius and to numerous others who were in similar circumstances (cf. 111.6) suggests that being unregistered (*incensus*) was no longer seen as extraordinary or reprehensible. It is also possible that Annius was one of the flood of new citizens resulting from the settlement after the Social War and that his absence from the rolls was due to the failure of the Roman government to conduct a complete census of the new citizens in the eighties and seventies. Cf. Wiseman (1), 60-69. Astin, 185-86.

legal bar: the *Lex Voconia* prescribed that anyone who was registered at the last census as having a property rating above a certain amount, probably 100,000 sesterces (Ps. Asconius 247, Stangl), could not name a woman as heir. It also prescribed that no legacy from such a testator should exceed the amount left to the heir or heirs. Since Annius, though clearly rich, was not on the census rolls, he was not, according to the letter of the law, precluded from making his daughter his heir. Verres, however, attempted to draw him within the scope of the *Lex Voconia* by inserting a retrospective provision in his edict making the prohibition against female heirs apply to all whose wealth exceeded the limit specified in the law, whether their names appeared on the census rolls or not.

105. secret overtures: *submittere* was sometimes used elliptically in the sense of sending a secret message or messenger to someone.
106. without risk: guardians could be called to account for mismanagement of a ward's property. Cf. 90n.

repeated demands: translates *saepe appellati*, a phrase that illustrates Cicero's common use of participles in place of adverbial clauses. They helped achieve conciseness and compression of sense, which were important in achieving a brisk, gripping narrative. Cicero also used participles for variety, especially in complex narrative sentences with multiple subordinate clauses. Cf. *efflagitatus* 92.8. For a detailed study of Cicero's use of participles cf. E. Laughton, *The Participle in Cicero* (Oxford 1964).

Who would have believed: Cicero digresses from his point, as mention of Verres' citation of an anti-feminist law creates the opportunity for a mocking allusion to Verres' reputed fondness for women and slavish infatuation with Chelidon. He prolongs the ridicule in a series of ironic references to Verres' pretensions and abilities as a jurist. Cicero had a well-known penchant and high reputation for barbed witticisms (cf. Plutarch, *Cic*. 27. Quint. 6.3.3), and the amusement of the audience at the expense of one's opponent he considered a most important aspect of the art of persuasion. Cf. *De Or*. 2.216-27, 236; 3.203. *Orator* 138.

praetorian law: cf. 104n.

Postumius: A. Postumius Albinus and Q. Fulvius Flaccus were censors in 174. Voconius obviously decreed that his law should apply to people on the census lists drawn up by these censors. This led the Epitomator of Livy to date the *Lex Voconia* in 174, but Cicero (*Sen.* 14) clearly gives 169 as the date. There were censors elected in 169, but Voconius chose understandably to refer in his law to the last completed census rather than to one that had not yet happened. Cf. Broughton (1), I.427.

107. safeguarded against illegality: the meaning is that Annius could not provide against violating laws or edicts that did not as yet exist. Cicero's basic contention in relation to this incident is that Annius' action, at the time it was taken, violated neither law nor justice. There were, therefore, no legitimate grounds on which Verres could interfere with it. Cicero also makes an important secondary argument that, even if Annius' action had some reprehensible aspect and some new point of law were needed to deal with it, such a legal innovation should not be applied retrospectively. He maintains that Roman law had never admitted the idea of retrospection except in relation to actions that were intrinsically evil, and even then only in rare instances.

duty to family: *testamentum inofficiosum* was a formal legal term in later Roman law designating a will that ignored the duties of *pietas* by failing to make provision for the testator's nearest relatives. The law granted such relatives a remedy (*querella*) against the designated heirs. It is unlikely, however, that this form of legal action existed at the time of the trial of Verres. Cf. Schulz, 275-78.

You should then have imitated: Cf. 54n.

108. Cornelian law: the *Lex Cornelia de falsis*, also known as the *Lex Cornelia testamentaria* or *nummaria*. It was an omnibus bill, covering all forms of forgery and counterfeiting, and was part of the comprehensive package of criminal legislation enacted by Sulla in 81-80, defining major crimes and establishing standing courts to deal with them. Cf. Mommsen, 667-81.

the people should have the right: translates *ad populum pertineat, pertinere* used in the sense of "belonging by right", "being the property of". For other examples cf. *OLD*, 1360.

109. Atinian, Furian: a *Lex Atinia* of the second century B.C. prescribed that ownership of stolen property could not be acquired by *usucapio*, i.e. uninterrupted

possession for a fixed period, which, according to the Twelve Tables, was two years for immovables, one year for other property. Cf. Watson (4), 24ff. The *Lex Furia*, which preceded the *Lex Voconia*, attempted, like the latter, to limit the size of legacies, fixing a maximum amount of one thousand asses except where the legatees were the spouse or nearest relatives. Cf. Watson (3), 163ff. Nothing is known of a *Lex Fusia* and the word *Fusias* in the text may have originated in an unintentional repetition of *Furias* by a copyist. Such dittography is not uncommon in the text of the Verrines.

lasts for a year: cf. 104n.

If the first of January: Quintilian cites this passage (5.10.76) as an example of an *argumentum ex consequentibus*, where something is presented as necessarily following from something else.

110. bequeaths more: cf. 104n. Cicero accuses Verres of inconsistency, since he has made the *Lex Voconia* apply to *incensi* in regard to the naming of a woman as heir, but not in regard to the size of legacies.

same category: i.e. the same category as the provision relating to female heirs.

suspect: Peterson prefers *discrimen*, the reading of *V*, to *dubium*, the reading of *SDP*. *Dubium*, however, gives a far more satisfactory sense. Cicero has been contending that the edict had a special motive, to overturn a pre-existing will. If the edict had no retrospective force, its motives could not be thus impugned, since no one would have violated it and no one could therefore be its target. For the phrase *in dubium venire* cf. *Att.* 11.15.2. *Quinct.* 5, 67.

111. in the same situation: this translates the reading of *V*. All the other manuscripts read *multi testamenta eodem modo fecerunt*: "many people made their wills in the same fashion". But the relevant point is not the kind of wills they made but their circumstances as wealthy citizens absent from the census rolls. The reading of *V* therefore seems preferable, though the very different tradition of the other manuscripts remains difficult to explain. A.E. Douglas has suggested to me that an incorrect explanatory note may have replaced a more obscure text.

112. line of defence: the argument is highly compressed. Cicero is making the point that the clause in Verres' urban edict relating to the *Lex Voconia* was so blatantly unjust and indefensible that he omitted it from his Sicilian edict. He did, however, indicate that, if any cases relating to this and other omitted clauses arose, he would decide them in accordance with the provisions of the urban edict. Cicero says this was an attempt by Verres to leave open for himself the defence that the omitted provisions had not been invented to deal with individual cases, but were regarded by him as valid general prescriptions that he was prepared to apply in Sicily, if necessary. Cicero dismisses this line of defence, insisting the deletion of the clauses implied repudiation of them and undermined any attempt to justify them. The other omitted clauses are dealt with by Cicero in sections 17-18.

I have no doubt: another obvious use of *pathos*, as Cicero dwells on the theme of the special love of fathers for their daughters and belabours the particular cruelty of Verres in robbing a daughter of the possessions her father had lovingly left her. The usual devices of the rhetorical question, anaphora, apostrophe, hyperbole, the tone of *iracundia* and *obiurgatio* are used to heighten the emotional effect.

who have a daughter: Cicero's devotion to his daughter Tullia is very apparent in his references to her throughout his Correspondence. She was born around 79 B.C. and was married three times, the last two marriages ending unhappily in divorce. Her premature death early in 45 left Cicero overwhelmed with grief and forced him into solitude in search of consolation from study and writing. Cf. *Att.* 12.13-20.

113. toga praetexta: this purple-bordered *toga* was worn by free-born children, up to about age fourteen in the case of boys, who then assumed the *toga virilis*, and up to the time of marriage in the case of girls. It was a symbol of free birth (*ingenuitas*), and the implication of Cicero's question is that Verres might as well remove even the symbols of the girl's free-born status, since he has deprived her of her basic rights and all her possessions.

Syracuse: Cicero's allegation of a secret, hurried departure by Verres from Syracuse had particular point, since the city was supposedly friendly to Verres and was the only Sicilian community besides Messana that had not sent a deputation to Rome to support the prosecution. Cf. *In Caec.* 14. *Verr.* 2.2.35-50; 2.4.15-17, 136-51.

114. last wish: *voluntas* used with reference to the dead carried the meaning of "last wish". Cf. below 124.10. *De Or.* 1.242.

 legal rule: this tralatician rule relating to inheritance is fully discussed by Watson (3), 71ff. It gave possession of an inheritance, in cases where no written will could be found, to the person who would have become heir if no will had been made. The grant of possession was provisional, however, and did not affect the title to the estate. Anyone claiming to be the testamentary heir could pursue the claim under the procedure of the civil law, and, if successful, would gain title to the inheritance.

115. fount of knowledge: the irony, while amusing the jury, also helped promote the impression of persistent manipulation and perversion of the law by Verres.

 was to go: *veniebat* is an example of the imperfect used to indicate an action about to happen in past time, the so-called *futurum in praeterito*.

 Minucian clan: since no will was produced, possession should have been granted in accordance with the rights established by the law of intestate succession. Under this law the foremost claim to an inheritance belonged to the *sui heredes*, i.e. those who were in the *potestas* of the deceased at the time of his death. Next in the line of succession were the *proximi agnati*, the closest category of agnates. If there were no *sui heredes* or *proximi agnati*, as was clearly the situation in the case of Minucius, the inheritance went to the *gentiles*, the members of the clan. Cf. Watson (3), 176ff.

 he could take: Cicero here alludes to two forms of civil procedure, *legis actio sacramento in rem* and *per sponsionem*, by which a claim to an inheritance (*petitio hereditatis*) could be pursued. The procedures are described by Gaius (4.91-96), and discussed by Greenidge (1), 188-90. The procedure *per sponsionem* required the defendant to provide security guaranteeing, in case of defeat, restoration of the thing in dispute (*lis*) and of its fruits (*vindiciae*). Cf. Gaius 4.95.

116. He has composed: Cicero is accusing Verres of having once again, in return for a bribe, composed a section of

his edict to serve the interests of an individual, in this case the man claiming to be Minucius' heir. Cicero's basic charge is that Verres omitted from his edict the provisions of the *edictum tralaticium* (outlined in 114) in relation to rights of possession in cases where no written will was produced, and substituted a statement that he would grant possession to the person who happened to be in possession, provided he was laying claim to being the testamentary heir. Cicero proceeds in 117 to show the absurdity of this provision, and adduces two further proofs of its dishonesty that he had used earlier in regard to the case of Annius, namely that no subsequent praetor adopted the provision and Verres himself omitted it from his Sicilian edict.

118. what can one say: an example of the figure of *dubitatio*, the pretence by the speaker that he cannot find the right word or does not know where to begin or what to say. Cf. Quint. 9.2.19. *Ad Her*. 4.40.

But the decrees: Cicero has skilfully moved his argument through a number of ludicrous or indefensible explanations of Verres' behaviour to the caustic and neatly antithetical conclusion that Verres had omitted the infamous decrees issued in Rome for pay to avoid infamy in the province for no pay.

119. contrary to the provisions: there was no legal obligation on praetors at this time to abide by the terms of their edicts in issuing judgements, and the evidence suggests there were many besides Verres who failed to do so. The abuse was finally remedied in 67, when the tribune C. Cornelius enacted a law specifically requiring praetors to administer the law in accordance with their edicts. Cf. Asconius 59, Clark. Dio 36.40.3.

L. Piso: L. Calpurnius Piso Frugi was in all probability *praetor peregrinus* in 74 B.C. On the evidence of this passage he not only used his right of veto (*intercessio*) as a magistrate of equal power (*par potestas*) to block decisions of Verres, but went so far as to deal with the vetoed cases himself. His right to do so was apparently unquestioned, and presumably arose from the fact that both the urban and peregrine praetors retained the full power of *iurisdictio*, while normally accepting a division of duties in their exercise of it. Cf. Jones (3), 72-73.

showers of stones: stone-throwing (*lapidatio*) was a common means of expressing public anger in antiquity, and a common feature of the demonstrations and political violence that became increasingly common in the late Republic. Cf. *Verr.* 2.4.95. *Sest.* 34, 77. *Dom.* 14. *Q.F.* 2.1.2. *De Or.* 2.197.

wisdom of Piso: the extended alliteration joined with the anaphora and assonance of the tetracolon following provide a striking and forceful description of the contrasting character and conduct of Piso.

120. consulted: legal experts began to emerge in the Roman world in the third century B.C., when knowledge of the law and its procedures ceased to be a monopoly of the College of Pontiffs. These jurisconsults had a critical, though informal influence on the operation and development of the *ius civile*. They helped citizens in the drafting of legal documents and advised magistrates in the drafting of their edicts. They gave legal opinions (*responsa*) on matters of law submitted to them, and their services in this regard were constantly sought by litigants, advocates, judges, and jurisdictional magistrates (cf. *Topica* 65-66). Their legal writings and published collections of their *responsa* further helped shape the course of Roman jurisprudence. Finally, they played a vital role in legal education by accepting students, who accompanied them and listened to them expounding the law and delivering *responsa* (*Brut.* 306). Since there were no law schools in Rome during the Republic, this was the only form of practical legal training available to those interested in the law. Until the time of Augustus jurisconsults had no official status. They were consulted because they had recognised legal skills. They gave their advice free of charge, and it could be accepted or rejected. Cf. Watson (2), 101-10. Rawson, 201-14. Kunkel, 92-116.

121. boar-pig's justice: there is possibly a play on both *ius* and *verrinum*. *Ius* could mean justice or broth or soup; *verrinum* was an adjective formed from *verres*, which, besides being a proper name, signified a boar-pig. *Ius verrinum* could therefore mean "justice of the Verrine variety" or "the broth of a boar-pig".

Sacerdos: Verres' immediate predecessor in the urban praetorship, whose name meant "priest", and who was reviled because he had not sacrificed the swine about to succeed him. Cicero apologises for the low quality of these puns on proper names, and is careful to attribute them to others, but similar jests recur at *Verr.* 2.2.52 and 2.4.53, 57, 95, and in general Cicero shows a weakness for this as for all other forms of word-play. Cf. Plutarch, *Cic.* 7.4-5, and Quintilian's remarks (6.3.4, 55) on these jokes and on double entendres (*amphibolia*) in general.

122. arrogance: *superbia* was the mark of the tyrant, the quality in rulers the Romans considered most incompatible with the notions of *libertas* and *respublica*. Cf. *Rep.* 2.46. Sallust, *Cat.* 6.7. Livy 9.46.8; 28.42.22.
to beat: the right of appeal (*provocatio*), which had been firmly established in Roman law by the *Lex Valeria* of 300 B.C. and the *Leges Porciae* of the second century, protected Roman citizens from the more severe forms of magisterial coercion (*coercitio*), including flogging. Cicero records (*Rab.* 12) that a *Lex Porcia* removed the rod from the bodies of all Roman citizens. Cf. *Verr.* 2.5.163. Sallust, *Cat.* 51.21. Livy 10.9.4. Lintott (2), 249-53.

123. proscribed: according to Valerius Maximus (9.2.1) Sulla had proscribed 4700 of his opponents in his *Lex de proscriptione* passed in 82. Those named in the law lost their rights to life and property, and it became a capital offense to help or harbour them. In addition, their sons and grandsons were debarred from public office. Cf. Plutarch, *Sulla* 31.
unconscionable: the irony is subtle but unmistakeable. *Egenti* and *fraternis* reveal the callous hypocrisy behind Verres' concern to uphold the law.
committing a crime: freedmen remained closely bound to their former masters, who became their patrons on manumission. They normally had a specific obligation to provide a certain amount of free labour (*operae*), but as well had a general obligation, based on *fides*, to show loyalty and generosity towards their patrons and to respect their wishes and protect their interests. Disregarding a patron's testamentary instructions might well therefore be seen by a conscientious freedman as a serious breach of *officium*. Cf. Treggiari, 68-81, 215-17.

124. I grant: making concessions and confessions seemingly unfavourable to one's case but designed to prove

something still more unfavourable to one's opponent or to enhance the credibility of one's other claims and arguments was a common rhetorical device. Cf. Quint. 9.2.51-52.

disapproving: the two rhetorical questions with their concise parallelism provide a compelling statement of the freedman's two-fold obligation to carry out the terms of the will, and they demolish any moral or legal argument Verres might offer for his refusal to allow him to do so. Cicero goes on to give the real reason behind Verres' action, his abhorrence of the idea that a freedman should inherit from a Roman knight.

125. countless: translates *sescenta*, the numeral commonly used to indicate an indefinitely large number.

There was a man: Cicero's account of this episode provides further illustration of his effective use of the plain style in narration. The facts, carefully coloured by the general tone, the slanting of motives and responses, the brief, sharp characterizations, and the occasional direct comment, are presented with a vigorous, compact directness, devoid of any obtrusive rhetorical or literary accountrement. The pace is quickened by a staccato sentence structure and asyndeton. Other notable examples of this narrative technique occur in the story of the ward Junius, notably in the description of the expedition by Junius' guardians to the house of Chelidon (137-38). Cf. 34n.

M. Octavius Ligus: he and his brother Lucius had become senators by 75 B.C. They most likely came from Forum Clodii in Etruria, one of many new families from municipalities who used their talents and resources to break into politics in the capital in the seventies and gain access to the expanded senate of the post-Sullan era. Cf. Wiseman (2), 24-32. Gruen (2), 201ff.

controversy: the will made by Sulpicius, who was a freedman, had obviously conformed to existing praetorian law relating to the property of freedmen (*de bonis libertorum*). Under this law the patron had a right to half the estate of a freedman who had no natural heirs. If the patron was dead, the right was held by his male descendants. Verres had extended the law by introducing a new clause into his edict giving a claim to the patron's female as well as male descendants. Sulpicius' patron

obviously had no male offspring, but he did have a daughter who proceeded to claim a part of Sulpicius' estate. Verres was prepared, in characteristic fashion, to apply his new regulation retrospectively and admit her claim. Cf. Watson (5), 231-35.
L. Gellius: consul in 72 and censor in 70. He later served under Pompey against the pirates and was an ally of Cicero in the Catilinarian crisis in 63.
126. authoritative position ... influence: *auctoritas* denoted the moral authority and power derived from one's personal qualities and achievements and from one's general social status and resources. Cf. *Topica* 73. *Gratia* represented the favour and regard and resulting influence derived above all from benefits conferred and services rendered (*beneficia* and *officia*). Cf. *Mur.* 42. *Planc.* 46-47. Hellegouarc'h, 150-70, 295-361.
127. any doubt: Cicero returns to the main theme of the section, Verres' *superbia* towards the lower classes, and for his concluding reassertion of the charge he resorts to a form of inductive argumentation (*inductio*) described by Quintilian as the inferring of the greater from the lesser (*maiora ex minoribus*). Cf. *Inv.* 1.51. Quint. 5.10.73, 86-87.
position etc.: a notable example of *congeries*. Cf. 34n.
repair of public buildings: cf. 103n.

128-154: *Verres' misconduct as a supervisor of the maintainance of public buildings.*

128. Q. Titinius: a wealthy senator, possibly a Sullan appointee, who does not appear to have gone on to any of the higher magistracies. Cicero makes several allusions to him in his Letters, and they were apparently friends. Cf. *Att.* 5.21.5; 7.18.4; 9.6.6. Gruen (2), 197.
Q. Tadius: a P. Tadius, probably a brother, had served as a legate of Verres in Sicily. Cf. *Verr.* 2.2.49; 2.5.63. The family was equestrian.
129. what should I say: *dubitatio* once more. Cf. 118n. Its purpose here is to convey the impression of an offense that defies description. The *exclamatio* of the following sentence, interrupted by the tricolon detailing the particularly public nature of the scene of Verres'

215

misconduct, further develops the image of indescribable audacity.
temple of Castor: according to tradition, the *aedes Castoris* in honour of the Dioscuri, Castor and Pollux, was dedicated in Rome in 484 B.C. in fulfillment of a vow made by the Roman commander, A. Postumius, during the battle of Lake Regillus, in which the Romans defeated the Latins. Cf. Livy 2.20.12; 42.5. The temple stood in the south-east end of the Forum and from early times had a platform in front which was used by the censors for their review of the parade of *equites* during the census. When the temple was restored by Metellus Delmaticus in 117 (cf. 154n), the platform was made an integral part of the building and the temple became a common site for *contiones* and legislative *comitia*. Cf. Taylor (3), 28, 108.
legal counselling: *advocationes* denoted the consultative services offered by the *iuris consulti*. Cf. *Fam.* 7.10.2.
130. **L.Sulla and Q. Metellus:** consuls in 80 B.C.
L. Octavius and C. Aurelius: consuls in 75 B.C. They had, in the absence of censors, re-let the contracts for the maintenance of temples, but inspection and approval of the work was not completed in 75, and the task was passed on by senatorial decree to two of the praetors for 74, Verres and Caelius.
131. **stated:** the frequentative form *dictitare* combined with the generic subjunctive and the unusually pronounced alliteration and assonance provide a colourful and potent representation of Verres' motives that is typical of Cicero's skill in moulding a narrative to excite prejudice or achieve a particular emotional effect.
132. **without any loss:** *intertrimentum* literally meant "damage due to wear and tear" (cf. Livy 32.2.2), but came to represent loss or damage in general. Ps. Asconius (Stangl, 251) explains its force in the present passage as follows: *intertrimentum vero ad utrius partem spectat, dantis et accipientis*: "it is concerned with the interests of both sides, the giver and receiver."
133. **He paid a visit:** Cicero once more makes good use of the mode of vivid description he called *sub oculos subiectio* (cf. 75n.). He switches to the historic present and provides a detailed word-picture of Verres inspecting the beautifully finished building, and pacing about in

frustration as he searched for some means of making a profit. The imaginary dialogue (*sermocinatio*) lends further vividness and realism to the scene and enables him to portray the unscrupulous greed of Verres and his lackeys with greater immediacy and more devastating effect. Cf. 141.6ff.

plumb: the Greeks believed columns should have a slight inward incline, a concept obviously not in vogue in 1st century Rome or Cicero would have stressed the unaesthetic as well as the unreasonable aspects of Verres' demand. The task of insuring the columns were perpendicular could have involved a great deal of work, since the temple had a huge colonnade completely surrounding the inner shrine, and any columns found not to be plumb would have to be stripped of their stucco, wholly dismantled and rebuilt and replastered.

134. contract: *lex* was the usual term for a contract for the performance of public works. Cf. below 143ff.
135. M. Marcellus: aedile in 91 and father of the consuls of 51 and 49. For the role of his family in the prosecution of Verres cf. Intro. p.11.
136. he was a man: the parenthesis provides another example of *frequentatio*, gathering together the various flaws in Verres' character that finally drove decent men to the desperate and humiliating expedient of seeking help from a prostitute. These summarizing reminders of major points, inserted at crucial stages in a *narratio* or *argumentatio*, are an important feature of Cicero's rhetorical method. Cf. 71n.
137. approached Chelidon: the tricolon with its solemn anaphora, the *exclamatio*, the rhetorical question, the image of duty compelling acceptance of the shame all show Cicero resorting once more to *pathos*, as he continues to exploit the emotive image of honourable and respected citizens forced to supplicate a prostitute.

they made their way: cf. 125n.
138. not ungracious: the litotes, as usual, lends emphasis to a point by means of understatement. Chelidon showed a surprising *humanitas*, the word Cicero used to describe the refining and humanizing effects of a liberal education. It represented the nature of man at his most civilized and, as applied to manners, described the urbane gentility, graciousness, and civility that accompanied the

development by education of man's intellectual, social, and moral faculties. Cf. Clarke, 135-45. The *humanitas* of the prostitute, of course, all the more starkly revealed the brutish rapacity of Verres.

139. has recounted: cf. 74n.
L. Domitius: L. Domitius Ahenobarbus, an arch-conservative of the highest nobility, whose wealth and connections made him, in Cicero's words, destined for the consulship from the day he was born. He was a staunch supporter of Cicero in the sixties, during the latter's campaigns for the praetorship and consulship. Cf. *Att.* 1.14; 4.8a.2. *Mil.* 22.
defending advocate: Mustius was a well-connected member of the *publicani*, the powerful class of businessmen that took public contracts. Cicero had tried hard from the beginning of his public life to win the political support of this important group, and by 70 could claim that he had spent a great deal of his life *in causis publicanorum*. Cf. *Verr.* 2.2.181. *Fam.* 13.9.2. *Q.F.* 1.1.32.

140. Are you not ashamed: Cicero has built Domitius' modest reluctance even to mention the name of Chelidon into an elaborate form of *comparatio* to heighten further the shameless depravity of Verres' subservience to her.

141. taking of bids: contracts were publicly auctioned on a basis of competitive bidding. Bids were registered by raising the finger (*digitum tollere*; cf. *Verr.* 2.3.27). It was standard, if not required, practice for the magistrate in charge to give formal notice of the day of the auction (*diem edicere*). Cf. Livy 23.38.12. Badian (2), 16ff. Verres auctioned the contract around the Ides of September (148.12) when the *Ludi Romani*, which extended from September 5th to the 19th, were at their height.
decked out: cf. 49n.
and what was it: a form of *sustentatio*, delaying to create suspense, and then relating something far more serious or far less serious than the build-up has led the audience to expect. Cf. Quint. 9.2.22-23.

142. If the contract: the device of *prosopopoeia* or *sermocinatio* once more. Cf. 103n. and below. This instance exemplifies one of the figure's chief functions, described by Quintilian (9.2.30) as "the disclosure of the inner thoughts of our adversaries, as if they were talking

to themselves".
property and land: *praes* meant a person who acted as surety, but could also denote the property offered as security. Cf. *Phil.* 2.78. *Praedium* specifically meant landed securities. According to Ps. Asconius (253, Stangl) *bonus* was a regular epithet of *praedia*, presumably meaning the pledges were sound and adequate.
Is there someone: the *prosopopoeia* adds to the directness and immediacy of the description of the ward's complaint against Verres. Cicero makes three main points: Junius, by long-established convention, had a special claim to the contract; he had given adequate security to insure the work would be done to Verres' satisfaction; even if Verres did not think the security adequate, this did not entitle him to adopt a course that would insure Junius' ruin. What Cicero meant by this last point is made clear in 143.16. Rather than taking an action that would ruin Junius, Verres should have sought greater security, which would have been readily offered.
143. something of this sort: Cicero's point was, of course, that Verres' innovations had a very different intent; they were specifically framed, like his edict on inheritances, to bring Verres profit from a particular case.
L. Marcius and M. Perperna: censors in 86. It was apparently from them that Junius' father had originally got the contract for the maintenance of the temple of Castor.
adequate security: *locuples* in contexts relating to undertakings and guarantees meant being wealthy enough to give reliable pledges. For examples cf. *OLD*, 1039.
144. If at this point: cf. 71n.; 136n.
145. aedileship: Cicero lists the duties of aediles in *Verr.* 2.5.36. Among them was *sacrarum aedium procuratio*, the care of sacred buildings, a task which, like many other aedilician duties, obviously involved some expenditure of personal funds.
146. apprehended damage: *damnum infectum* meant damage not actually done, but in danger of being done. Since Habonius was the man who had taken over from the original contractor and was also the man Verres intended to get the new contract, this clause was, in effect, asking Habonius to give security to himself.

should have protected: the praetor was, in Cicero's words, *iuris civilis custos*, the custodian of the civil law (*Leg.* 3.8), and, as such, had a special obligation to protect the rights of an orphaned minor.

147. some stone: this passage has caused some difficulty. Cicero has argued all along that the only work involved consisted in dismantling the sections of stone and rebuilding them, and he states clearly that no stone or other material had to be brought in. What then is the sense of the clause *lapis aliqui caedendus et adportandus fuit machina sua*? Some editors take *lapis* to mean marble or small pieces of stone and *saxum* to mean large sections. Cf. Greenwood, 281. Long, 163. But it is difficult to justify this distinction between *lapis* and *saxum*, both of which are commonly and apparently synonymously used to mean stone for building, and, besides, Cicero is unequivocal in his claim that no expense, great or small, was incurred in materials. Other editors regard the clause as interrogative, but the language of the following phrase, *nam illo* etc., does not provide a satisfactory form of response. It seems preferable to take the clause to mean some of the dismantled sections of stone had to be reshaped and then returned by means of the *machina* to their proper place. This dismantling and replacing of the sections of the columns is specifically stated in 145.3 to be the sole purpose for which the *machina* was required. *Nam*, in slightly elliptical fashion, explains that nothing more was involved, since no new materials were brought in.

    such as those: *illas* here represents things pointed out by the speaker, "those over there". Cf. *OLD*, 823. The columns of the temple would have been clearly visible to the members of the court.

    impluvium: cf. 61n.

148. it may be suggested: *at enim* commonly introduces a supposed objection in Cicero. Cf. *Cael.* 10. *Dom.* 5.

149. had sealed: cf. 50n.

    in order to have: *haberet* is the reading of the MSS, emended by Peterson to *ageret*. But *minus* does not combine easily with either verb, and the text must be considered suspect.

150. he had indeed: for the force of the *cum ... tum* clauses cf. 41n.

he repaid: the cost of the new contract, which came to five hundred and sixty thousand was charged to Junius and had to be paid by D. Brutus, who had acted as Junius' main surety. Brutus, an influential *nobilis* and former consul of 77, contested the matter and forced Verres to repay him one hundred and ten thousand. Since the repayment was made after all the details of the new contract had been settled and Verres should no longer have been involved, Cicero argues that the repayment shows the money had gone to Verres, not Habonius.

151. dressed as a minor: Cicero had brought Junius into court conspicuously dressed in the *toga praetexta* of an underage youth in an attempt to arouse the jury's sympathy. Such appeals to pity (*miseratio* or *commiseratio*) were considered the most powerful form of *pathos* (cf. Quint. 6.1.23), and were a notable feature of Roman trials. Defendants regularly appeared wearing mourning and in a general state of dishevelment. Parents, wives, and children of the accused or of his victims were brought in looking similarly unkempt and mournful. Blood-stained weapons, clothing, and other gory exhibits were commonly on show. Even vivid paintings of crimes were sometimes displayed. Such visual inducements to pity were, of course, supplemented by vivid verbal pictures of the pitiable circumstances of the accused or of the cruel nature and consequences of his wrongdoing. The ancients, however, recognised that there were high risks in such high-powered emotional appeals. If overdone, the effect was lost (*nihil enim lacrima citius arescit*), if ineptly done, the tears became laughter. Cf. Quint. 6.1.23-45; 11.3.170. *Ad Her.* 2.50. *Inv.* 1.106-09. *De Or.* 2.195-96. Cicero excelled in the techniques of *miseratio* and was notorious for his use of them. Cf. *Orator* 130-31. *Planc.* 83. Clarke (2), 70.

7 a Gracchus or a Saturninus: Cicero regularly lists the Gracchi and Saturninus as the great examples of demagogic *populares* who had aroused unjust political and economic expectations in the people and had broadened the divide between the ruling aristocracy and the *plebs*. Cf. *Cat.* 1.29; 4.4. *Dom.* 82. *Har. Resp.* 41, 43. *Sest.* 101, 105. *Vat.* 23. *Brut.* 224. *Leg.* 3.20.

152. locket: the *bulla* was a golden locket, containing an amulet, that was worn around the neck by free-born

children. Boys ceased wearing them when they assumed the *toga virilis*. Cf. Propertius 4.1.131.

153. **that affects us all:** another example of *thesis*, as Cicero extends the argument from the particular to the general, thereby magnifying the implications of Verres' misdeeds and the need to deal resolutely with them. Cf. 37n.

154. **L. Metellus:** L. Caecilius Metellus Delmaticus, consul in 119, led a war against the Dalmations and was awarded a triumph in 117. He used his spoils from the war to restore the temple of Castor. Cf. Appian, *Illyr*. 11. Asconius 28, Clark.

    Vortumnus: the god of gardens and fruit. He had a bronze statue in the Vicus Tuscus (Varro, *LL* 5.46), which led south-west from the forum, the route along which the procession of religious images and dignitaries travelled from the Capitol to the Circus Maximus for the inauguration of *Ludi*.

    Is anyone to imagine: an argument from incompatibles or contraries (*ex repugnantibus* or *ex contrariis*), a form of reasoning that used an accepted or clearly proven proposition to show the falsehood of a conflicting or opposite proposition. It was a type of enthymeme, the rhetorical or incomplete syllogism, which drew its conclusions from premises that were implied rather than stated, or probable rather than certain. Cf. Quint. 5.10.2-3; 5.14.1-4. *Ad Her*. 4.25. The rhetorical questions at the beginning of the section might also be described as enthymemes, though their mode of argument is the inferring of *maiora ex minoribus*. Cf. 127n.

155-58: *Verres' misconduct in the trials of Opimus and Oppianicus.*

155. **Q. Opimius:** Sulla had severely limited the right of tribunes to exercise the veto. Opimius during his tribunate in 75 had attempted to defy these limitations. He was prosecuted the following year by leading members of the Sullan oligarchy, named by Ps. Asconius (255, Stangl) as Catulus, Hortensius, and Scribonius Curio. The charge was disobedience to a law; the penalty was a fine, and the mode of enforcement a quasi-criminal *iudicium*, presided over by the urban praetor. Cf. Greenidge (1), 12-13.

<u>a few arrogant individuals</u>: such disparaging allusions to leaders of the Sullan oligarchy more likely reflect a conventional attempt by Cicero to arouse *invidia* against his opponents in the trial than any antipathy to the Sullan system or its *principes*.

157. <u>Junius</u>: C. Junius, aedile in 75, was appointed president (*quaesitor*) of the *quaestio de sicariis* in 74. One of the cases that came before him was that of S. Albius .Oppianicus, who was convicted on a charge of poisoning amid suspicions that the jury had been bribed. His chief *patronus*, the demagogic tribune P. Quinctius, used the conviction to denounce senatorial oppression and corruption, and, as part of his campaign, launched a prosecution against Junius, alleging that he had failed to take the required oath and that the records of the urban praetor showed he had failed to fill vacancies in the jury. Cicero here implies that Verres had tampered with the records to insure Junius' conviction and to deflect popular indignation from himself. Cf. *Cluent*. 73-77, 89-96.

158. <u>supplementary selection</u>: cf. Intro. p. 10. If the *decuria* of jurors assigned to a particular case could not supply enough jurors, the additional number required was drawn by lot (*subsortitio*) from the *decuria* next in line to serve. Verres was hoping that, by means of such a *subsortitio*, his friend Q. Curtius, who was president of a criminal court in 70, would remove from the *decuria* due to hear his own case the jurors most likely to be unsympathetic.

The speech ends abruptly with these relatively mild and tentative allegations of jury-tampering. There is no amplification to dramatize the wrongdoing and its implications, and no form of peroration. This has led some scholars to suspect the speech is incomplete, but it must be seen as part of a larger whole, and the ending fits well with the opening of *Verr*. II.2, where Cicero emphasizes there is much that must be omitted so that he may finally come to his main concern, the cause of the Sicilians.

INDEXES

References are to page numbers.

A. Names

Acilius Glabrio, M'., 8, 14, 49, 166, 177.
Aemilius Paulus, L., 69, 187.
Aemilius Scaurus, M., 182, 201-02.
Annius Asellus, P., 111, 115, 117, 119, 123, 207.
Caecilius Metellus, L., 6.
Caecilius Metellus, M., 6, 9, 12, 204.
Caecilius Metellus Creticus, Q., 6, 9, 12, 198, 204.
Caecilius Metellus Delmaticus, L., 153, 216, 222.
Caecilius Niger, Q., 8, 168.
Calpurnius Piso Frugi, L., 125, 211.
Chelidon, 111, 113, 125, 139-41.
Claudius Marcellus, M., (cos. 214), 33, 69, 166.
Claudius Marcellus, M., (aedile 91), 137-39, 145, 153, 217.
Claudius Nero, C., 65, 83-91, 95.
Cornelius Dolabella, Cn., 5, 57-63, 67, 75, 85-89, 99, 101, 105-06, 182, 201-02.
Cornelius Scipio Africanus Aemilianus, P., 33, 165.
Cornelius Scipio Asiaticus, L., (cos. 190), 69, 187
Cornelius Sisenna, L., 6.
Cornelius Sulla, L., 4-5, 55-59, 169, 179, 181, 197, 213, 222.
Curtius Postumus, Q., 157, 223.
Domitius Ahenobarbus, L., 11, 141, 218.
Fabius Hadrianus, C., 83.
Gellius Publicola, L., 129-31, 215.
Habonius, L., 135-37, 141-43, 149, 151.
Hortensius Hortalus, Q., 5-6, 8-9, 12, 43, 83, 151, 173-74, 198, 204, 222.
Junius, C., 157, 223.
Junius, P., 135-40.
Junius Brutus, D., 145, 151, 221.
Licinius Lucullus, L., 5.
Licinius Murena, L., 99, 197-98.
Licinius Sacerdos, C., 45, 111, 125, 129, 135, 176, 212.
Lutatius Catulus, Q., 5-6, 11, 222.
Malleolus, C., 57, 101-03, 182.

Mustius, C., 137-41, 218.
Mummius Achaicus, L., 69, 187.
Octavius Ligus, M., 129-33, 214.
Opimius, Q., 6, 155-56, 222.
Papirius Carbo, Cn., 5, 31, 51-59, 89, 101, 165.
Philodamus, 76-88, 93.
Pompeius Magnus, Cn., 4, 10, 12, 16, 186.
Pupius Piso, M., 55, 181.
Quinctius Flamininus, T., 69, 187.
Servilius Glaucia, C., 45, 175.
Servilius Vatia Isauricus, P., 69-70, 187.
Sulpicius Olympus, C., 129, 214.
Tullia, 209.
Tullius Cicero, M.,
 quaestorship, 7, 37;

aedileship, 9, 35, 39, 147, 167-68, 170;
conduct of Verrine prosecution, 8-10, 25, 27, 35-39, 43, 47, 49, 111, 161;
motives for prosecuting Verres, 7-8, 10-12, 27, 35, 39, 41;
view of empire, 195;
attitude towards prosecutors, 202.
Verres, C.,
 parentage, 5-6, 179, 203;
 political affiliation, 5-6, 11;
 quaestorship, 5, 31, 51-57, 107;
 legateship, 57-99, 107;
 proquaestorship, 101-05;
 praetorship, 5-6, 107-57, 202-03;
 events of his trial, 6-10, 37, 39, 49, 109, 203-04;
 death, 10.

B. Subjects

accusatio perpetua, 10, 173-74, 177, 185.
Aediles, 167, 185, 219.
album, 2, 4.
amicitia, 182, 202.
ampliatio, 3-4, 44, 86, 175-76.
argumentum ex consequentibus, 208.
Ariminum, 53, 55, 179.
artes liberales, 184.
Asia, 65, 75, 85, 87, 184.
asylia, 95, 196.
auctoritas, 215.
audacia, 160, 181.
Booty, 69-71, 153, 186.

bulla, 221-22.
Burdens on provincials, 183, 201.
calumnia, 2.
Census, 205.
Challenging of jurors, 4, 9, 37, 162, 170.
Cilicia, 59, 182-83, 198.
comitium, 65, 71, 184-85.
comperendinatio or
 comperendinatus, 10, 42, 44, 159, 174-76.
Corinth, 69, 187.
Contracts, 204-05, 216, 218.
conventus civium Romanorum, 191.

decuria, 4, 9, 14, 223.
Delos, 61-63, 184.
dignitas, 180.
divinatio, 8.
divisores, 5, 177, 203.
Edict, 111-33, 205, 211.
Embezzlement court, 33, 165, 185.
equites, 2, 172, 175.
existimatio, 170.
Extortion court, 1-6, 163, 171, 174, 185, 195.
Freedmen, 127-31, 213-14.
Friends and allies, 168.
frugalitas, 203.
frumentum cellae nomine, 105, 201.
Grain-tithe, 165.
gratia, 215.
Greeks, 190.
Guardians, 101-103, 113, 135, 137-47, 198-99, 206.
Host-guest relationship, 191.
humanitas, 217-18.
illustris accusatio, 7, 160, 168, 202.
impluvium, 149, 188.
inquisitio, 2-3, 8.
Jurisconsults, 125, 212, 216.
ius praetorium, 112, 120, 205.
Lampsacum, 75, 81, 91, 93, 119, 190.
Laodicea, 87, 193.
lapidatio, 212.
Latona, 184.
Legates, 95-97, 182, 194.
iudicium populi, 167.
Lex Acilia, 1-4, 44, 163, 175-76.
Lex Atinia, 114, 207.
Lex Aurelia, 4-5, 11, 15, 172.
Lex Calpurnia, 1, 3.
Lex Cornelia de repetundis, 4, 163.
Lex Cornelia de proscriptione, 126, 213.
Lex Cornelia testamentaria, 114, 207.
Lex Furia, 114, 207.
Lex Fusia, 114, 207.
Lex Julia, 183.
Lex Junia, 14.
Lex Porcia, 167, 213.
Lex Sempronia, 167.
Lex Servilia Glauciae, 3, 175-76.
Lex Servilia Caepionis, 3.
Lex Valeria, 213.
Lex Voconia, 112, 114, 116, 206-09.
litis aestimatio, 3.
ludi, 9, 167-68, 218, 222.
luxuria, 179, 203.
Miletus, 97-99, 197.
Money-lending, 192.
negotiatores, 2.
nominis delatio, 2, 8, 161.
novus homo, novitas, 7-8, 179.
optimates, 181.
patroni, 1-2, 161.
peculium, 102, 200.
Pirates, 99, 197-98.
populares, 181.
possessio, 120-22, 210-11.
postulatio, 8.
potentia, 161.
Praetors, 1, 4, 14, 204-05, 211, 220, 222.
provocatio, 163, 213.
publicani, 2, 14, 172, 218.
pudor, 168-69.
Quaestors, 178, 181, 185.
Quarries, 35, 167.
recuperatores, 1, 3.
religio, 162.

Rewards in Roman criminal law, 171.
Rostra, 185.
sodalis, 100, 102, 156, 199, 201.
sors, sortitio, 181.
subscriptor, 168.
subsortitio, 10, 156, 223.
Syracuse, 209-10.
tabula Bembina, 2, 14.

Temple of Castor, 133-37, 153-54, 216-17, 220, 222.
testamentum inofficiosum, 207.
toga praetexta, 119, 209, 221.
tribuni aerarii, 4, 15.
Treason court, 33, 165.
vicarius, 102, 200.
virtus, 161, 203.
Vortumnus, 222.

C. Literary Terms

adiectio, 159, 161.
Alliteration, 162, 170, 212, 216.
amphibolia, 213.
Amplification, 164, 176, 186.
Anacolouthon, 164, 173, 203.
Anaphora, 176-77, 193-94, 196, 199, 201, 209, 212, 217.
anteoccupatio, 180, 186.
Antithesis, 164, 170, 174, 177, 192, 195.
Apostrophe, 180, 183, 194, 209.
argumentatio, 194.
argumentum ex repugnantibus, 222.
Assonance, 162, 170, 212, 216.
Asyndeton, 166, 176, 194, 214.
Chiasmus, 181, 193, 195.
clausula, 192, 197.
commiseratio, 221.
commoratio, 173.
comparatio, 180, 185-86, 188, 218.
congeries, 178, 215.
coniectura, 194.
dubitatio, 211, 215.
Enthymeme, 222.
Ethos, 193.
exclamatio, 180, 183, 186, 193-94, 217.

exordium, 172.
expolitio, 180, 196.
exemplum, 186-87.
frequentatio, 192, 196, 217.
geminatio, 159.
Grand style, 163, 183, 201.
Hendiadys, 192.
Homoeoteleuton, 164, 177, 194.
hyperbaton, 169, 187.
Hyperbole, 194, 209.
inductio, 215.
iracundia, 183, 209.
Irony, 179, 188, 190, 210, 213.
Isocolon, 164, 192.
Litotes, 217.
maiora ex minoribus, 215, 222.
narratio, 179, 188-90, 193, 214, 217.
obiurgatio, 183, 209.
Parallelism, 162, 170, 192, 197, 214.
Paralipsis, 178, 184, 188, 193, 204.
Parenthesis or *digressio*, 164-65, 217.
paronomasia, 160, 186, 213.
Pathos, 193, 201, 209, 217, 221.
Periodic sentence, 169, 183, 192, 197, 203.

permissio, 200.
Plain style, 179, 214.
probatio, 193.
prosopopoeia, 201, 204, 218-19.
Redundancy, 159.
repetitio, 173, 176.
Rhetorical question, 164, 171, 183, 188, 194, 201, 209, 214, 217.
sermocinatio, 204, 217-18.
sibi ipsi responsio, 195.
sub oculos subiectio, 193, 216-17.
sustentatio, 218.
thesis, 180, 222.
translatio, 198.
Tricolon, triad, 161, 171, 176, 183, 191, 199, 217.
Wit, 206.
Zeugma, 166.